Sport, Sponsorship and Public Health

This book examines the development of sport sponsorship and its impact on global public health. It argues that sport governing bodies should not continue to treat fans solely as consumers, and that a more ethical approach should be taken to sport sponsorship.

Drawing on research from sport studies, marketing and public health, the book presents a brief history of advertising and marketing in sport, including the importance of tobacco in the development of sport sponsorship, before exploring key aspects of the contemporary relationship between sport and corporate sponsors, including mega-events, digital technologies and brand engagement. It offers an in-depth case study of sponsorship in the English Premier League – one of the world's most successful sporting properties – before considering how sport might be better regulated, now and in the future, to better protect the interests of fans and other stakeholders from a health perspective. The book features a number of insightful images showcasing sport sponsorship in connection with tobacco, mega-events, alcohol, junk food and drink, and gambling over the years.

Addressing a topical and hugely important issue, this is important reading for students, researchers, practitioners and policy makers with an interest in sport business and management, the ethics of sport, physical activity and health, event studies, marketing or public health.

Robin Ireland is Honorary Research Fellow in the College of Medical Veterinary and Life Sciences affiliated to the School of Health and Wellbeing, University of Glasgow, UK. He is also Honorary Director of Research with the European Healthy Stadia Network. He was awarded his PhD by the University of Glasgow in 2021. His thesis was on the Commercial Determinants of Health in Sport. He was elected Member of the UK Faculty of Public Health through Distinction in 2015.

Routledge Research in Physical Activity and Health

The *Routledge Research in Physical Activity and Health* series offers a multi-disciplinary forum for cutting-edge research in the broad area of physical activity, exercise and health. Showcasing the work of emerging and established scholars working in areas ranging from physiology and chronic disease, psychology and mental health to physical activity and health promotion and socio-economic and cultural aspects of physical activity participation, the series is an important channel for groundbreaking research in physical activity and health.

Technology in Physical Activity and Health Promotion
Edited by Zan Gao

Physical Activity and the Abdominal Viscera
Responses in Health and Disease
Roy J. Shephard

Obesity: A Kinesiologist's Perspective
Roy J. Shephard

The Politics of Physical Activity
Joe Piggin

Physical Activity and Rehabilitation in Life-threatening Illness
Amy J. Litterini and Christopher M. Wilson

Sport, Sponsorship and Public Health
Robin Ireland

For more information about this series, please visit: https://www.routledge.com/sport/series/RRPAH

Sport, Sponsorship and Public Health

Robin Ireland

Routledge
Taylor & Francis Group
LONDON AND NEW YORK

First published 2023
by Routledge
4 Park Square, Milton Park, Abingdon, Oxon OX14 4RN

and by Routledge
605 Third Avenue, New York, NY 10158

Routledge is an imprint of the Taylor & Francis Group, an informa business

© 2023 Robin Ireland

The right of Robin Ireland to be identified as author of this work has been asserted in accordance with sections 77 and 78 of the Copyright, Designs and Patents Act 1988.

All rights reserved. No part of this book may be reprinted or reproduced or utilised in any form or by any electronic, mechanical, or other means, now known or hereafter invented, including photocopying and recording, or in any information storage or retrieval system, without permission in writing from the publishers.

Trademark notice: Product or corporate names may be trademarks or registered trademarks, and are used only for identification and explanation without intent to infringe.

British Library Cataloguing-in-Publication Data
A catalogue record for this book is available from the British Library

Library of Congress Cataloging-in-Publication Data
Names: Ireland, Robin, author.
Title: Sport, sponsorship and public health / Robin Ireland.
Description: Abingdon, Oxon ; New York, N.Y. : Routledge, 2023. | Series: Routledge research in physical activity and health | Includes bibliographical references and index. |
Identifiers: LCCN 2022046633 | ISBN 9781032145181 (hardback) | ISBN 9781032145198 (paperback) | ISBN 9781003239734 (ebook)
Subjects: LCSH: Sports sponsorship—Moral and ethical aspects. | Corporate sponsorship—Moral and ethical aspects. | Public health. | Sports and globalization—Economic aspects. | Soccer—Economic aspects—Great Britain. | F.A. Premier League.
Classification: LCC GV716 .I74 2023 | DDC 796.06/98—dc23/eng/20221122
LC record available at https://lccn.loc.gov/2022046633

ISBN: 978-1-032-14518-1 (hbk)
ISBN: 978-1-032-14519-8 (pbk)
ISBN: 978-1-003-23973-4 (ebk)

DOI: 10.4324/9781003239734

Typeset in Goudy
by codeMantra

Contents

List of figures vii
List of table xi
Acknowledgements xiii

1 Introduction 1

2 Public health and sport 7

3 An introduction to advertising and marketing in sport 22

4 The tobacco industry and the development of sport sponsorship 40

5 Mega-events and sponsorship 53

6 The commodification of modern sport 75

7 The commercialisation and globalisation of football in England 93

8 Sport and brand engagement 112

9 The regulation of sport 130

10 Conclusions and discussion 144

Index 151

Figures

2.1	Strategies that determine the commercial determinants of health	9
3.1	Sponsorship pyramid of an English Premier League club	28
3.2	The sport sponsorship promotional assemblage	30
7.1	Shirt sponsorship of clubs that have participated in the English Premier League	99

Tobacco Sponsorship

1. Badge for Virginia Slims Circuit (women's professional tennis). "You've come a long way, baby". 1972. *Source: R. Ireland.*
2. Embassy World Professional Darts Championship 25th Anniversary (1978–2002) dart flights. 2002. *Source: R. Ireland.*
3. WD & HO Wills Scissors Cigarette Cards (Sporting Girls series). 1913. *Source: R. Ireland.*
4. John Player Special League Official Programme and Scorecard. Essex v Kent. 1985. *Source: R. Ireland.*
5. The Park Drive Book of Football. 1970. *Source: R. Ireland.*
6. Honus Wagner, Pittsburgh Pirates. Reproduction of T206 Piedmont cigarette card. Originally issued in 1909. *Source: R. Ireland.*
7. G.L. Garnsey, New South Wales. Capstan cigarette card (Prominent Australian and English Cricketers series). 1907. *Source: R. Ireland.*
8. B.L. Osler, South Africa. United Tobacco Cos. cigarette card (Springbok Rugby and Cricket Teams series). 1931. *Source: R. Ireland.*
9. FC Bayern Snuff. 2022. *Source: R. Ireland.*

Mega-Events Sponsorship

1. Budweiser 2002 FIFA World Cup Keyring, Japan and South Korea. *Source: R. Ireland.*
2. Budweiser 2014 FIFA World Cup Scarf 'Tous Ensemble' Spain, Brazil. *Source: R. Ireland.*

3   Budweiser 2018 'Light Up the FIFA World Cup' glass, Russia. *Source: R. Ireland.*
4   Torch Relay Coca-Cola Towel, Tokyo 2020 Olympics (postponed). *Source: R. Ireland.*
5   Romania v Albania Coca-Cola cup, UEFA EUROs, 19 June 2016. *Source: R. Ireland.*
6   Coca-Cola Commemorative Badge, Los Angeles Olympics, 1932. *Source: R. Ireland.*
7   Coca-Cola Cricket World Cup Cards, India, 1996. *Source: R. Ireland.*
8   Reemsta Olympia #194 Television Recording Equipment and #103 Torch Ceremony, Berlin 1936 Olympics. *Source: R. Ireland.*

Alcohol Sponsorship

1   Huddersfield Town FC, The John Smith's Stadium, 2017/2018. *Source: R. Ireland.*
2   Guinness Six Nations Official Rugby Cap, 2022. *Source: R. Ireland.*
3   France v Wales (Rugby Union) Official Programme, 1948. *Source: R. Ireland.*
4   England v Belgium (Women's International Football) Official Programme, 1978. *Source: R. Ireland.*
5   Reproduction of Norwich City FC shirt, 1986/1987. *Original image with kind permission of G. Parry.*
6   Kevin Harvick, Budweiser Chevrolet, NASCAR Sprint Cup Series, 2013. *Source: R. Ireland.*

Junk Food and Drink Sponsorship

1   Jeff Astle, West Bromwich Albion FC, A & BC Gum (Footballers Series), 1969. *Source: R. Ireland.*
2   Michael Owen, Cadbury Legend Sticker, Panini Premier League 2020 Collection. *Source: R. Ireland.*
3   Ian Wright, Cadbury Legend Sticker, Panini Premier League 2020 Collection. *Source: R. Ireland.*
4   Cadbury Dairy Milk Limited Club Edition, 360 grams, Official Partner of Liverpool FC, 2021/2022. *Source: R. Ireland.*
5   Tom Westerman (aged six years), Milo cricket, Australia, 2013. *Original image with kind permission of L. and T. Westerman.*
6   Kellogg's swimming badges, 2002. *Source: R. Ireland.*
7   Red Bull Racing Formula One Team – 1:43 Scale Model, 2017. *Source: R. Ireland.*
8   Coca-Cola English Premier League Trophy Tour, Liverpool, 23 March 2019. *Original image with kind permission of E. Boyland.*

9   Scoreboard, FC Valur, Reykjavik, 1998. *Original image with kind permission of B. Sweeney.*
10 Dyson Heppell, Essendon, AFL Team Coach, 2021. *Source: R. Ireland.*

Gambling Sponsorship

1   Littlewoods' Football Pools Coupon, 30 January 1932. *Source: R. Ireland.*
2   Ashley Barnes, Burnley FC. English Premier League Panini Trading Card, 2019/2020. *Source: R. Ireland.*
3   Fulham FC shirt (Betfair), 2002/2003. *Original image with kind permission of P. Terry.*
4   St. Andrews Trillion Trophy Stadium, Birmingham City FC, 2021/2022. *Original image with kind permission of The Big Step.*
5   Bet365 Stadium, Stoke City FC, 2018/2019. *Source: R. Ireland.*
6   Front and back of Daniel Farke mask (Manager, Norwich City FC). Circulated at Arsenal v Norwich City Carabao Cup, 25 October 2017. *Source: R. Ireland.*

Table

5.1 FIFA commercial partners at the 2018 World Cup 58

Acknowledgements

This book evolved from my experiences and discussions whilst being Chief Executive of the Health Equalities Group (formerly Heart of Mersey), a charity based in Liverpool. My thanks go out therefore to staff and colleagues as well as trustees of the charity during my 14 years in this post. I was then able to develop and refine my thinking whilst I was fortunate enough to study for and complete a doctorate at the University of Glasgow in the Commercial Determinants of Health in Sport. My PhD supervisors (Dr Chris Bunn, Dr Stephanie Chambers and Professor Gerda Reith) and my examiners (Professor Andy Smith and Professor Ilona Kickbusch) contributed considerably to my research and ideas.

The original book proposal developed from a conversation with Simon Whitmore of Routledge whilst we were attending the Football Collective Conference held at Sheffield United FC in November 2019.

I must thank many friends, colleagues and fellow sports fans, who helped by suggesting research links, were kind enough to read and comment on versions of book chapters at various stages, and who provided help with the images used in the book: Bill Bellew, Emma Boyland, Beth Bradshaw, Graham Brewster, Simon Capewell, Mike Carey, Stephanie Chambers, Kathryn Curran, Richard Glendenning, James Grimes (The Big Step), Alex Jackson (National Football Museum), Andrew Kirk, Malcolm O'Neill, Geraint Parry, Matthew Philpott, Andy Smith, Brian Sweeney, Paul Terry, Carol Thomas, Michael Viggars and Lucy Westerman.

My particular thanks to Bob Bennett for the hours he spent in reading early drafts of the book, and to Alan Ward, whose generosity with his time and his help with the book images were invaluable.

Finally, I need to thank those who have put up with me whilst I was researching and writing this book: my daughters, Boglarka and Flora, and my partner, Rebecca.

Chapter 1

Introduction

Introduction

This book seeks to address the development of sport sponsorship from a health perspective. Commercial brands have always used the passion and excitement of sport to sell their products to fans, but modern-day commodification has taken this to a new level. It has been argued that the tobacco industry helped create modern sponsorship in the 1970s by using sport to display its brands when other means of advertising were denied to it by regulation. Other purveyors of unhealthy commodities such as gambling, alcohol, and food and beverages which are high in fat, salt or sugar have followed the same approach as tobacco, in using sport as a means to market their brands to mass audiences. At the same time as fans are encouraged to consume more, they are also being told to behave responsibly in their consumption.

As far as I am aware, this is the first book to consider sport sponsorship and its potential impact on public health. By drawing on texts from a wide range of disciplines, I synthesise modern approaches to sponsorship and examine exactly how transnational corporations promote unhealthy brands to sports fans. Key case studies are included throughout the book.

Personal perspective

Sport and health are rarely considered together unless in an individualised 'sport as medicine' approach (Krustrup and Parnell 2020). My working experience in public health has led me to directly question how sport can be a force for better health. I established the Healthy Stadia initiative in 2004 in Merseyside (Ashton 2020; Viggars et al. 2020) in order to consider how sports stadia settings may be able to promote health. The original concept remains:

> Healthy Stadia are ... those which promote the health of visitors, fans, players, employees and the surrounding community ... places where people can go to have a positive, healthy experience playing or watching sport.
> (European Healthy Stadia Network 2020)

DOI: 10.4324/9781003239734-1

My public health practice has led me to believe in the importance of working at a collective level to improve environments and policies rather than blaming individuals for their ill health (Baum 2015). In considering commercial determinants of health in sport (Ireland et al. 2019), my public health perspective in this book will argue that corporate behaviour in sport promotes profits at the expense of fans' well-being. I have been fortunate enough to explore this further both in my Master of Public Health degree (2007) and my PhD thesis (Ireland 2021). This book has enabled me to develop my thoughts further and to explore more widely the marketing of unhealthy brands in sport and its potential impact on health.

I am acutely aware of my personal position as a researcher, however. King's observation of over 20 years ago (quoted below) correctly noted that many sociologists writing in the 1990s adopted the position of male fans who attend football matches.

> Sociologists of football are, in this country, overwhelmingly white and male, and they have adopted the position of a large majority of white, male fans who also attend matches.
>
> (King 2002 p.11)

King argued that by taking this socially and gender-specific position, these sociologists adopted a critical populist approach to what he called the "new consumption of football in the 1990s" (2002 p.11). King referenced Haynes (1995) and Taylor (1992) in describing what he considered to be a romanticised notion of football fans, which influenced their sociological enquiries. More recently, popular football writers such as John Nicholson have described their experiences on football terraces in the 1970s, invoking a mystical authentic community in which football clubs become "a sort of secular holy place" (2019 p.14). For myself, however, I have no wish to return to the dangerous, decrepit and often unwelcoming – particularly to women and supporters of colour – British football stadia of the 1970s and 1980s.

As a football fan, I have supported Norwich City FC for 50 years, a period during which football itself has been transformed. I attended the FA Cup semi-final between Norwich City and Everton at Villa Park in 1989. The tragic events at the semi-final at Hillsborough between Liverpool and Nottingham Forest on the same day had an enormous impact on football and its governance that persists to the present, as Adrian Tempany, a Liverpool fan and Hillsborough survivor, has written (Tempany 2016). As a spectator at Villa Park, and a resident of Liverpool between 1984 and 2018, I directly shared some of the distressing memories of that day and felt some closure with the people of Liverpool when the inquests into the deaths of the men, women and children at Hillsborough concluded in 2016 that the fans were "unlawfully killed" (Conn 2016). Perhaps these experiences have protected me from any undue sentimentality in my own consumption of sport. Certainly, they have led me to question the authority of those who provide leadership in sport and to challenge any notion of a 'sporting family'. As this book argues, the organisation of professional sport reflects economic and social interests within neoliberal capitalism.

These personal experiences colour my perception, but I have striven to prevent them from lessening my academic clarity. However, just as Tempany's experience of being a Hillsborough survivor has directly contributed to his overall view of football, it would be disingenuous of me to claim that my research has not been affected in some way by my own experiences of watching sport in person or on television. Numerato argues that "a reflexive football fan is not an actor who reflects upon his or her own individuality and position, but an actor who, in the first instance, critically scrutinises football culture" and considers "the development of football and its socio-cultural aspects" (Numerato 2018 pp.58,59). As a reflexive football fan, I experience the emotion and passion that accompanies my support for Norwich City and recognise that I am a consumer of its brand.

The sociology of sport has largely adopted this populist male perspective, but the situation has at least improved, with researchers reflecting a more diverse range of backgrounds and interests in the twenty-first century. Women's participation in sport has certainly, and rightly so, received much more attention, for example.

As Cashmore wrote, there is often resistance to writing about sport "on any other terms other than those of the fan, the reporter or the athlete" (2010 p.3). Those of us who work in public health are used to charges of puritanism or of acting as the 'fun police' when we seek to question commercial activity which damages health. And yet why should sport get a free ride from critical investigation? The term 'sportwashing' has become much more prevalent as it is recognised that sport is of course political, and that staging a World Cup in Russia or Qatar, or the Olympics in China, is not an altruistic decision. As a sports sociologist and a public health practitioner and activist, I have attempted to draw not only on the body of theory and practice from these disciplines but also those of many other fields such as history, economics, marketing, philosophy and psychology. I hope that this book achieves its primary purpose, to provide an overview of sport sponsorship, its potential impact on public health and a consideration of what, if anything, should be done about the relationship between sport and unhealthy brands.

What is not in the book

This book does not pretend to be comprehensive. Although it attempts to take a global view of public health and sport sponsorship, this is inevitably from a white, male, British sport sociologist's perspective. In one sense, of course, that simply mirrors modern sport, which some historians say was largely invented in Victorian Britain. Putting that argument aside, perhaps too much attention has been given to football and cricket and the sports developing from them in America and Australia. However, modern sport has been commodified mostly under Western capitalism, and sport sponsorship follows this pattern.

There are some obvious omissions. Taking a public health perspective, I have focused on sports governing bodies, competitions and clubs, and professional sport, rather than individuals. This means I have left out any major discussion of the celebrity endorser from Sir Stanley Matthews promoting cigarettes in the 1950s to British ex-footballers promoting gambling in 2022. Perhaps this is for another book.

Navigating the book

The book is organised principally to describe and explain how and why transnational companies use sport sponsorship to promote unhealthy consumption. The book can be read as a whole, but particular chapters can also be read individually depending on a reader's specific interest. References are provided at the end of each chapter.

The next chapter (Chapter 2) explores why sport sponsorship should be considered more closely by those who are concerned about people's health. The leading causes of death worldwide are non-communicable diseases, and yet those responsible for professional sport have allowed their nominally healthy activities to be colonised by those hawking junk food, sugary drinks, alcohol and tobacco. With mental health becoming of increasing concern, the rise of gambling marketing in sport has raised more recent issues. The chapter describes how commercial interests frame the argument that ill health is the responsibility of the individual, while underplaying the business practices which promote unhealthy consumption. The chapter concludes with a brief case study of Mountain Dew.

Chapter 3 describes how, although sport has always been commercial, the arrival of television led to new levels of commodification. This chapter provides an introduction to marketing in sport, provides definitions of key terms and introduces sports sponsorship. A description of the commercialisation of Australian Rules football over the last 50 years is provided for illustration.

Some academics argue that modern sport sponsorship was largely developed by the alcohol and tobacco industries. Both industries are certainly guilty of using sport to avoid regulations that prevented them from marketing their brands in more traditional ways. The tobacco industry in particular, having been banned from advertising on first British and then American television, used sport to continue to promote its brands until the World Health Organization's Framework Convention on Tobacco Control stopped this in 2005. Chapter 4 describes the impact and reach of tobacco sponsorship globally and its role in the development of modern sport sponsorship. It concludes with a case study of the Virginia Slims sponsored Women's Tennis Association events between 1970 and 1995.

The Olympics and the Fédération Internationale de Football Association (FIFA) World Cup have helped create the modern world of sport sponsorship. As mega-events, they also have attracted most attention from researchers and scholars. Chapter 5 examines the Olympics and the World Cup from a public health perspective, showing how brands such as Coca-Coca and Budweiser (part of AB InBev) have used these global extravaganzas to drive consumption of their products. As women's sport is now receiving more attention, the development of the women's World Cup is provided as an example of the growing commercialisation of women's football.

Chapter 6 takes a sociological approach to consider the commodification of modern sport and how this might impact on public health. The growth in value of broadcasting rights internationally is based on increased income from sport sponsorship and advertising and has led to the commodification of all elements of professional sport. In turn this has led to the transformation of the sports fan into a consumer. The chapter includes examples of unhealthy sponsorship from various sports including English football, New Zealand rugby union and NASCAR racing in the United States. It concludes with a more detailed economic and sociological consideration of the transformation of cricket internationally.

The establishment of the FA Premier League (now known as the English Premier League) in the 1992/1993 football season in the United Kingdom established a new business model and took professional football in Britain to new levels of exposure. It provided opportunities to commodify all aspects of the game. Since it was launched, the EPL has become the richest, most broadcast (and therefore watched) sports league in the twenty-first century. Chapter 7 provides a detailed case study of the Premier League and its member clubs. Gambling brands are the most prominent in club sponsorships, whilst the Premier League's own relationships with Coca-Cola and Cadbury (part of Mondelez International) are considered.

Chapter 8 describes the evolution of sports marketing from static signage to a wide variety of on- and off-site digital activations. Sport sponsorship is usually supplemented by related marketing activities which often cost more than the sponsorship itself. This chapter describes international marketing practices by the alcohol, gambling and food and beverage industries that are designed to increase the consumption of unhealthy products by developing strong relationships with sports fans through verbal and visual references to the emotion and passion of sport. It concludes with a case study of Red Bull, a brand which was launched in Austria in 1997 and has used a wide range of sports to promote consumption of its highly caffeinated and sugary soft drink.

In Chapter 9, I consider how and why sport should not be left to the commercial marketplace to self-regulate. The chapter includes a consideration of the ethics of sports sponsorship and marketing. Whilst it is recognised that sports governing bodies traditionally resist interference, claiming that sport and politics do not mix, and that governments collude in an imagined view of the past, there are opportunities and indeed requirements for regulation, particularly when sport is used so blatantly to promote the consumption of gambling, alcohol and food and beverages which are high in fat, salt and sugar. The reasons why those who hold economic capital in sport (club owners) might take a different position towards sport sponsorship from those who possess the cultural capital (fans) are considered. This chapter concludes with recommendations for the regulation of sport which should be considered by the World Health Organization, national governments and governing bodies of sport.

In the final chapter of the book, I make some closing remarks and consider briefly what healthy sport sponsorship might look like, with a brief consideration of other possible funding models.

References

Ashton, J. (2020) *Practising Public Health. An Eyewitness Account*, Oxford: Oxford University Press.

Baum, F. (2015) *The New Public Health*, Fourth ed., Melbourne: Oxford University Press.

Conn, D. (2016) 'Hillsborough inquests jury rules 96 victims were unlawfully killed', *The Guardian*, 26 April 2016, available: https://www.theguardian.com/uk-news/2016/apr/26/hillsborough-inquests-jury-says-96-victims-were-unlawfully-killed [accessed 18 May 2020].

European Healthy Stadia Network (2020) *Healthy Stadia Concept*, available: https://healthystadia.eu/healthy-stadia-concept/ [accessed 9 July 2020].

Haynes, R. (1995) *The Football Imagination: The Rise of Football Fanzine Culture*, Aldershot: Arena.

Ireland, R. (2021) *Commercial Determinants of Health in Sport. The Example of the English Premier League*, unpublished thesis (PhD), University of Glasgow.

Ireland, R., Bunn, C., Reith, G., Philpott, M., Capewell, S., Boyland, E. and Chambers, S. (2019) 'Commercial determinants of health: Advertising of alcohol and unhealthy foods during sporting events', *Bulletin of the World Health Organization*, 97, 290–295.

King, A. (2002) *The End of the Terraces. The Transformation of English Football in the 1990s*, Revised ed., London: Leicester University Press.

Krustrup, P. and Parnell, D. eds. (2020) *Football as Medicine. Prescribing Football for Global Health Promotion*, Abingdon: Routledge.

Nicholson, J. (2019) *Can We Have Our Football Back?*, Head.

Numerato, D. (2018) *Football Fans, Activism and Social Change*, Abingdon: Routledge.

Taylor, R. (1992) *Football and Its Fans. Supporters and Their Relations with the Game, 1885–1985.*, Leicester: Leicester University Press.

Tempany, A. (2016) *And the Sun Shines Now. How Hillsborough and the Premier League Changed Britain*, London: Faber & Faber.

Viggars, M., Curran, K. and Philpott, M. (2020) 'Tobacco-free stadia: A case study at the 2016 UEFA European Championships in France' in Krustrup, P. and Parnell, D., eds., *Football as Medicine. Prescribing Football for Global Health Promotion*, Abingdon: Routledge, 229–247.

Chapter 2

Public health and sport

The rise of non-communicable diseases

As life expectancy has increased, the leading cause of mortality in almost all countries in the world has become non-communicable diseases (NCDs) (Mathers and Bonita 2009; World Health Organization 2018b). These NCDs or chronic diseases include heart attacks and strokes, cancers, respiratory disease and diabetes. Mental illnesses are also increasingly prevalent, affecting physical health and potentially leading to depression, loneliness and anti-social behaviour (Whiteford et al. 2010; World Health Organization European Office 2019). The World Health Organization has estimated that NCDs kill 41 million people per year (World Health Organization 2018b). In contrast, on 4 January 2022, the WHO reported nearly 5.5 million deaths due to the coronavirus pandemic (World Health Organization 2022), albeit this is likely to be an underestimate as a result of the under-reporting of data. Further, many of those with chronic diseases are likely to experience worse effects from the virus (Nikoloski et al. 2021).

An understanding that medical care is not the principal driver of health (McKeown 1979) has accompanied the increase of NCDs. Two-thirds of NCD deaths are the result of tobacco and alcohol use, poor nutrition and insufficient physical activity (World Health Organization 2018b). Further, there is a social gradient in these deaths, with health being related to social position, and standards of health declining from the top to the bottom of society (Marmot and Wilkinson 2006). In considering the growing health inequalities experienced between countries, the WHO established a Commission on the Social Determinants of Health (CSDH 2008) to examine the social and economic policies which shaped the conditions in which people live and die. The Commission took a holistic view of health and argued that the social gradient of health between and within countries was caused by the "unequal distribution of power, income, goods, and services" (CSDH 2008 p.1). Given limited success in addressing these social determinants of health, some attention has moved to the activities of commercial interests under neoliberalism. Modern capitalism contributes to the burden of disease by the aggressive marketing of tobacco, alcohol and unhealthy food (Bakan 2005; Freudenberg 2021), leading to an increased consumption of these unhealthy commodities (Lencucha and Thow 2019).

DOI: 10.4324/9781003239734-2

The rise in the prevalence of NCDs has been accompanied by a global implementation of free-market economic policies, including the development of a capitalist culture featuring increasing commodity production and consumption (Sell and Williams 2020). Sport is an intrinsic part of this culture, being embedded in the social, political and economic structures of capitalism (Sage 1998; Scambler 2005; Smart 2007; Collins 2013; Lavalette 2013).

Industries such as alcohol and tobacco can impact on health not only through the direct marketing of their brands but also through their lobbying for sympathetic regulatory environments for their products (Lee et al. 2004; Savell et al. 2015). In low- and middle-income countries where public health regulation is weak, commodities such as tobacco, alcohol and ultra-processed food contribute directly to poor health (Islam and Hossain 2015). Thus, health harms caused by industrial epidemics of unhealthy commodities (Jahiel and Babor 2007; Jahiel 2008; Gilmore et al. 2011; Stuckler et al. 2012; Moodie et al. 2013; Collin and Hill 2016) are spread by transnational corporations using global markets. Whilst free-market advocates espouse the virtues of competition, it is increasingly the case that transnational corporations establish an oligopolistic position, such as Coca-Cola and Pepsi in the soft drinks industry (Harvey 2007), and seek to maintain their position in the marketplace using extensive marketing.

Poor diet, smoking and alcohol consumption are directly linked to non-communicable diseases such as heart disease, respiratory disease, common cancers and type 2 diabetes, which are the leading causes of premature death globally (Stuckler and Basu 2011; World Health Organization 2018b). Mental disorders are associated with major NCDs (World Health Organization European Office 2019), with the harmful use of alcohol a risk factor (World Health Organization 2018a). In addition, disordered gambling has become increasingly prevalent, contributing to poor mental health (Shaffer and Korn 2002; Wardle et al. 2019; Gambling Related Harm All Parliamentary Group 2020). The social determinants of health, or the conditions in which people live as affected by wider forces such as economic and social policies, are responsible for differences in individual health status (World Health Organization 2019). These forces include globalisation, or the ways in which businesses and people are becoming more connected, enabling the global promotion of unhealthy brands that leads to many negative health impacts (Labonté and Schrecker 2006).

The commercial determinants of health: the practices of transnational corporations and how they impact on health

> Health outcomes are determined by the influence of corporate activities on the social environment in which people live and work: namely the availability, cultural desirability, and prices of unhealthy products. The environment shapes the so-called lifeworlds, lifestyles, and choices of individual consumers – ultimately determining health outcomes.
>
> (Kickbusch et al. 2016 pp.e895–896)

The role of transnational corporations and their impact on health (Baum et al. 2016) has come under increasing scrutiny, with many transnational corporations having turnovers larger than national states' GDP (Baum 2015). A growing literature has examined the practices of transnational corporations and the commercial determinants of health (CDOH). Two of the first papers to use the term "commercial" or "corporate" determinants of health were Kickbusch (2012) and Millar (2013). The former described how corporate power combined with global marketing influenced political decision-making at the highest levels. In this example, FIFA overruled a Brazilian law prohibiting the sale of alcohol at sporting events by insisting on the sale of beer at the 2014 World Cup on behalf of its sponsor, Budweiser (Kickbusch 2012). Millar's description of corporate determinants of health included a wide variety of businesses that damaged health or the environment, including tobacco, alcohol, unhealthy foods and beverages, resource extraction and the electronic media. Millar argued for government intervention where he saw a "failure in market mechanism" (Millar 2013 p.327) in controlling the overconsumption of sugar, fat and salt resulting from the actions of the food and beverage sector, for example.

Developing the paradigm, Kickbusch et al. (2016) went on to define CDOH as "strategies and approaches used by the private sector to promote products and choices that are detrimental to health". As shown in Figure 2.1, corporate influence is exerted through four channels: marketing, supply chain, lobbying and corporate citizenship. In considering how transnational corporations use sport to promote unhealthy products and choices, this book focuses on marketing and sports sponsorship where sports fans may be considered as consumers (Da Silva and Las Casas 2017). Unhealthy commodity industries (UCIs) are able to market their brands through sport, using sponsorship to increase the cultural desirability and consumption of sugary drinks or gambling (Ireland and Viggars 2019). Corporate marketeers also direct their marketing at politicians and policymakers as well as consumers in order to ensure that the business environment is sympathetic to their interests (Hastings 2015).

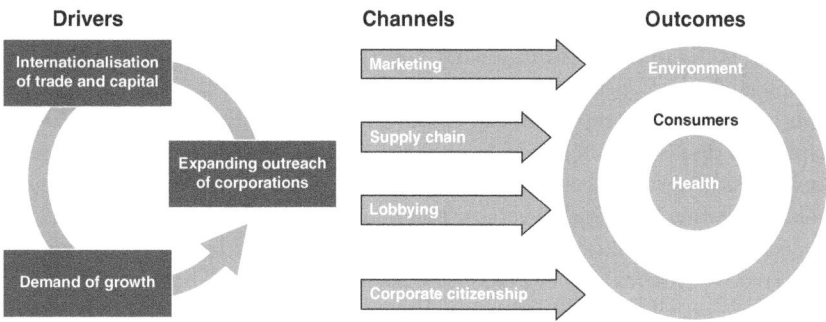

Figure 2.1 Strategies that determine the commercial determinants of health.
Source: Kickbusch et al. (2016).

The marketing of unhealthy brands to sports fans

de Lacy-Vawdon and Livingstone (2020) and Mialon (2020) wrote that research into CDOH has focused on the activities of the food, alcohol and tobacco industries. This is understandable when deaths from NCDs are attributable to 19 leading risk factors, of which five of the top eight are related to diet (high blood pressure, high blood glucose, obesity, high cholesterol and alcohol use), and the second highest risk factor is tobacco use (Stuckler and Basu 2011). Reports by Sir Michael Marmot undertaken both for the World Health Organisation (Commission on Social Determinants of Health 2008) and the UK government (The Marmot Review 2010) demonstrated that the unequal disease burden from these diseases was determined by "a toxic combination of poor social policies and programmes, unfair economic arrangements, and bad politics" (Commission on Social Determinants of Health 2008 p.1). A further report a decade later showed that, if anything, things had got worse in the United Kingdom (Marmot 2020). Whilst the public health approach adopted by governments is often focused on behaviours thought of as 'lifestyle' (Katikireddi et al. 2013), our choices are influenced by circumstances beyond our control, "not to mention billions spent on advertising and marketing seeking to influence our choices" (Marmot 2015 p.75).

30 years ago, Crompton (1993) wrote that the sponsors of sport were alcohol and tobacco companies which were using an association with healthy lifestyles to promote and normalise their products. The advertising and promotion of tobacco products in sport has largely been halted following extensive campaigning (Arnott et al. 2007) and effective national and international policies (Shibuya et al. 2003) including the WHO's Framework Convention on Tobacco Control (World Health Organization 2003). However, the tactics used by other industries such as 'Big Food', 'Big Soda' or 'Big Alcohol' are very similar to those used by 'Big Tobacco' (Freeman and Sindall 2019). Petticrew et al. (2017) referenced the tobacco industry when examining the tactics of the food, beverage, alcohol and gambling industries in using the concept of complexity to undermine effective public health policies. UCIs argue that the aetiology of NCDs is too complex to allow individual products to be blamed and that policy interventions cannot be effective in addressing complex problems.

There is discussion regarding what constitutes UCIs and indeed what conditions might be considered as NCDs, with this category now being expanded from four chronic diseases (cancer, cardiovascular disease, diabetes and chronic respiratory disease) to include mental health (Herrick 2020). Freudenberg, in his book *Lethal but Legal*, considered the corporate practices of the alcohol, automobile, firearms, food and beverage, pharmaceutical and tobacco industries. He argued that these industries had a profound influence on health behaviour and promoted what he called "hyperconsumption" (2016 p.xi). This he defined as a pattern of consumption directly linked to premature mortality and preventable diseases and contributing to "global epidemics of chronic disease and injuries" (2016 p.37).

de Lacy-Vawdon and Livingstone (2020) found that CDOH literature referenced the food, tobacco and alcohol industries most frequently. Five of the 32 texts they identified discussed the gambling industry. Knai *et al.* (2018) noted that whilst the gambling industry has received less attention than other UCIs as a driver of NCDs, it is associated with other risk factors such as alcohol consumption and that disabilities associated with gambling harms are similar to those associated with alcohol. A number of mental health disorders are often co-morbid with gambling problems (Shaffer and Korn 2002). Whilst there are contested medicalised discourses of addiction around gambling (Reith 2019), there is a growing consensus that gambling should be treated as a public health issue (*Lancet* 2017; Wardle *et al.* 2019; Cassidy 2020) and as a UCI with no agreed safe level of consumption. As with food, soft drinks and processed foods that are high in fat, sugar, salt and alcohol, the emphasis has been on addressing individual behaviour ('responsible gambling') rather than the environment which has led to gambling addictions (Reith 2019; Cassidy 2020; Orford 2020).

According to some commentators, the focus on tobacco as a product with a unique ability to cause harm has detracted from a wider understanding of the CDOH and their impact on the consumption of unhealthy products (Casswell 2013; West and Marteau 2013). A systems thinking approach (Meadows 2009) to inform policy action on unhealthy commodities is being called for, in contrast to traditional individual risk commodity approaches which can be fragmented and piecemeal (Knai *et al.* 2018). Milsom *et al.* (2020) argued that there is a challenge to achieve greater policy coherence for NCD prevention given that public health practitioners have often focused on individual behaviour change to reduce the consumption of unhealthy products rather than higher-level supply-side regulations. This book takes a systems approach to the potential harms caused by the marketing practices of UCIs in sport and will consider the practices of Big Tobacco, Food, Alcohol and Gambling.

As I have argued, the marketing strategies of UCIs impact on consumption and public health (Hawkins *et al.* 2018). These strategies include branding, advertising, promotion and the creation of new markets to increase sales (The Health Foundation 2020). Hastings (2012) argued that marketing textbooks lionise consumption at the expense of our health. Marketing includes public relations, merchandising and sponsorship as well as the promotion of brand consciousness and loyalty to develop brand relationships and relationship marketing (Hastings 2015). Hastings suggested that the increase in all forms of sports sponsorship in recent years shows "the power of innocence by association" (Hastings 2015 p.1051), whereby corporate marketers wish to add an emotional and psychological value to their brand through an association with sport. Relationship marketing is a perfect practice for sport, where clubs focus on their fans, treating them as customers/consumers, in order to improve their commercial income whilst reducing their dependence on success in the sporting field. These relationships have always existed in sport where owners and directors focus on establishing a close bond between fans and club (Bühler and Nufer 2013).

Sport has proved a willing vehicle for the marketing and globalisation of unhealthy brands by transnational corporations, whilst tobacco and alcohol executives have sought to circumvent marketing restrictions placed on them by governments wishing to address the social and health costs caused by the consumption of these legal products (Cornwell 1997, 2020). Collin (2003) has written of the globalisation of the tobacco industry and how it used technological developments to circumvent regulation and increase awareness of its brands, with its sponsorship of motor racing as an example of its tactics. Whilst tobacco industry sponsorship has been largely removed from sport, there is still considerable sport sponsorship by the alcohol, gambling, fast food and sugary drinks industries, which raises public health concerns (Kelly *et al.* 2010; Carter *et al.* 2013; Bunn *et al.* 2018; Dixon *et al.* 2019; Ireland *et al.* 2019). The London Olympic Games was criticised for its 'junk food' sponsors including Coca-Cola, McDonald's and Cadbury at a time of growing global obesity rates (Garde and Rigby 2012). Hastings noted the corporate takeover of the Olympics – "an event that should be a beacon of healthy activity not another shopping opportunity" (Hastings 2012 e5124).

Despite sport sponsorship being a key component of the marketing of UCIs, it receives little mention in the CDOH and public health literature. Ireland *et al.* (2019) described how the appeal of sport is used to promote brands and products that harm health. Hastings (2015) argued that brand exposure through entertainment (sport and screen-based entertainment) provided business benefits including publicity, favourable brand associations and promotional opportunities. Knai *et al.* (2018) gave the example of the shirt sponsorship of English Premier League teams by gambling companies as UCIs building alliances with others beyond their core business to create an appearance of larger support. The increase of all sports and entertainment sponsorship by corporate marketeers illustrates the marketing value of association with large sporting events. Jernigan (2009), in his consideration of the global alcohol industry, argued that public health research has not kept up with the ability of the industry to innovate in its marketing.

Commercial determinants, structure and agency

Lee and Crosbie (2020) argued that commercial interests have framed the argument that ill health is the responsibility of the individual, what Rose refers to as "responsibilization" (Rose 1999), deflecting attention away from the business practices and policies which create health inequalities (Schrecker and Bambra 2015; Douglas 2016).

Freudenberg (2016) described how multi-national consumer corporations have established an ideology through key public messaging which argues that individuals, not companies or governments, are responsible for their health and consumption choices. In this "corporate consumption ideology" (Freudenberg 2016 p.126), personal choice (described as 'lifestyle' in public health literature) is the major determinant of health; corporations are only responding to consumer demand; education is key to making informed choices; and government has no role in regulation. Corporate practices promote the consumption of unhealthy commodities through their marketing (Kickbusch et al. 2016) and any attempt to curtail the operation of free markets is commonly positioned as unnecessary regulation (Allen 2021). Whilst the environment we live in promotes unhealthy consumption, such as through marketing in sport, defenders of neoliberal capitalism argue that people are responsible for their health and should be blamed for their consuming practices (Baum 2015; Schrecker and Bambra 2015). Neoliberal society individualises responsibilities and requires individuals to manage their own risks (Rose 1999). Maani et al. (2020) argued that whilst the use of unhealthy commodities is strongly influenced by factors such as availability and advertising as part of a marketing mix, the focus in health policies is on individual 'lifestyles', as for example in UK obesity policy (Theis and White 2021). Greenfield (2011) described how a focus on personal responsibility enables industries to avoid their own responsibilities. These standpoints play well in neoliberal regimes such as in the United States, United Kingdom and Australia, where a focus on individual freedoms has constrained moves to protect health by introducing regulations to control the marketing of unhealthy commodities (Allen 2021). Individual choice and personal responsibility are, of course, desirable, but as we have seen in the example of tobacco industry marketing, choices are made in a constructed space where such choices may be manufactured and manipulated (Greenfield 2011).

Academics have compared the practices of the tobacco and food industry (Brownell and Warner 2009; Malik 2010) and argue that the tobacco industry had a strategy or "playbook" (Brownell and Warner 2009 p.259). This involved a series of actions which included influencing public opinion and lobbying against legislation and regulation. UCIs seek to promote the consumption of their brands whilst emphasising personal responsibility in this consumption. The tobacco industry's playbook will be explored in more depth in Chapter 4.

Case Study: Sugary drinks, sports sponsorship and health: the example of Mountain Dew

This book will provide many examples of 'unhealthy' sports sponsorship drawn from each of the UCIs identified previously. Sugary drinks are one of the greatest sources of added sugars in American (Harris et al. 2013), British (Public Health England and Food Standards Agency 2021) and most other global diets, contributing to the growing prevalence of diabetes, obesity and tooth decay internationally (World Health Organization 2017). The WHO reported that reduced consumption of sugary drinks would lead to savings in healthcare costs and that taxing sugar-sweetened beverages has been shown to benefit low-income households and children most (World Health Organization 2017). And yet food and beverage companies use sport to target consumers who often fall into these categories. Coca-Cola has a long history of associating its brands with sport, which is documented throughout this book (see Chapter 5 for the corporation's association with the Olympics, which began in 1928). In the United States, companies such as Coca-Cola (including Sprite, Powerade and Fanta), Dr Pepper Snapple Group (including 7 Up and Sunkist), Kraft Food (including Capri Sun) and PepsiCo (including Gatorade and Mountain Dew) contributed 63 per cent of all full-calorie soda and energy drinks advertisements appearing on American television in 2010 that were associated with sports sponsorship (including athletes, teams, leagues and events) (Harris *et al.* 2013). In 2013, Coca-Cola and PepsiCo spent a combined US$640 million on sponsorship in the United States alone; 84 per cent of PepsiCo's sponsorship expenditure went on sport (Nestle 2015). Industry reports on sponsorship evaluation are hard to come by, but an American report on NASCAR (National Association of Stock Car Auto Racing) sponsorship by a soft drink brand showed an increase in average weekly consumption (DeGaris and West 2012).

Mountain Dew is a lemon and lime sugary drink, originally trademarked in 1948, which became a PepsiCo product in 1964. Harris (2009), an Appalachian law professor, has written an excellent short history of the drink titled 'Undoing the Damage of the Dew'. She noted that between 1947 and 1996, Americans went from consuming on average two soft drinks per week to two per day. The population health effects of this increased consumption have been described above, and Harris documented the particular effect of Mountain Dew on teeth; the dental harm it causes has become known as 'Mountain Dew Mouth' (Gameau 2015). A single 12 fluid ounce can of Mountain Dew contains 46 grams (11 teaspoons) of added sugar (PepsiCo 2022). This is more than the daily amount of sugar recommended for an adult American male (37.5 grams or nine teaspoons) or female (25 grams or six teaspoons) (CDC 2021). The same-sized can contains 54milligrams of caffeine (equivalent to just under half that contained in a standard cup of coffee) with some research linking caffeine use to depression and anxiety in American schools (Luebbe and Bell 2009).

The marketing of Mountain Dew includes the sponsorship of action sports events to target young males in particular (Bennett *et al.* 2009). PepsiCo has sponsored the Dew Tour from 2005, a showcase of action sports ranging from BMX riding to snowboarding (Belzer 2014). The sponsorship works. Browne asserted that increasing sales of Mountain Dew can be linked to its association with these non-traditional extreme sports (Browne 2004). Further, Dees *et al.* (2010) explored the effects of fan loyalty, goodwill and brand attitude on the purchase intentions of fans at a Dew Action Sports Tour held in Orlando, Florida. As the sponsors (Mountain Dew and Sony PlayStation) no doubt hoped, the event's spectators developed positive feelings and attitudes towards their products, increasing their intentions to purchase. Mountain Dew's focus on a targeted male audience is reinforced by its sponsorship of the North American Basketball League (NBA) (Carp 2021), of which 63 per cent of American men claim to be fans in contrast to 38 per cent of women (Gough 2021). Sport's traditional male audience is consistently targeted by soft drink and energy drink companies, and this will be returned to throughout this book. Red Bull, in particular, has a very similar marketing strategy to Mountain Dew (Tejwani 2020).

References

Allen, L.N. (2021) 'Commercial determinants of global health' in Kickbusch, I., Ganten, D. and Moeti, M., eds., *Handbook of Global Health*, Cham: Springer International Publishing, 1275–1310.

Arnott, D., Dockrell, M., Sandford, A. and Willmore, I. (2007) 'Comprehensive smoke-free legislation in England: How advocacy won the day', *Tobacco Control*, 16, 423–428.

Bakan, J. (2005) *The Corporation. The Pathological Pursuit of Profit and Power*, London: Constable.

Baum, F. (2015) *The New Public Health*, Fourth ed., Melbourne: Oxford University Press.

Baum, F.E., Sanders, D.M., Fisher, M., Anaf, J., Freudenberg, N., Friel, S., Labonté, R., London, L., Monteiro, C., Scott-Samuel, A. and Sen, A. (2016) 'Assessing the health impact of transnational corporations: Its importance and a framework', *Globalization and Health*, 12(27).

Belzer, J. (2014) 'Action sports sponsorship the life blood of mountain dew', *Forbes*, 16 December 2014, available: https://www.forbes.com/sites/jasonbelzer/2014/12/16/action-sports-sponsorship-the-life-blood-of-mountain-dew/?sh=49b5cd922fdf [accessed 6 January 2022].

Bennett, G., Ferreira, M., Lee, J. and Polite, F. (2009) 'The role of involvement in sports and sport spectatorship in sponsor's brand use: The case of Mountain Dew and action sports sponsorship', *Sport Marketing Quarterly*, 18(1), 14–24.

Browne, D. (2004) *Amped: How Big Air, Big Dollars, and a New Generation Took Sports to the Extreme*, New York: Bloomsbury.

Brownell, K.D. and Warner, K.E. (2009) 'The perils of ignoring history: Big tobacco played dirty and millions died. How similar is big food?', *The Millbank Quarterly*, 87(1), 259–294.

Bűhler, A. and Nufer, G. (2013) *Relationship Marketing in Sport*, Abingdon: Routledge.

Bunn, C., Ireland, R., Minton, J., Holman, D., Philpott, M., & Chambers, S. (2018) 'Shirt sponsorship by gambling companies in the English and Scottish Premier Leagues: Global reach and public health concerns'. *Soccer and Society*, 20(6), 824–835.

Carp, S. (2021) 'NBA and PepsiCo renew sponsorship deal ahead of All-Star Weekend', *SportsProMedia*, 2 March 2021, available: https://www.sportspromedia.com/news/nba-pepsico-sponsorship-deal-renewal-all-star-weekend/ [accessed 6 January 2022].

Carter, M.-A., Signal, L., Edwards, R., Hoek, J. and Maher, A. (2013) 'Food, fizzy and football: Promoting unhealthy food and beverages through sport - a New Zealand case study', *BMC Public Health*, 13(126), 1–7.

Cassidy, R. (2020) *Vicious Games. Capitalism and Gambling*, London: Pluto Press.
Casswell, S. (2013) 'Vested interests in addiction research and policy. Why do we not see the corporate interests of the alcohol industry as clearly as we see those of the tobacco industry?', *Addiction*, 108, 680–685.
CDC (2021) *Get the Facts: Added Sugars*, Washington, DC, available: https://www.cdc.gov/nutrition/data-statistics/added-sugars.html [accessed 6 January 2022].
Collin, J. (2003) 'Think global, smoke local: Transnational tobacco companies and cognitive globalization' in Lee, K., ed., *Health Impacts of Globalization. Towards Global Governance*, Basingstoke: Palgrave Macmillan.
Collin, J. and Hill, S. (2016) 'Industrial epidemics and inequalities: The commercial sector as a structural driver of inequalities in non-communicable diseases' in Smith, K. E., Hill, S. and Bambra, C., eds., *Health Inequalities. Critical Perspectives*, Oxford: Oxford University Press.
Collins, T. (2013) *Sport in Capitalist Society. A Short History*, Abingdon: Routledge.
Commission on Social Determinants of Health (2008) *Closing the Gap in a Generation. Health Equity through Action on the Social Determinants of Health*, Geneva: World Health Organization.
Cornwell, T.B. (1997) 'The use of sponsorship-linked marketing by tobacco firms: International public policy issues', *The Journal of Consumer Affairs*, 31(2), 238–254.
Cornwell, T.B. (2020) *Sponsorship in Marketing. Effective Partnerships in Sports, Arts and Events*, Second ed., Abingdon: Routledge.
Crompton, J.L. (1993) 'Sponsorship of sport by tobacco and alcohol companies: A review of the issues', *Journal of Sport & Social Issues*, 73, 148–167.
CSDH (2008) *Closing the Gap in a Generation: Health Equity through Action on the Social Determinants of Health. Final Report of the Commission on Social Determinants of Health*, Geneva: World Health Organization.
Da Silva, E.C. and Las Casas, A.L. (2017) 'Sport fans as consumers: An approach to sport marketing', *British Journal of Marketing Studies*, 5(4), 36–48.
de Lacy-Vawdon, C. and Livingstone, C. (2020) 'Defining the commercial determinants of health: A systematic review', *BMC Public Health*, 20(1), 1022, available: http://dx.doi.org/10.1186/s12889-020-09126-1.
Dees, W., Hall, T., Tsuji, Y. and Bennett, G. (2010) 'Examining the effects of fan loyalty and goodwill on consumer perceptions of brands at an action sports event', *Journal of Sponsorship*, 4(1), 38–50.
DeGaris, L. and West, C. (2012) 'The effects of sponsorship activation on the sales of a major soft drink brand', *Journal of Brand Strategy*, 1(4), 403–412.
Dixon, H., Lee, A. and Scully, M. (2019) 'Sports sponsorship as a cause of obesity', *Current Obesity Reports*, 8, 480–494.
Douglas, M. (2016) 'Beyond 'health': Why don't we tackle the cause of health inequalities?' in Smith, K. E., Hill, S. and Bambra, C., eds., *Health Inequalities. Critical Perspectives*, Oxford: Oxford University Press.
Freeman, B. and Sindall, C. (2019) 'Countering the commercial determinants of health: Strategic challenges for public health', *Public Health Research & Practice*, 29(3), e2931917.
Freudenberg, N. (2016) *Lethal but Legal. Corporations, Consumption and Protecting Public Health*, Oxford: Oxford University Press.
Freudenberg, N. (2021) *At What Cost. Modern Capitalism and the Future of Health*, New York: Oxford University Press.

Gambling Related Harm All Parliamentary Group (2020) *Final Report of the Inquiry into Online Gambling Harm*, London, available: http://www.grh-appg.com/wp-content/uploads/2020/06/Online-report-Final-June16-2020.pdf [accessed 12 October 2020].

Gameau, D. (2015) *That Sugar Film*, Australia, available http://www.samuelgoldwynfilms.com/wp-content/uploads/2017/01/That-Sugar-Film_USPressNotes.pdf [accessed 6 January 2022].

Garde, A. and Rigby, N. (2012) 'Going for gold - Should responsible governments raise the bar on sponsorship of the Olympic Games and other sporting events by food and beverage companies?', *Communications Law*, 17(No 2), 42–49.

Gilmore, A.B., Savell, E. and Collin, J. (2011) 'Public health, corporations and the new responsibility deal: Promoting partnerships with vectors of disease?', *Journal of Public Health*, 33(1), 2–4.

Gough, C. (2021) *NBA Interest Level in the U.S. 2021, By Gender*, available: https://www.statista.com/statistics/1098381/national-basketball-association-interest-gender/ [accessed 6 January 2022].

Greenfield, K. (2011) *The Myth of Choice: Personal Responsibility in a World of Limits*, Yale University Press.

Harris, J.L., Schwartz, M.B. and Brownell, K.D. (2013) *Sugary Drinks Food Advertising to Children and Teens Score. Evaluating Sugary Drink Nutrition and Marketing to Youth*, Yale Rudd Center for Food Policy & Obesity, available: http://milfordyouthcenter.org/wp-content/uploads/2013/07/SugaryDrinkFACTS_ReportSummary.pdf [accessed 6 January 2022].

Harris, P.N. (2009) 'Undoing the Damage of the Dew', *Appalachian Journal of Law*, 9(1), 53–120.

Harvey, D. (2007) *A Brief History of Neoliberalism*, Oxford: Oxford University Press.

Hastings, G. (2012) 'Why corporate power is a public health priority', *British Medical Journal*, 345(7871), 26–29.

Hastings, G. (2015) 'Public health and the value of disobedience', *Public Health*, 129, 1046–1054.

Hawkins, B., Holden, C., Eckhardt, J. and Lee, K. (2018) 'Reassessing policy paradigms: A comparison of the global tobacco and alcohol industries', *Global Public Health*, 13(1), 1–19.

Herrick, C. (2020) 'The optics of noncommunicable diseases: From lifestyle to environmental toxicity', *Sociology of Health & Illness*, 42(5), 1014–1059.

Ireland, R., Bunn, C., Reith, G., Philpott, M., Capewell, S., Boyland, E. and Chambers, S. (2019) 'Commercial determinants of health: Advertising of alcohol and unhealthy foods during sporting events', *Bulletin of the World Health Organization*, 97, 290–295.

Ireland, R. and Viggars, M. (2019) 'Is football bad for your health? How English Premier League clubs are used to promote energy drinks, booze and betting', available: https://healthystadia.eu/is-football-bad-for-your-health/ [accessed 14 April 2020].

Islam, S. and Hossain, T. (2015) *Social Justice in the Globalization of Production*, London: Palgrave Macmillan.

Jahiel, R.I. (2008) 'Corporation-induced diseases, upstream epidemiologic surveillance, and urban health', *Journal of Urban Health*, 85(4), 517.

Jahiel, R.I. and Babor, T.F. (2007) 'Industrial epidemics, public health advocacy and the alcohol industry: Lessons from other fields', *Addiction*, 102, 1335–1339.

Jernigan, D.H. (2009) 'The global alcohol industry: An overview', *Addiction*, 104 (Suppl. 1), 6–12.

Katikireddi, S.V., Martin, H., Smith, K.E. and Williams, G. (2013) 'Health inequalities: The need to move beyond bad behaviours', *Journal of Epidemiology and Community Health*, 67(9), 715–716.

Kelly, B., Halford, J.C., Boyland, E.J., Chapman, K., Bautista-Castaño, I., Berg, C., Caroli, M., Cook, B., Coutinho, J.G., Effertz, T., Grammatikaki, E., Keller, K., Leung, R., Manios, Y., Monteiro, R., Pedley, C., Prell, H., Raine, K., Recine, E., Serra-Majem, L., Singh, S. and Summerbell, C. (2010) 'Television food advertising to children: A global perspective', *American Journal of Public Health*, 100(9), 1730–1736.

Kickbusch, I. (2012) 'Addressing the interface of the political and commercial determinants of health', *Health Promotion International*, 27(4), 427–428.

Kickbusch, I., Allen, L., & Franz, C. (2016) 'The commercial determinants of health'. *The Lancet Global Health*, 4(12), e895–e896.

Knai, C., Petticrew, M., Mays, N., Capewell, S., Cassidy, R., Cummins, S., Eastmure, E., Fafard, P., Hawkins, B., Jensen, J.D., Katikireddi, S.V., Mwatsama, M., Orford, J. and Weishaar, H. (2018) 'Systems thinking as a framework for analyzing commercial determinants of health', *The Milbank Quarterly*, 96(3), 472–498, available: http://dx.doi.org/10.1111/1468-0009.12339.

Labonté, R. and Schrecker, T. (2006) *Globalization and Social Determinants of Health: Analytic and Strategic Review Paper*, Ottawa: Institute of Population Health, available: https://www.who.int/social_determinants/resources/globalization.pdf?ua=1 [accessed 12 October 2020].

Lancet (2017) 'Problem gambling is a public health concern', *Lancet*, Sep 2; 390 (10098), 913. doi:10.1016/S0140-6736(17)32333-4.

Lavalette, M. ed. (2013) *Capitalism and Sport: Politics, Protest, People and Play*, London: Bookmarks.

Lee, K. and Crosbie, E. (2020) 'Understanding structure and agency as commercial determinants of health. Comment on "How Neoliberalism Is Shaping the Supply of Unhealthy Commodities and What This Means for NCD Prevention"', *IJHPM*, 9(7), 315–318.

Lee, K., Gilmore, A.B. and Collin, J. (2004) 'Looking inside the tobacco industry: Revealing insights from the Guildford Depository', *Addiction*, 99, 394–397.

Lencucha, R. and Thow, A.M. (2019) 'How neoliberalism is shaping the supply of unhealthy commodities and what this means for NCD prevention', *International Journal of Health Policy and Management*, 8(9), 514–520.

Luebbe, A.M. and Bell, D.J. (2009) 'Mountain Dew® or mountain don't?: A pilot investigation of caffeine use parameters and relations to depression and anxiety symptoms in 5th- and 10th-grade students', *The Journal of School Health*, 79(8), 380–387, available: http://dx.doi.org/10.1111/j.1746-1561.2009.00424.x.

Maani, N., McKee, M., Petticrew, M. and Galea, S. (2020) 'Corporate practices and the health of populations: A research and translational agenda', *The Lancet*, 5(February 2020).

Malik, R. (2010) *Catch Me If You Can: Big Food Using Big Tobacco's Playbook? Applying the Lessons Learned from Big Tobacco to Attack the Obesity Epidemic*, Internal Harvard Library Report, unpublished.

Marmot, M. (2015) *The Health Gap. The Challenge of an Unequal World*, London: Bloomsbury Publishing.

Marmot, M. (2020) 'Health equity in England: The Marmot review 10 years on', *BMJ*, 368, m693, available: http://dx.doi.org/10.1136/bmj.m693.

Marmot, M. and Wilkinson, R.G. eds. (2006) *Social Determinants of Health*, Second ed., Oxford: Oxford University Press.

Mathers, C. and Bonita, R. (2009) 'Current global health status' in Beaglehole, R. and Bonita, R., eds., *Global Public Health. A New Era*, Oxford: Oxford University Press.

McKeown, T. (1979) *The Role of Medicine: Dream Mirage or Nemesis?*, Oxford: Basil Blackwell.

Meadows, D., H. (2009) *Thinking in Systems*, Abingdon: Earthscan.

Mialon, M. (2020) 'An overview of the commercial determinants of health'. *Globalization and Health*, 16(1), 1–7.

Millar, J.S. (2013) 'The corporate determinants of health: How big business affects our health, and the need for government action!', *Canadian Journal of Public Health*, 104(4), e327–e329.

Milsom, P., Smith, R. and Walls, H. (2020) 'A systems thinking approach to inform coherent policy action for NCD prevention: Comment on "How Neoliberalism Is Shaping the Supply of Unhealthy Commodities and What This Means for NCD Prevention".', *International Journal of Health Policy and Management*, 9(5), 212–214.

Moodie, R., Stuckler, D., Monteiro, C., Sheron, N., Neal, B., Thamarangsi, T., Lincoln, P. and Casswell, S. (2013) 'Profits and pandemics: Prevention of harmful effects of tobacco, alcohol, and ultra-processed food and drink industries', *Lancet*, 381, 670–679.

Nestle, M. (2015) *Soda Politics. Taking On Big Soda (and Winning)*, Oxford: Oxford University Press.

Nikoloski, Z., Alqunaibet, A.M., Alfawaz, R.A., Almudarra, S.S., Herbst, C.H., El-Saharty, S., Alsukait, R. and Algwizani, A. (2021) 'Covid-19 and non-communicable diseases: Evidence from a systematic literature review', *BMC Public Health*, 21(1), 1068, available: http://dx.doi.org/10.1186/s12889-021-11116-w.

Orford, J. (2020) *The Gambling Establishment. Challenging the Power of the Modern Gambling Industry and Its Allies*, Abingdon: Routledge.

PepsiCo (2022) *The Facts about Your Favorite Beverages (US): MTN DEW*, available: https://www.pepsicobeveragefacts.com/Home/Product?formula=44316*01*01-10&form=RTD&size=12 [accessed 6 January 2022].

Petticrew, M., Katikireddi, S.V., Knai, C., Cassidy, R., Hessari, N.M., Thomas, J. and Weishaar, H. (2017) '"Nothing can be done until everything is done": The use of complexity arguments by food, beverage, alcohol and gambling industries', *Journal of Epidemiology and Community Health*, 71, 1078–1083.

Public Health England and Food Standards Agency (2021) *National Diet and Nutrition Survey: Diet, Nutrition and Physical Activity in 2020. A Follow Up Study during COVID-19*, London, available: https://assets.publishing.service.gov.uk/government/uploads/system/uploads/attachment_data/file/1019663/Follow_up_stud_2020_main_report.pdf [accessed 27 June 2022].

Reith, G. (2019) *Addictive Consumption. Capitalism, Modernity and Excess*, Abingdon: Routledge.

Rose, N. (1999) *Powers of Freedom: Reframing Political Thought*, Cambridge: Cambridge University Press.

Sage, G.H. (1998) *Power and Ideology in American Sport*, Second ed., Champaign: Human Kinetics.

Savell, E., Fooks, G. and Gilmore, A.B. (2015) 'How does the alcohol industry attempt to influence marketing regulations? A systematic review', *Addiction*, 111, 18–32.

Scambler, G. (2005) *Sport and Society. History, Power and Culture*, Maidenhead: Open University Press.
Schrecker, T. and Bambra, C. (2015) *How Politics Makes Us Sick. Neoliberal Epidemics*, London: Palgrave Macmillan.
Sell, S.K. and Williams, O.D. (2020) 'Health under capitalism: A global political economy of structural pathogenesis', *Review of International Political Economy*, 27(1), 1–25.
Shaffer, H.J. and Korn, D.A. (2002) 'Gambling and related mental disorders: A public health analysis', *Annual Review of Public Health*, 23(1), 171–212.
Shibuya, K., Ciecierski, C., Guindon, E., Bettcher, D.W., Evans, D.B. and Murray, C.J.L. (2003) 'WHO framework convention on tobacco control: Development of an evidence based global public health treaty', *BMJ*, 327, 154–157.
Smart, B. (2007) 'Not playing around: Global capitalism, modern sport and consumer culture' in Giulianotti, R. and Robertson, R., eds., *Globalization and Sport*, Oxford: Blackwell Publishing.
Stuckler, D. and Basu, S. (2011) 'Evaluating the health burden of chronic diseases' in Stuckler, D. and Siegel, K., eds., *Sick Societies. Responding to the Global Challenge of Chronic Disease*, Oxford: Oxford University Press.
Stuckler, D., McKee, M., Ebrahim, S. and Basu, S. (2012) 'Manufacturing epidemics: The role of global producers in increased consumption of unhealthy commodities including processed foods, alcohol, and tobacco', *PLoS Medicine*, 9(6), e1001235.
Tejwani, K. (2020) *Wings of Change: How the World's Biggest Energy Drink Manufacturer Made a Mark in Football*, Worthing: Pitch Publishing.
The Health Foundation (2020) *Rapid Evidence Review: The Commercial Determinants of Health*, Internal Report, unpublished.
The Marmot Review (2010) *Fair Society, Healthy Lives*, available: www.ucl.ac.uk/marmotreview [accessed 30 August 2020].
Theis, D.R.Z. and White, M. (2021) 'Is obesity policy in England fit for purpose? Analysis of government strategies and policies, 1992–2020', *The Milbank Quarterly*, 99(1), 126–170, available: https://dx,doi.org/10.1111/1468-0009.12498.
Wardle, H., Reith, G., Langham, E. and Rogers, R.D. (2019) 'Gambling and public health: We need policy action to prevent harm', *BMJ*, 365, l1807, available: http://dx.doi.org/10.1136/bmj.l1807.
West, R. and Marteau, T. (2013) 'Commentary on Casswell (2013): The commercial determinants of health"', *Addiction*, 108, 686–687.
Whiteford, H.A., Degenhardt, L., Rehm, J., Baxter, A., Ferrari, A.J., Erskine, H.E., Charlson, F.J., Norman, R.E., Flaxman, A.D., Johns, N., Burstein, R., Murray, C.J.L. and Vos, T. (2010) 'Global burden of disease attributable to mental and substance use disorders: Findings from the Global Burden of Disease Study 2010', *The Lancet*, 382(9904), 1575–1586.
World Health Organization (2003) *WHO Framework Convention on Tobacco Control*, Geneva: WHO, available: https://www.who.int/fctc/text_download/en/ [accessed 23 August 2020].
World Health Organization (2017) *Taxes on Sugary Drinks: Why Do It?*, Geneva, available: https://apps.who.int/iris/bitstream/handle/10665/260253/WHO-NMH-PND-16.5Rev.1-eng.pdf;sequence=1#:~:text=People%20who%20consume%20sugary%20drinks, consume%20such%20drinks(5).&text=The%20number%20of%20people%20with, million%20in%202014(6). [accessed 6 January 2022].

World Health Organization (2018a) *Alcohol: Fact Sheet*, Geneva, available: https://www.who.int/news-room/fact-sheets/detail/alcohol [accessed 12 October 2020].

World Health Organization (2018b) *Noncommunicable Diseases. Fact Sheet*, available: https://www.who.int/news-room/fact-sheets/detail/noncommunicable-diseases [accessed 30 June 2020].

World Health Organization (2019) *Social Determinants of Health*, Geneva, available: https://www.who.int/social_determinants/sdh_definition/en/ [accessed 12 October 2020].

World Health Organization (2022) *WHO Coronavirus (COVID-19) Dashboard*, available: https://covid19.who.int/ [accessed 5 January 2022].

World Health Organization European Office (2019) *Mental Health: Fact Sheet*, available: https://www.euro.who.int/__data/assets/pdf_file/0004/404851/MNH_FactSheet_ENG.pdf?ua=1 [accessed 30 June 2020].

Chapter 3

An introduction to advertising and marketing in sport

The commercial origins of sport

Sport has been commercial since "people would pay to see a performance" (McComb 2004 p.108), and brands were using sport to market their products in the nineteenth century. The historical origins of all sports are contested, with narratives sometimes chosen to suit (Vamplew 2021); rugby is an obvious example through the origin myth developed around William Webb Ellis (Allison and MacLean 2012). Academics such as Collins (2013; 2019) argue that sport was a product of capitalism developed as a part of the commercialised leisure industry of the nineteenth century. Across Britain, North America and Australia, sport developed following industrialisation, accompanied by urban growth and better transport infrastructure (Pomfret 2016). An early argument in British football might be characterised as an initial struggle between the keepers of the sport as leisure and those who wanted to make the game commercial (Mason (1980). At the end of the nineteenth century, as football grew rapidly in popularity, there were tensions between the 'Corinthian' principles of the south of England (Horne et al. 1999) as personified by the 'Gentleman Amateur' (Holt 1992) and the industrialists and property owners in the North and Midlands (Giulianotti 1999). The latter sought to pay their players and faced with a dangerous division, the Football Association voted to legalise professionalism in 1885 (Collins 2013; Russell 2013).

Football clubs from Lancashire and the Midlands began to draw in large enough crowds to justify erecting stands and enclosures and charging for admission (Russell 2013). The FA Cup final of 1872 had a crowd of 2,000; in 1888, there were 17,000 spectators at Kennington Oval. When the final was held at Crystal Palace, crowds rose from 45,000 in 1895 to 69,000 in 1900, and, further, to 120,000 in 1913 (Walvin 1994). The size of crowds was solely limited by the capacity of stadiums (Walvin 1994). Baseball went through a similar process of transition from amateur to professional as gate money gradually transformed it after the American Civil War into what Seymour called a "commercialized amusement business" (1989 (1960) p.3). Advertisers were quick to see the benefits of promoting their products to what was then a largely male audience of sports fans.

DOI: 10.4324/9781003239734-3

The actual point at which sports sponsorship began is arguable. If it is considered a form of philanthropy or patronage, it can be traced back to Roman times when rulers provided entertainment in amphitheatres as public spectacle (Gruneau 2017). Cricket has been seen as a pioneer in sport sponsorship, and the first example of modern sponsorship is often given as the Australian catering company Spiers and Pond, which supported the first England cricket tour of Australia in 1861/1862. It is claimed that the company made a profit of £11,000, a considerable sum in those days (The Central Council of Physical Recreation 1983).

Unhealthy commodity industries were already seeing opportunities for marketing to the large following that British football was attracting over a hundred years ago. The strategy of claiming health benefits for food products (a common technique in today's marketing) was advanced in 1898 when Bovril (a salty meat extract product developed in the 1870s) drew heavily on its claimed sporting benefits in promoting its association with Nottingham Forest, the FA Cup winners in 1898 (Hadley 1970). A testimonial from the club stated, "During our training for the ENGLISH CUP TIES we used Bovril very freely. We consider it was A VERY IMPORTANT FACTOR in giving our men strength and staying power" (Hadley 1970 p.88). Bovril used endorsements from sportsmen of all kinds for many years in linking its 'fluid extract of beef' to athletic prowess and good health, and the warming drink is still available at the majority of British football grounds to this day. Gaining endorsements from athletes and celebrities is still a very simple form of advertising which has remained popular. Wheaties, an American breakfast cereal which is relatively high in salt content, has used Babe Ruth, Joe DiMaggio, Jackie Robinson, Chris Evert, Michael Johnson, Tiger Woods and Serena Williams to promote its 'breakfast of champions' from the 1920s to the present day (Masterman 2011).

Gambling has long been associated with recreational pastimes and was popular in the British leisure culture of the eighteenth and nineteenth centuries amongst all classes (Clapson 1992). Mason (1980) argued that the ex-public schoolboys and middle-class professionals who dominated the FA at the end of the nineteenth century were concerned to avoid any concerns about betting and corruption, and players and officials were thus banned from betting on games in 1892 (Inglis 1988). Despite this ban, there was a growing practice amongst the sporting press of offering the opportunity to forecast the results of matches for a small stake in the hope of a big cash prize (Mason 1980; Clapson 1992). This coupon-betting, based on bookmakers issuing coupons, developed rapidly in the first decade of the twentieth century in particular areas of England such as Lancashire and Yorkshire (Mason 1980; Clapson 1992).

The expansion of football coupon-betting met opposition. Hill wrote that politicians and religious leaders regarded "betting by working people as an irrational and feckless pursuit liable to lead to poverty" (2002 p.39). Football administrators were concerned about the impact of gambling on the image and probity of football. By 1910, betting was banned in British football grounds and any player or official taking part in coupon-betting was permanently suspended (Inglis 1988). Newspapers continued to promote coupon-betting to boost their circulation until this was also banned in 1928 (Inglis 1988). Clapson (1992) characterised the time between the early to mid-nineteenth century and the mid-twentieth century as an evolution from a pre-industrial sporting and betting culture into a mass commercialised gambling market based on bookmakers and newspapers (the 'sporting press').

The alcohol business was also closely involved in British football from a very early stage (Mason 1980; Collins and Vamplew 2002). Public houses played an important part in the origin of some football clubs, both in terms of providing changing facilities for players before a game, and in offering fields to play on. Pubs provided these spaces, as well as prizes and gambling facilities, in return for the opportunity to sell beer (Collins and Vamplew 2002). Sports stadiums offered locations for advertising aimed at the growing crowds attending matches. In British football, signage began to appear on stands and gradually on perimeter boards. Tobacco company brands were quick to associate themselves with sport and might be considered the early innovators in exploiting the potential of its mass cultural appeal (this is fully explored in the next chapter). But the alcohol industry also emphasised a relationship between sport and beer drinking, in particular. In the early years of professional baseball, American beer barons bought clubs both to advertise their products and to find community approval. Jacob Ruppert Jr, of the brewing company of the same name, owned the New York Yankees from 1915 to 1939 and notably opposed his fellow tycoon, William Wrigley, buying into baseball's National League in case his ownership commercialised chewing gum (Michener 1976). August A. Busch Jr, the president of the Anheuser-Busch brewery, purchased the St Louis Cardinals baseball team in 1953 (Stainback 1997), with the stadium being named Busch Stadium in 1954 (Carruthers 2014), an early example of struggles between fans seeking to retain the cultural heritage of their team and owners seeking to maximise the commercial potential of stadium naming rights. Between 1953 and 1978, Anheuser-Busch brewery sales grew from under 6 million to 35 million barrels (Stainback 1997), growth partly attributed to the corporation's association with baseball (Johnson 1988). In the NFL, the 'Bud Bowl' was created as an advertising gimmick by Anheuser-Busch in 1989, using the Super Bowl to launch an advertising campaign featuring a mock football game between bottles of Bud and Bud Lite (Crepeau 2020). This proved very successful as Super Bowl television audiences soured. Anheuser-Busch's (now AB InBev) advertising spend in sport has continued until today and the relationship between the alcohol industry and sport will be regularly considered throughout this book.

Sport's commercial potential grew after the Second World War, with television and sponsorship opening up new economic possibilities in the 1960s (Whannel 1986). Television ownership grew rapidly; only 9 per cent of Americans owned a television set in 1950, but 93 per cent had one by 1965 (McComb 2004). Having been resistant initially to football being broadcast live on television, the Football

League in England and Wales gave in to commercial pressures and permitted the screening of live football in 1983, which in turn encouraged shirt sponsorship, increasing the sponsorship potential of the elite clubs (Whannel 1986, 2002). The relationship between the media and sport has been apparent since the nineteenth century when newspapers first brought reports of matches and sporting events to the public, thus boosting their own readership (Domeneghetti 2017). The development of television technology and televised sport helped to shape the media industry structure (Gratton et al. 2012). ABC launched the first networked sports division in the United States in 1959, taking it the top of viewer ratings by 1976.

Shirt (also called uniform or jersey) sponsorship, in which a brand name and/or logo is displayed on the front of players' shirts, has become a lucrative source of income for clubs and the principal marketing outlet in football (Chanavat et al. 2017). Other sports, such as motor racing, have also been quick to display logos on equipment as well as uniforms (Carey 2020). A brand is more fully described below but, in its simplest and earliest form, it was a sign of ownership, such as denoting that an animal belonged to someone by placing a mark either directly or indirectly on to it. When used to designate people, as by the Nazis or by slaveowners, branding is stigmatised and considered abhorrent (Bastos and Levy 2012). It is worth remembering this when considering the story of Uruguayan football legend Obdulio Varela, a man of colour born in a poor area of Montevideo. Varela was captain of the first football club to have a sponsor's name on its shirt, Peñarol of Montevideo (Allen 2014), in 1954/55. He refused to wear the new shirt, saying, "They used to drag us blacks around by rings in our noses. Those days are gone" (Galeano 2013 (1995) p.108). Peñarol took the field with ten players wearing the sponsored shirts, whilst Varela wore an old shirt. He did, however, agree to a sponsorship proposal from the National Beer Factory during a strike over players' freedom on movement and wages in 1948/1949. The money was donated to poor children (Bassorelli 2012 pp.58–71). Sports stars have also refused to wear sponsored shirts in more recent times, such as Sonny Bill Williams, a former New Zealand international rugby player, who refused to wear shirts displaying any branding relating to banks, alcohol or gambling (*BOL News* 2020), most recently in 2019.

In Europe, an alcohol company, Jägermeister, was the first sponsor to have a logo on a football team's shirt, and the German Bundesliga club Eintracht Braunschweig carried the liquor brand in 1973 (Unlucan 2015). Following initial opposition from the Football Association, shirt sponsorship was permitted in England from 1977, with Liverpool signing a £100,000 two-year shirt-sponsorship deal with Hitachi, the Japanese electrical company, in 1979 (Planet Football 2017). By the 1980s and 1990s, alcohol companies were commonly represented on club shirts in England; examples included Holsten Pils (Tottenham), Fosters (Norwich City) and Shipstones (Nottingham Forest) (Billingham 2015). Shirt sponsorship came much later to the United States, with the National Basketball Association (NBA), for example, only allowing such sponsorship in 2017 (Carey 2020).

The alcohol, fast food, gambling and tobacco industries have always been involved in sport, but it is the commodified sport of today which takes unhealthy marketing to an entirely new level. Every space in stadia and on athletes' playing uniforms is considered an opportunity to display a brand logo, whilst corporations pay large sums to have their advertisements accompany sporting events. Sport is now a key component of globalisation (Giulianotti and Robertson 2007) built upon huge increases in broadcasting revenue. The simple advertising of brands in newspapers and on billboards in the latter stages of the nineteenth century and the first half of the twentieth century has been replaced by a slick assemblage of digital marketing techniques (Einstein 2017), all designed to persuade sports fans and followers to consume. And the consumption of many of these advertised products is likely to have a negative impact on our health.

Marketing in the new globalised entertainment sports industry

In the beginning there was advertising. Stillerman (2016) provided a helpful overview of the sociology of consumption and the various theories included in this. Stillerman argued that brands and advertising came along in tandem. Brands were symbols and slogans, developed by manufacturers to distinguish their products from their competitors (Aaker 1991). And advertising was a way to promote these brands via newspapers, postcards (including cigarette cards) and other printed materials. The means for advertising brands have become more complex, as it is increasingly hard to get a brand seen (Thompson 1995) and corporate brands need to find a way to stand out in an overcrowded marketplace (Goldman and Papson 2006). Sport offers an opportunity for transnational corporations to raise global awareness of their brands whilst promoting commodity consumption (Smart 2007).

Marketing has therefore evolved from static signage to a wide variety of on-site activations (Dees et al. 2019) accompanied by the exponential growth of sport sponsorship in the last 40 years (Cornwell 2020). At the same time there has been an increased commercial value of broadcast rights for leagues such as the English Premier League and the Australian Football League (the AFL is described in detail at the end of this chapter) (Fujak and Frawley 2016).

Shirt sponsorship and LED pitchside advertising are the most common mechanisms employed to market brands. However, sport sponsorship is much more than simply attaching a brand name to an event, a competition or a club. Corporations pay large sums for access to fans domestically and globally (Maguire 2020) and want to see a return on their investment, which is usually measured against brand awareness and, if possible, product sales (O'Keefe et al. 2009). They typically supplement their sponsorship with related marketing activities which may cost more than the sponsorship itself (Keller 2013). Sponsorship arrangements are complex and are likely to be individually negotiated between recipient and corporation to meet the needs of both parties and the brand in particular. It is seen as important that there is a fit or congruence based on the shared attributes of sponsor and sponsee (Cornwell 2019). Thus, tobacco industry sponsorship was always open to justified criticism that an obviously unhealthy and carcinogenic product was deliberately associating itself with health and fitness as promoted through sport (Carrigan and Carrigan 1997).

There has been discussion and debate about the definition of commercial sponsorship. It may be defined as a direct partnership and/or commercial transaction between an organisation or a brand and another organisation (Chanavat et al. 2017). Semens argued that modern sponsorship "with an overtly commercial element" (2019 p.111) was conceived of in the late 1970s through the construction of sponsorship rights packages which were sold to partners in non-competing business sectors. Whilst sponsorship may be defined as a "single payment made for advertising" (Chanavat et al. 2017 p.112), it has become considerably more complex in its objectives (Meenaghan 2005). Chanavat et al. (2017) described the key factors for successful sponsorship as coherence, objectives, duration and meaning of content. Coherence (sometimes called congruence) relates to whether a company's brand values are in harmony with the sponsees. This will be explored later. Public health advocates would question whether an association between a perceived healthy activity such as football and the consumption of fast food can ever be described as brand coherence. The use of McDonald's child player escorts at the 2018 World Cup was heavily criticised, for example (Ashraf 2018). Ashraf contested the motives of the McDonald's programme, which claimed to be supporting a healthy and balanced lifestyle whilst promoting the consumption of fast food, high in fat, sugar and salt, that is associated with obesity, type 2 diabetes and heart disease.

Meenaghan (2005) provided examples of the objectives of brand sponsorship. Whilst increased sales of a product might be the most obvious, there might be much more complex (and thus harder to evaluate) objectives, such as the creation of a positive image, promoting brand attractiveness and platforms for lobbying. The duration of a sponsorship is also important in order to maintain the visibility of a brand image amongst other brands competing for the public's attention. Finally, the content of a sponsorship programme is a key factor. By telling a story about the brand, sponsorship can strengthen public support and encourage brand awareness and brand preference (Chanavat et al. 2017). The complexity of modern sponsorship will be explored in much more detail in Chapter 8.

Professional club websites reserve space for their sponsors (Kriemadis et al. 2010) and typically illustrate a version of what might be described as the sponsorship pyramid (Bühler and Nufer 2013) – see Figure 3.1. A football jersey, with the brand of the club's leading sponsor on the front, might be considered a key sign value in consumption, helping to develop both club and sponsor's client base (Millward 2011). The main sponsor, as well as having its logo on the shirt, will have other opportunities made available to it, such as perimeter advertising during live matches and public relations opportunities provided by the club (Bühler and Nufer 2013). The manufacturers of football kits pay considerable sums to be associated with an English Premier League club (Unlucan 2014), which they hope to recoup from the sale of replica shirts, revenue from which they share with the

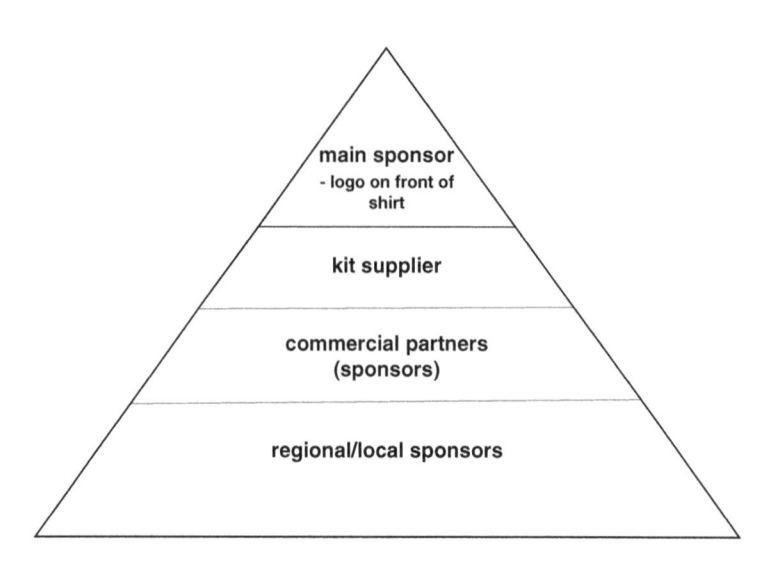

```
         /\
        /  \
       / main sponsor \
      / - logo on front of \
     /       shirt         \
    /------------------------\
   /      kit supplier        \
  /----------------------------\
 /    commercial partners       \
/        (sponsors)              \
----------------------------------
/     regional/local sponsors     \
------------------------------------
```

Figure 3.1 Sponsorship pyramid of an English Premier League club.
Source: After Bűhler and Nufer (2013 p.94).

retailer and the club (Szymanski and Kuypers 1999). The name and brand of the kit supplier usually follows that of the main sponsor on the club website.

The names of a number of other commercial partners appear on the next level of the sponsorship pyramid (Bűhler and Nufer 2013). Once again, their brands are likely to appear on perimeter advertising. Some might sponsor the club's training kit or even the sleeve or reverse of the shirt. Finally, the lowest level of the pyramid lists regional and/or local sponsors. They will pay less than the other sponsors and will receive smaller and possibly more targeted benefits. Chapter 5 includes a description of the tiered structure of partnership that FIFA uses, which is another way of visualising the sponsorship pyramid as described above. All sponsorship packages are tailored to the needs of sponsor and sponsee, with fees determined by the relative success and profile of the club, including the size of its fan base (Bűhler and Nufer 2013). The club website therefore acts as part of the network which a sponsor utilises to promote its brands. It is an appropriate point of contact between club, sponsors and fans through which to establish the full range of commercial partnerships an individual club might hold.

Since the 1980s, the internet has radically changed the way that organisations interact with the public, and it enables sports clubs to enhance their marketing activities and communications directly to their supporters and customers (Beech *et al.* 2000). Websites help revenue streams and gather data on supporters whilst being critical to fan communication (Whiteside 2014). With more powerful and easily accessible technologies, websites include audio and video files and podcasts enabling more user interaction (Ioakimidis 2010) and more potential for commercial partners. Club websites are a key component of contemporary sporting culture in engaging with fans as both supporters and consumers (Cleland et al. 2018). They help clubs practise relationship marketing in developing relationships with remote supporters to promote and distribute products and services globally (Kriemadis et al. 2010).

Manchester United's seven-year sponsorship deal with Chevrolet, part of the General Motors Corporation, was worth around US$560 million when it was signed in July 2012 (Rowe and Zemanek 2014). That translates to around £44.75 million per year (Mirror Football 2012). The car company's press release claimed that the sponsorship deal would enable it to reach Manchester United's 659 million followers around the world (Chevrolet Pressroom 2012). Unusually, a breakdown of the sponsorship detail was included in a peer-reviewed academic journal. Rowe and Zemanek (2014) drew on a report from Kantar Media which claimed that there were 325 million fans of Manchester United in the Asia-Pacific region, including 108 million in China alone. The report argued that the potential audience for Chevrolet included 138 million followers of football in China (45 per cent of the adult population), 43 million in Brazil (68 per cent of the adult population) and 17 million in South Korea, where 43 per cent of the adult population follow football.

The study included the detail of a major sponsorship deal. As well as Chevrolet's logo being placed on the front of the official Manchester United shirt, it also appeared on the chairs where the players and manager sat during matches, on an interactive stadium crowd photo where fans could tag themselves, on the LED perimeter boards at home games and as part of the backdrop during pre- and post-game interviews. Other on-site promotions were activated when Manchester United toured China in 2013 and 2016 (Sheen 2016). The sponsorship programme was supported by a website (www.chevroletfc.com), a Facebook page, a YouTube channel and a Twitter account. Chevrolet's marketing team looked for interaction on their social networks, which was particularly successful in Asia where fans were given access to the football club, football shirts and other goods, and even match tickets and travel expenses in a few cases.

Carrigan and Carrigan (1997) referenced a series of studies that identified sport sponsorship as a tactic developed by the tobacco and alcohol industries to avoid legal restrictions imposed on advertising (Cornwell 1997; Amis and Cornwell 2005). Sport sponsorship increases brand awareness, drives positive consumer perception (Kelly et al. 2011a) and is associated with increased levels of consumption of unhealthy products (Brown 2016). Further, associating unhealthy brands with sport can also provide a 'health halo' effect whereby fast food, for example, can benefit from an association with healthier lifestyles (Whalen et al. 2018). Sport sponsorship can promote a sponsor's community standing (Carrigan and Carrigan 1997) and has the potential for societal benefit. It can also be used by UCIs to divert public attention from their associated harms (Ireland and Boyland 2019).

As has been described, marketing literature emphasises that for sport sponsorship to be successful, it needs to be mixed with other promotional tools (Bühler and Nufer 2013). Marketeers use a number of methods to 'activate' their brand, with these linking strategies illustrated in Figure 3.2. Some of these methods, such as pitch perimeter advertising and brand logos displayed on the front of players' shirts, have been described previously.

This chapter concludes with a case study of Australian Rules football to illustrate how the development of television coverage of the sport has enabled the growth of sponsorship packages, including many that feature unhealthy commodity industries.

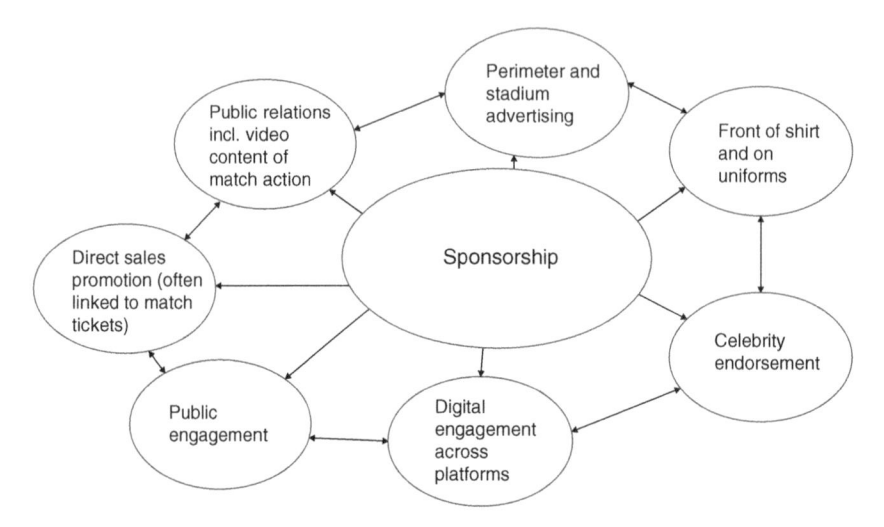

Figure 3.2 The sport sponsorship promotional assemblage.
Source: Adapted from Bühler and Nufer (2013 p.99).

Case Study: The commercialisation of Australian Rules football

Sport plays a major role in Australian culture (Vamplew 2021) and there are growing concerns and numerous studies about unhealthy marketing in Australian sport. Academics have considered this marketing in clubs, leagues and competitions, and across sports (Sherriff et al. 2009; Kelly et al. 2011b; Carter et al. 2013; Lindsay et al. 2013; Pettigrew et al. 2013; Macniven et al. 2014; Bestman et al. 2015; Kelly et al. 2015; Parry et al. 2017), together with business interests in sports marketing and sponsorship (Quester 2007).

Australian Rules football has been described as a barometer of the Australian national identity (Collins 2019) and its great national game (Blainey 2003). It is a football code specific to Australia, and its early history in the late nineteenth century and first half of the twentieth century was of isolated and separate development through an Australian state-based competition (Vamplew 2021). As the sport developed into the Victorian Football League, its progress was driven economically from a semi-professional metropolitan concern into a national, fully commercialised league (Andrews 2000). As the League sought revenue to meet increased player payments, it secured its first major sponsorship deal with the tobacco company W.D. & H.O. Wills in 1968 (Andrews 2000). Wills paid A$12,000 for the signage and associated promotions in the AFL (the governing body of Australian Rules football launched in 1990 from the Victorian Football League) final series (Phillips et al. 2005). Direct advertising of tobacco products on Australian television was banned from 1976, but tobacco companies used sport to bypass this legislation and continued to provide product exposure. Wills had quadrupled its sponsorship of the AFL by 1975 (Nadel 1998) and, even in 1989, the tobacco industry provided A$20 million dollars to rugby league in New South Wales and A$14 million to Australian cricket (May 2020). The involvement of the tobacco industry in sport, so critical to our understanding of how transnational corporations exploit sports fans' love of the game, will be explored in the next chapter.

As in other parts of the world, elite Australian sport changed after the introduction of live television broadcasts in the 1970s (Adair 2009), together with the introduction of colour television in 1975 (Hutchins and Phillips 1997). The AFL benefited considerably from the impact of broadcasting and the consequent exposure of its member clubs (Turner and Shilbury 2005), which in turn resulted in the increased commercialisation and opportunities for sponsors to reach greater audiences. As in Britain, the change to greater commercialisation was not welcomed by everyone in the sport. The Australian journalist and former politician, Bob Santamaria, was quoted in 1990 as saying that Australian football was "now a highly capitalised business played by professionals, not for a sporting public, composed of families, but for television audiences financed by television channels and sponsors" (reproduced in Whimpress 1994 p.38).

The expansion of the AFL was specifically designed to attract greater revenue from broadcasting rights, marketing activities and sponsorship. League revenue rose swiftly from A$20.6 million in 1986, to A$68 million in 1995 and A$186.3 million in 2004. Total spectator attendance in the AFL also increased from 5.4 million in 1994, to 6.6 million ten years later, whilst the Grand Final (the play-off match determining the club champion for the season) was reported as being watched by 3 million viewers in 2004 (Turner and Shilbury 2005 p.171). In 2019, and before the coronavirus pandemic, the Annual Report of the AFL provided a clear picture of the extent of commercialisation of the sport (AFL 2019). Total AFL viewership was reported as over 110 million across free-to-air and subscription channels, with club membership growing steadily, especially across the national women's league (AFLW) which was established in 2017. AFL matches were broadcast to 100 countries including China (seen as a key market), demonstrating the desire to reach a global audience. Total AFL revenue was reported at A$793.9 million (a staggering 3,754 per cent increase from 1986, without even accounting for changes in the value of the Australian dollar). Sponsorship models reflected the tiered approach adopted in other major sports globally and reported in this book. In 2019, the men's league had Coca-Cola and Gatorade (a PepsiCo brand) as 'major' partners, and Bet Easy, McDonald's, Mars, Milo and Jim Beam as 'official partners'. The sponsorship structure of the AFLW is similar to that of the men's game, although the 'partners' are slightly different, including both Gatorade and McDonald's with the addition of Special K.

The AFL's Annual Report details very clearly the close relationship of the league with its sponsors, with brand engagement a critical element. For example, Carlton United Breweries provided fans of the winners of the 2019 Grand Final (Richmond Football Club) with a special beer can featuring a QR code that sent fans to a landing page showing highlights of their club's win. Pump, a sweetened bottled water brand owned by Coca-Cola, provided fans of all AFL clubs with bespoke bottles 'to support their team' (AFL 2019 p.46). McDonald's had a suite of engagement offers including the production and distribution of Captains' Cards, with more than 400,000 collectors' cards distributed in-store. In 2021, it was reported that the AFL had signed a ten-year extension to its sponsorship agreement with McDonald's, having first partnered with the fast-food company in 2014 (SportBusiness 2021). The agreement included the McDonald's logo being carried on the match ball, sponsorship of both the AFL and AFLW, together with the Macca's Kick 2 Kick programme, which provides access to a draw to win match tickets.

Sartori *et al.* (2018) carried out a study on the AFL clubs in 2017 and found that 56 out of 453 sponsors (12 per cent) could be classified as unhealthy. The authors used a traffic light system to categorise sponsors. Those classified as red included all alcohol sponsors, wagering companies and casinos (gambling), and food and beverage sponsors according to nutrient criteria. Food and beverage brands (46 per cent) were the most common category of red sponsorship in the AFL, followed by alcohol (43 per cent). Coca-Cola had the highest number of sponsorship partnerships, sponsoring 13 of 18 clubs (72 per cent), with Carlton Draught (a beer producer) sponsoring six clubs (33 per cent). The authors noted the popularity of the AFL, measured by match attendance by game. Given that excess weight and obesity affect two-thirds of Australian adults (Australian Institute of Health and Welfare 2020) and that one in six adult Australians drink alcohol at a level that puts them at risk of an alcohol-related disease or injury during their lifetime, the Australian study raised concerns about the level of unhealthy sponsorship on AFL club websites and on playing uniforms. The authors advocated for a coordinated approach to remove unhealthy sponsors from sport in Australia, similar to that used to remove tobacco sponsorship. An earlier study carried out in 2012 on the sponsorship of Australian national and state sports organisations showed similar results, with Australian Football having the highest number of gambling sponsors (Macniven et al. 2014).

Further research (Nuss et al. 2019) considered unhealthy marketing in the television broadcast of the 2017 AFL Grand Final. This study used a content analysis to examine instances of unhealthy food and sugary drinks, alcohol and gambling marketing. This indicated extensive and similar branding during what is described as the highest-rating sporting event in Australia. The study of the Grand Final only considered marketing instances during the game and did not include pre- or post-match footage (they included the commercial breaks within the match quarters but not at half-time). The researchers found 559 instances of unhealthy marketing, with viewers being exposed to 4.4 unhealthy marketing episodes per minute. The majority (81 per cent) of these episodes were for fast food, soft drink and sports drink brands, with promotions for McDonald's making up just over half (51 per cent) of these. This was mainly due to McDonald's having its branding on the goalposts.

An earlier Australian study (Lindsay et al. 2013) investigated alcohol, gambling and unhealthy food marketing during the Australian National Rugby League 2012 State of Origin three-game series. The authors noted that marketing for 'risky products' "saturated the game coverage" (page 8). Alcohol brands had on-field placements (such as players' jerseys and painted logos on the pitch) and off-field placements (including scoreboard advertising and drink coolers), all contributing to the high frequency of marketing.

Studies show that children who are exposed to the promotion of junk food, alcohol and gambling products in Australian sport are easily able to recall shirt sponsors, for example (Bestman et al. 2015). Further, another study shows that children's exposure to unhealthy food marketing in sport influences their food knowledge, preferences and consumption (Kelly et al. 2011a). To paraphrase Bob Santamaria from over 30 years ago, Australian football is now a highly capitalised business designed primarily for television audiences, and based on encouraging fans, including children, to buy junk food, drink alcohol and gamble. But those business interests mirror mediated sport globally.

Conclusions

This chapter described the early advertising of unhealthy products and brands in sport by the gambling, alcohol, food and beverage, and tobacco industries, and introduced and defined sport sponsorship. The concept of brand coherence was used to ask whether unhealthy brands should ever be associated with sport. The tobacco industry used sponsorship as a means of avoiding regulations on the advertising of tobacco products, and this is discussed in more detail in the following chapter. Modern sponsorship is part of a number of promotional tools, in which brands are displayed on players' uniforms and pitch perimeters. The evolution of sports marketing is further discussed in Chapter 8, which considers sport and brand engagement. Finally, this chapter used a case study of Australian Rules football to illustrate how television coverage and sponsorship have transformed this sport, whilst enabling junk food and alcohol companies to market their brands to fans.

References

Aaker, D.A. (1991) *Managing Brand Equity. Capitalizing on the Value of a Brand Name*, New York: The Free Press.

Adair, D. (2009) 'Australian sport history: From the founding years to today', *Sport in History*, 29(3), 405–436, available: http://dx.doi.org/10.1080/17460260903043351.

AFL (2019) *AFL: 2019 Annual Report*, Melbourne, available: https://resources.afl.com.au/afl/document/2020/03/18/925fd047-a9b6-4f7d-8046-138a56ba36f4/2019-AFL-Annual-Report.pdf [accessed 13 January 2022].

Allen, S. (2014) 'A brief history of jersey sponsorship', *Mental Floss*, 20 March 2014, available: https://www.mentalfloss.com/article/27776/brief-history-jersey-sponsorship [accessed 11 January 2022].

Allison, L. and MacLean, R. (2012) 'There's a deathless myth on the close tonight: Re-assessing Rugby's place in the history of sport', *The International Journal of the History of Sport*, 29(13), 1866–1884, available: http://dx.doi.org/10.1080/09523367.2012.708612.

Amis, J. and Cornwell, T.B. (2005) 'Sport sponsorship in a global age' in Amis, J. and Cornwell, T. B., eds., *Global Sports Sponsorship*, Oxford: Berg.

Andrews, I. (2000) 'From a club to a corporate game: The changing face of Australian Football, 1960–1999' in Mangan, J.A. and Nauright, J., eds., *Sport in Australasian Society*, Abingdon: Frank Cass.

Ashraf, A. (2018) 'Irony of fast food at FIFA World Cup: McDonald's sponsors Player Mascots to promote healthy living, but what about trans fats?', available: https://www.firstpost.com/world/irony-of-fast-food-at-fifa-world-cup-mcdonalds-sponsors-player-mascots-to-promote-healthy-living-but-what-about-trans-fats-4740681.html [accessed 15 July 2020].

Australian Institute of Health and Welfare (2020) *Australia's Health. Overweight and obesity*, available: https://www.aihw.gov.au/reports/australias-health/overweight-and-obesity [accessed 13 January 2022].

Bassorelli, G. (2012) *El Negro Jefe. Héroes de Peñarol*, Montevideo: Editorial Fin de Siglio.

Bastos, W. and Levy, S.J. (2012) 'A history of the concept of branding: Practice and theory', *Journal of Historical Research in Marketing*, 4(3), 347–368

Beech, J., Chadwick, S. and Tapp, A. (2000) 'Surfing in the premier league: Key issues for football club marketers using the Internet', *Managing Leisure*, 5, 51–64.

Bestman, A., Thomas, S., Randle, M. and Thomas, S.D.M. (2015) 'Children's implicit recall of junk food, alcohol and gambling sponsorship in Australian sport', *BMC Public Health*, 15(1022), 1–9.

Billingham, G. (2015) 'A brief history of shirt sponsorship', *The Football Pink*, available: https://footballpink.net/2018-10-22-a-brief-history-of-football-shirt-sponsorship/ [accessed 11 January 2022].

Blainey, G. (2003) *A Game of Our Own. The Origins of Australian Football*, Melbourne: Black.

BOL News (2020) 'Sonny Williams, Muslim Legend refuses to wear shirt with betting firm logo', *BOL News*, 24 January 2020, available: https://www.bolnews.com/trending/2020/01/sonny-williams-muslim-legend-refuses-to-wear-shirt-with-betting-firm-logo/ [accessed 11 January 2020].

Brown, K. (2016) 'Association between alcohol sports sponsorship and consumption: A systematic review', *Alcohol and Alcoholism*, 51(6), 747–755.

Bühler, A. and Nufer, G. (2013) *Relationship Marketing in Sport*, Abingdon: Routledge.

Carey, R. (2020) *A History of Sponsorship*, available: https://museumofjerseys.com/2020/05/19/a-history-of-sponsorship/ [accessed 11 January 2022].

Carrigan, M. and Carrigan, J. (1997) 'UK sports sponsorship: Fair play or foul?', *A European Review*, 6(2).

Carruthers, J. (2014) 'Timeline of sports marketing', 19 January 2022, available: https://www.fastsigns.com/blog/detail/2014/09/25/sport-events-advertising-through-the-years [accessed

Carter, M.-A., Signal, L., Edwards, R., Hoek, J. and Maher, A. (2013) 'Food, fizzy and football: Promoting unhealthy food and beverages through sport – A New Zealand case study', *BMC Public Health*, 13(126), 1–7.

Chanavat, N., Desbordes, M. and Lorgnier, N. (2017) 'Sports sponsorship and professional football' in Chanavat, N., Desbordes, M. and Lorgnier, N., eds., *Routledge Handbook of Football Marketing*, Abingdon: Routledge.

Chevrolet Pressroom (2012) *Chevrolet Celebrates Debut on New Manchester United Shirt* [press release], available: https://media.chevrolet.com/media/us/en/chevrolet/news.detail.html/content/Pages/news/us/en/2014/Jul/0709-manu-shirt.html [accessed 15 September 2020].

Clapson, M. (1992) *A Bit of a Flutter. Popular Gambling and English Society, c.1823–1961*, Manchester: Manchester University Press.

Cleland, J., Doidge, M., Millward, P. and Widdop, P. (2018) *Collective Action and Football Fandom. A Relational Sociological Approach*, Cham: Springer Nature (for Palgrave Macmillan).

Collins, T. (2013) *Sport in Capitalist Society. A Short History*, Abingdon: Routledge.

Collins, T. (2019) *How Football Began. A Global History of How the World's Football Codes Were Born*, Abingdon: Routledge.

Collins, T. and Vamplew, W. (2002) *Mud, Sweat and Beers. A Cultural History of Sport and Alcohol*, Oxford: Berg.

Cornwell, T.B. (1997) 'The use of sponsorship-linked marketing by tobacco firms: International public policy issues', *The Journal of Consumer Affairs*, 31(2), 238–254.

Cornwell, T.B. (2019) 'Less "Sponsorship as Advertising" and More sponsorship-linked marketing as authentic engagement', *Journal of Advertising*, 48(1), 49–60.

Cornwell, T.B. (2020) *Sponsorship in Marketing. Effective Partnerships in Sports, Arts and Events*, Second ed., Abingdon: Routledge.

Crepeau, R.C. (2020) *NFL Football. A History of America's New National Pastime*, Urbana: University of Illinois Press.

Dees, W., Gay, C., Popp, N. and Jensen, J.A. (2019) 'Assessing the impact of sponsor asset selection, intangible rights, and activation on sponsorship effectiveness', *Sport Marketing Quarterly*, 28, 91–101.

Domeneghetti, R. (2017) *From the Back Page to the Front Room: Football's Journey through the English Media*, Second ed., Glasgow: Ockley Books.

Einstein, M. (2017) *Advertising. What Everyone Needs to Know*, New York: Oxford University Press.

Fujak, H. and Frawley, S. (2016) 'The relationship between television viewership and advertising content in Australian Football Broadcasts', *Communication & Sport*, 4(1), 82–101.

Galeano, E. (2013 (1995)) *Soccer in Sun and Shadow*, Fourth ed., New York: Nation Books.

Giulianotti, R. (1999) *Football. A Sociology of the Global Game*, Cambridge: Polity Press.

Giulianotti, R. and Robertson, R. eds. (2007) *Globalization and Sport*, Oxford: Blackwell Publishing.

Goldman, R. and Papson, S. (2006) 'Capital's brandscapes', *Journal of Consumer Culture*, 6(3), 327–353.

Gratton, C., Liu, D., Ramchandani, G. and Wilson, D. (2012) *The Global Economics of Sport*, Abingdon: Routledge.

Gruneau, R. (2017) *Sport & Modernity*, Cambridge: Polity.

Hadley, P. (1970) *The History of Bovril Advertising*, London: Ambassador Publishing.

Hill, J. (2002) *Sport, Leisure & Culture in Twentieth-Century Britain*. Basingstoke: Palgrave.

Holt, R. (1992) *Sport and the British. A Modern History*, Oxford: Clarendon Press.

Horne, J., Tomlinson, A. and Whannel, G. (1999) *Understanding Sport. An Introduction to the Sociological and Cultural Analysis of Sport*. London: Spon Press.

Hutchins, B. and Phillips, M.G. (1997) 'Selling permissible violence: The commodification of Australian Rugby League 1970–1995', *International Review for the Sociology of Sport*, 32(2), 161–176, available: http://dx.doi.org/10.1177/101269097032002004.

Inglis, S. (1988) *League Football. And the Men Who Made It*, London: Willow Books.

Ioakimidis, M. (2010) 'Online marketing of professional sports clubs: Engaging fans on a new playing field', *International Journal of Sports Marketing & Sponsorship*, 11(4), 2–13.

Ireland, R. and Boyland, E. (2019) 'Sports sponsorship and young people: Good or bad for health?', *BMJ Paediatrics Open*, 3(1), e000446.

Johnson, W.O. (1988) 'Sports and suds', *Sports Illustrated*, (6), 68–82.

Keller, K.L. (2013) *Strategic Brand Management. Building, Measuring, and Managing Brand Equity*, Fourth ed., Harlow: Pearson Education.

Kelly, B., Baur, L.A., Bauman, A.E., King, L., Chapman, K. and Smith, B.J. (2011a) '"Food company sponsors are kind, generous and cool": (Mis)conceptions of junior sports players', *International Journal of Behavioral Nutrition and Physical Activity*, 8(1), 1–7.

Kelly, B., Baur, L.A., Bauman, A.E., Smith, B.J., Saleh, S., King, L.A. and Chapman, K. (2011b) 'Role modelling unhealthy behaviours: Food and drink sponsorship of peak sporting organisations', *Health Promotion Journal of Australia*, 22(1), 72–75.

Kelly, S., Ireland, M., Alpert, F. and Managan, J. (2015) 'Young consumers' exposure to alcohol sponsorship in sport', *International Journal of Sports Marketing & Sponsorship*, 16(2), 2–21.

Kriemadis, T., Terzoudis, C. and Kartakoullis, N. (2010) 'Internet marketing in football clubs: A comparison between English and Greek websites', *Soccer & Society*, 11(3), 291–307.

Lindsay, S., Thomas, S., Lewis, S., Westberg, K., Moodie, R. and Jones, S. (2013) 'Eat, drink and gamble: Marketing messages about 'risky' products in an Australian major sporting series', *BMC Public Health*, 13(1), 1–11.

Macniven, R., Kelly, B. and King, L. (2014) 'Unhealthy product sponsorship of Australian national and state sports organisations', *Health Promotion Journal of Australia*, 26(1), 52–56, available: http://dx.doi.org/10.1016/j.jsams.2014.11.030.

Maguire, K. (2020) *The Price of Football. Understanding Football Club Finance*, Newcastle upon Tyne: Agenda

Mason, T. (1980) *Association Football and English Society, 1863–1915*, Brighton: The Harvester Press.

Masterman, G. (2011) *Sponsorship for a Return on Investment*, Abingdon: Routledge.

May, C. (2020) *Tobacco Sponsorship and Advertising in Sport*, available: https://www.clearinghouseforsport.gov.au/kb/tobacco-sponsorship-and-advertising-in-sport#tobacco_sponsorship_and_advertising_in_sport [accessed 20 January 2022].

McComb, D.G. (2004) *Sports in World History*, Abingdon: Routledge.

Meenaghan, T. (2005) 'Evaluating sponsorship effects' in Amis, J. and Cornwell, T.B., eds., *Global Sports Sponsorship*, Oxford: Berg.

Michener, J.A. (1976) *Sports in America*, New York: Random House.

Millward, P. (2011) *The Global Football League. Transnational Networks, Social Movements and Sport in the New Media Age*, Basingstoke: Palgrave Macmillan.

Mirror Football (2012) 'Va va vroom! United's shirt deal with Chevy is worth £357million', *Daily Mirror*, 4 August 2012, available: https://www.mirror.co.uk/sport/football/news/manchester-uniteds-chevrolet-sponsorship-is-worth-1215088 [accessed 15 September 2020].

Nadel, D. (1998) 'Colour, corporations and commissioners, 1976–1985', *More Than a Game: The Real Story of Australian Rules Football*, Melbourne University Press, Melbourne, 200–24.

Nuss, T., Scully, M., Wakefield, M. and Dixon, H. (2019) 'Unhealthy sport sponsorship at the 2017 AFL Grand Final: A case study of its frequency, duration and nature', *Australian and New Zealand Journal of Public Health*, 43(4), 366–372.

O'Keefe, R., Titlebaum, P. and Hill, C. (2009) 'Sponsorship activation: Turning money spent into money earned', *Journal of Sponsorship*, 3(1), 43–53.

Parry, K.D., Hall, T. and Baxter, A. (2017) 'Who ate all of the pies? The importance of food in the Australian sporting experience', *Sport in Society*, 20(2), 202–218.

Pettigrew, S., Rosenberg, M., Ferguson, R., Houghton, S. and Wood, L. (2013) 'Game on: Do children absorb sports sponsorship messages?', *Public Health Nutrition*, 16(12), 2197–2204.

Phillips, M.G., Hutchins, B. and Stewart, B. (2005) 'The media sport cultural complex: Football and fan resistance in Australia' in Nauright, J. and Schimmel, Kimberly S., eds., *The Political Economy of Sport*, London: Palgrave Macmillan, 85–103.

Planet Football (2017) *Why Man Utd, Chelsea and Co. Have Little Kettering Town to thank*, available: https://www.planetfootball.com/in-depth/man-utd-chelsea-co-little-kettering-town-thank/ [accessed 2 September 2020].

Pomfret, R. (2016) 'The evolution of professional team sports' in Pomfret, R. and Wilson, J.K., eds., *Sports through the Lens of Economic History*, Cheltenham: Edward Elgar.

Quester, P. (2007) 'Sport Marketing and Sponsorship: I cheer therefore I am', *Actes du XXIIIème Congrès International de l'AFM–31 mai & 1er juin*:

Rowe, W.J. and Zemanek, J.E. (2014) 'Chevrolet and Manchester United: A transformational sponsorship in a traditional industry', *Innovative Marketing*, 10(1), 40–48.

Russell, D. (2013) 'Kicking off: The origins of association football' in Steen, R., Novick, J. and Richards, H., eds., *The Cambridge Companion to Football*, Cambridge: Cambridge University Press.

Sartori, A., Stoneham, M. and Edmunds, M. (2018) 'Unhealthy sponsorship in sport: A case study of the AFL', *Australian and New Zealand Journal of Public Health*, 42(5), 474–9.

Semens, A. (2019) 'Football sponsorship' in Hughson, J., Moore, K., Spaaij, R. and Maguire, J., eds., *Routledge Handbook of Football Studies* (Paperback ed.), Abingdon: Routledge, 111–123.

Seymour, H. (1989) *Baseball. The Early Years*, New York: Oxford University Press.

Sheen, T. (2016) 'Manchester United pre-season tour to take place in China', *The Independent*, 22 March 2016, available: https://www.independent.co.uk/sport/football/premier-league/manchester-united-pre-season-tour-take-place-china-a6945946.html [accessed 15 September 2020].

Sherriff, J., Griffiths, D. and Daube, M. (2009) 'Cricket: Notching up runs for food and alcohol companies?', *Australian and New Zealand Journal of Public Health*, 34(1), 19–23.

Smart, B. (2007) 'Not playing around: Global capitalism, modern sport and consumer culture' in Giulianotti, R. and Robertson, R., eds., *Globalization and Sport*, Oxford: Blackwell Publishing.

SportBusiness (2021) 'AFL signs new long-term deal with McDonald's', *SportBusiness*, 17 September 2021, available: https://www.sportbusiness.com/news/afl-signs-new-long-term-deal-with-mcdonalds/?logged_in=1 [accessed 12 January 2022].

Stainback, R.D. (1997) *Alcohol and Sport*, Champaign: Human Kinetics.

Stillerman, J. (2016) *The Sociology of Consumption. A Global Approach*, Cambridge: Polity Press.

Szymanski, S. and Kuypers, T. (1999) *Winners and Losers. The Business Strategy of Football*, London: Viking.

The Central Council of Physical Recreation (1983) *Committee of Enquiry into Sports Sponsorship. "The Howell Report"*, London.

Thompson, J.B. (1995) *The Media and Modernity. A Social Theory of the Media*, Cambridge: Polity Press.

Turner, P. and Shilbury, D. (2005) 'Determining the professional sport broadcasting landscape: An Australian football club perspective', *Sport Management Review*, 8(2), 167–193.

Unlucan, D. (2014) 'Jersey manufacturers in football/soccer: The analysis of current jersey manufacturers of 1061 football/soccer clubs in top leagues of 72 countries', *Soccer & Society*, 15(3), 314–333.

Unlucan, D. (2015) 'Jersey sponsors in football/soccer: The industry classification of main jersey sponsors of 1147 football/soccer clubs in top leagues of 79 countries', *Soccer and Society*, 16(1), 42–62.

Vamplew, W. (2021) *Games People Played. A Global History of Sport*, London: Reaktion Books.

Walvin, J. (1994) *The People's Game. The History of Football Revisited*, Edinburgh: Mainstream Publishing.

Whalen, R., Harrold, J., Child, S., Halford, J. and Boyland, E. (2018) 'The health halo trend in UK television food advertising viewed by children: The rise of implicit and explicit health messaging in the promotion of unhealthy foods', *International Journal of Environmental Research and Public Health*, 15, 560–568.

Whannel, G. (1986) 'The unholy alliance: Notes on television and the remaking of British sport 1965–85', *Leisure Studies*, 5(2), 129–145, available: http://dx.doi.org/10.1080/02614368600390111.

Whannel, G. (2002) *Fields in Vision. Television Sport and Cultural Transformation*, London: Routledge.

Whimpress, B. (1994) 'Australian football' in Vamplew, W. and Stoddart, B., eds., *Sport in Australia. A Social History*, Cambridge: Cambridge University Press.

Whiteside, E.A. (2014) 'New media and the changing role of sports information' in Billings, A.C. and Hardin, M., eds., *Routledge Handbook of Sport and New Media*, Abingdon: Routledge.

Chapter 4

The tobacco industry and the development of sport sponsorship

Early tobacco industry advertising including celebrity endorsement

The first advertisement that I have been able to locate concerning cigarettes at a live sporting event was an advertising board placed on a stand at Burnley's stadium (Turf Moor) in a Mitchell and Kenyon (1902) film of the match between Burnley and Manchester United on 6 December 1902. This appears to be, coincidently, the earliest film of Manchester United in action. The board is advertising Bulldog Flake pipe tobacco to the fans attending the match. At this time, football crowds were almost entirely male, and companies were already identifying a market for their products. Perhaps this early advertising represented the coming struggle between tobacco manufacturers for market share and offers an example of what would follow across the twentieth century, with sport providing easy access to potential new consumers.

Always innovators in their advertising and marketing, tobacco companies developed cigarette cards as a useful advertising device in the early days of codified sport and of mass rolled cigarette production (Brandt 2007). These cards were issued by tobacco manufacturers to stiffen cigarette packaging and to promote their brands. Originating in the United States in the 1870s, they featured many sports such as baseball and cricket. Interestingly, Honus Wagner of the Pittsburgh Pirates was reported to have objected to his portrait being used on a baseball card in 1909 which promoted an American Tobacco Company brand, as he hated smoking (Zoss and Bowman 1989). W.D. & H.O. Wills (a founding company of Imperial Tobacco) became the first British cigarette manufacturer to include cards in its packaging in 1887, and by 1896 the first football set of cigarette cards had been produced as a way to obtain brand loyalty (Simkin 2020). Collecting these cards was popular into the 1920s and 1930s, and they featured various sports. Although most of these cards depicted white male sports stars, a series of cards promoting Scissors cigarettes (owned by W.D. & H.O. Wills) was issued in 1913 entitled 'Sporting Girls'. Unlike most cards, these featured unnamed participants rather than identified athletes and included activities such as crochet and roller skating as well as women taking part in sports such as badminton and hockey.

Given the date of issue, it is probable that this advertising was aimed at a male market, but it could also be an early sign of a tobacco company identifying potential female customers. Brandt quotes the *New York Times* of 25 December 1888 in saying that cigarette cards were used both to entice youngsters to take up smoking and also to entice boys under 12 years to smoke more in order to complete their collections (Brandt 2007, see p.32).

In later years, many sports players were paid by companies to advertise their goods. Once again, the tobacco industry was an early innovator. Baseball stars such as Norman A. (Bub) McMillan of the Chicago Cubs promoted Chesterfield cigarettes (part of Philip Morris) in the 1920s. English football stars followed the same path to raise more income, with Dixie Dean promoting Carreras Clubs cigarettes in the 1930s, and Craven A capitalising on the fame of England footballer Stanley Matthews in the 1950s. An advertisement portraying Matthews, filtered cigarette in hand, in 1952 describes the brand as a "smooth" cigarette which was "kind to your throat". The tobacco industry was already trying to counter claims that cigarettes were unhealthy, and indeed were asserting that their products were good for you. Matthews was not a smoker but possibly earned more from his commercial endorsements than from his playing (Griffin 2012). Sadly, professional baseball player 'Babe' Ruth, one of the legends of American sporting culture and an enthusiastic endorser of Old Gold cigarettes ("smoother and better") (O'Keefe and Pollay 1996), died in 1948 at the age of 53 from nasopharyngeal cancer, brought on by heavy tobacco use in association with alcohol (Zoss and Bowman 1989).

When the health effects of smoking were widely understood by the 1970s and smoking amongst baseball players all but ended, tobacco companies aggressively promoted chewing tobacco and snuff as safe alternatives (Zoss and Bowman 1989). Not all athletes were happy to accept tobacco sponsorship, however. Whilst Brazilian football legend Pelé was very happy to accept commercial sponsorship (he was the first athlete to trademark his name) (O'Malley 2014), he refused to be associated with any alcohol or tobacco companies (Foer 2004; Pelé 2007; Harris 2018). In more recent history, other athletes have objected to unhealthy sponsorship being associated with them (although plenty have also been happy to benefit from associations with alcohol, sugary food and beverages, tobacco and gambling). For example, global football star Cristiano Ronaldo received plenty of media coverage when he pushed aside a bottle of Coca-Cola in favour of water at a press conference (Alton 2021).

The banning of commercial cigarette advertising on British television in 1965 led to major tobacco firms such as Benson and Hedges and Rothmans ploughing large sums into televised sports such as cricket, tennis and motor racing to maintain exposure for their brands (Whannel 1986, 2002). An exchange reported in Hansard, the official report of UK parliamentary debates, noted 66 tobacco-sponsored events and sports in the United Kingdom in 1983, including Embassy darts and Marlboro motor racing, amounting to 265 hours of televised cigarette-sponsored sport, "all designed to circumvent the ban on tobacco advertising on television" (raised by George Foulkes MP (now Baron Foulkes of Cumnock) and reported in Hansard 1983 p.795). English football was featured in branded annuals such as *Rothmans Football Yearbook*, which was published by the tobacco company from 1970 until 2002/2003, when it was withdrawn in advance of stronger UK legislation regarding tobacco sponsorship in sport. *The Park Drive Book of Football* was only available by collecting coupons issued by tobacco company Gallahers in their brand's Park Drive cigarette packets. The 1970 edition carried an article by Denis Howell MP, the then Minister for Sport. This may have indicated establishment acceptability, but the book's popularity was more likely to have been secured by pieces published under the names of famous footballers and managers of the time including George Best, Don Revie and Gordon Banks.

It was reported that the tobacco industry might have contributed as much as one third of all sport sponsorship in Britain in the early 1970s (Wilson 1988). In writing about 'The Sports Business' in 1988, the sportswriter Neil Wilson turned to the special events director of Gallahers to describe the foundations of the tobacco company's policy towards sponsorship. These included "Guaranteed national radio and national press", that "Events should be cost-effective" (they should provide a 'return') and that they should find the "Right target market" (Wilson 1988 pages 160, 161). These objectives would be familiar to any marketeer seeking to advance their brand through sport sponsorship in the twenty-first century (albeit an online presence would be an additional and indispensable objective). In the 1980s, the Gallahers' portfolio included Benson and Hedges branded cricket, snooker, tennis and golf. Sports sponsorships were as common in the United States. RJ Reynolds (the tobacco company was formed in 1875 and merged with British American Tobacco in 2004) sponsored eight different baseball teams in 1963, whilst American Tobacco sponsored six more (Pollay 1994). In 1971, RJ Reynolds was also the chief sponsor of NASCAR's Winston Cup Series, with teenage males being significant followers of American stock car racing (DeParle 1989). By the late 1980s, cigarette companies had advertisements in 22 of the 24 Major League ballparks in the United States (DeParle 1989).

As we have seen, the tobacco industry has long used athlete endorsements and sport sponsorship to promote its products – an approach still being used to promote smokeless tobacco in the United States amongst adolescent males today (Couch *et al.* 2019). The German football club Bayern Munich was still allowing its brand to be used to promote snuff (a form of smokeless tobacco) in 2022. Many sports advocates have always been unhappy that their sport, a "healthy product", was being used to market unhealthy brands. In 1989, for example, the UK Rugby Football League was criticised for its sponsorship by the brewing and tobacco industries, whose sponsorships were "hardly in keeping with the values the game is supposed to embody" (Gate 1989 p.144).

The next section explores how the tobacco industry developed a playbook in the 1970s to avoid government regulation even as the damaging effects of tobacco use were becoming widely known and understood. Later sections of the book will examine how the processed food, gambling and alcohol industries are adopting the same approaches in the twenty-first century as the damaging effects of unhealthy consumption fuel today's global epidemic of non-communicable diseases (Moodie *et al.* 2013).

The tobacco industry 'playbook'

The long-term benefits to transnational companies of linking a stigmatised product with a healthy sporting image is a theme throughout this book and was demonstrated originally by the tobacco industry (Polley 1998). As highly regulated industries, tobacco and alcohol were at the forefront of marketing initiatives, including the use of sport as an association with a healthy product (Sparks et al. 2005). The sport sponsorship strategies of today's alcohol, food and drink and gambling industries closely resemble the strategies developed during the tobacco industry's move into sport sponsorship in the 1960s (Cornwell 1997). For example, academics compare the practices of the tobacco and food industry (Brownell and Warner 2009; Malik 2010) and argue that the tobacco industry had a strategy or "playbook" (Brownell and Warner 2009 p.259). The playbook or script involves a series of actions used by unhealthy commodity industries, which include influencing public opinion through public relations and framing, lobbying against legislation and regulation and marketing products. Corporations seek to promote the consumption of their brands whilst emphasising personal responsibility in this consumption. This chapter continues by reviewing the use of this playbook by tobacco-industry executives and lobbyists in the field of sports sponsorship even when government regulations, both in the United States and the United Kingdom, had stopped the direct advertising of tobacco products on television, and when the health harms of tobacco use were widely known and understood.

Self-regulation, government regulation and global treaties

The health harms caused by tobacco have been widely known since the seminal report on smoking and health by the Royal College of Physicians of London in 1962. The US Surgeon General published similar findings in 1964. Both reports linked smoking with dangerous health effects including lung cancer, heart disease and chronic bronchitis. And yet sport continued to be a willing vehicle for the marketing and globalisation of cigarette brands by transnational corporations, whilst tobacco executives sought to circumvent marketing restrictions placed on them by governments wishing to address the social cost to health caused by consumption of these legal products (Cornwell 1997). Collin (2003) has described the globalisation of the tobacco industry and how it used technological developments to circumvent regulation and increase awareness of its brands, with the sponsorship of motor racing as an example of its tactics. Controls on the advertising of tobacco products in the 1960s and 1970s led tobacco companies to invest in sport to make up for lost advertising revenue (Dewhirst 2004). Sponsorship of Formula 1 motor racing was associated with tobacco advertising from 1968 and the industry continued with indirect marketing techniques even after the 2005 European Union Tobacco Advertising Directive (Grant-Braham and Britton 2011). Nevertheless, as in motor racing, sport has shown its ability to attract alternative sources of income.

Pollay (1994) has written comprehensively of how, following the restrictions placed on the advertising of cigarettes on US broadcast media, sponsorship of sports events and teams swiftly followed, creating new means for television exposure. Any hope of ethical behaviour by the tobacco industry was misplaced, as cigarette companies simply used sport to carry their message whilst denying that their methods targeted youth and other new smokers. British American Tobacco (BAT) launched its sports sponsorship programme in Thailand in 1987 amid advertising restrictions; BAT's events in 1989 included a visit by Manchester United to promote the 555 cigarette brand (MacKenzie et al. 2007).

Opportunities for tobacco advertising and sponsorship were severely limited because of the Framework Convention on Tobacco Control (FCTC) (WHO 2003). The FCTC was the first treaty negotiated under the auspices of the World Health Organization. Importantly, it addressed demand reduction strategies as well as supply issues. Thus, it considered price and tax measures as well as non-price measures such as tobacco advertising, promotion and sponsorship to reduce the demand for tobacco. The FCTC was based on the accumulation of scientific evidence of health harms caused by the use of tobacco and took an international collective approach to a threat to global public health (Shibuya et al. 2003). It implicitly recognised that without control over the marketing of transnational tobacco companies, they would continue to aggressively market their products, including to non-smoking women and children, resulting in increased rates of smoking (Connolly 1992). It should be noted that Philip Morris, the then largest US tobacco company, objected to many provisions in the FCTC including a ban on advertisements targeting children (this would have excluded sport sponsorship) (Waxman 2002). It should also be recorded that tobacco companies denied any link between smoking and health for many years, or that their marketing in sport targeted young people, despite the obvious evidence to the contrary (DeParle 1989).

Marketing works

Whilst the tobacco industry spent millions to promote its products, it argued that the public could make their own judgement about what brands to try. Brandt noted that attacks on marketing as a "manipulative evil" (Brandt 2007 p.74) could alienate the public. Surely, women and men could resist and even ignore such blandishments to consume? Even back in 1926, American President Calvin Coolidge was arguing approvingly that mass demand had been created almost entirely through advertising (quoted in Brandt 2007 p.74). Sixty years later, Red Bull created a demand for an entirely new product through aggressive marketing (see Chapter 8).

In discussing the marketing of cigarettes to women in the 1930s, Brandt described the creation of a product and a behaviour which "now possessed specific and appealing social meanings of glamour, beauty, autonomy, and equality" (2007 p.78). Transnational corporations use similar approaches in today's campaigns to promote fun and excitement amongst young male consumers in particular (gambling marketing), risky and edgy behaviours for both young men and women (energy drinks), rewards and treats for fans (chocolate), and social gatherings and celebrations for everyone (alcohol). Examples of these campaigns, facilitated through sports sponsorship, will be regularly described in this book, with glamour and equality being used to promote cigarettes to young female tennis fans in the case study provided later in this chapter.

Remarkably, though, the tobacco industry claimed first that it did not market its products to young people and children, and second, that advertising does not increase consumption. The tobacco industry's own documents, released through litigation and whistleblowing (Brandt 2007), showed otherwise (Bates and Rowell 2004). The companies sponsored motor racing, for example, to market directly to youth (Bates and Rowell 2004). The motivation for sports advertising and sponsorship was clear, as Wayne Robertson of RJR Tobacco was reported as saying in 1989: "We use sports as an avenue for advertising our products ... We can go into an area where we're marketing an event, measure sales during the event and measure sales after the event, and see an increase in sales" (Bates and Rowell 2004 p.45). In the US Surgeon General's report, also in 1989, it was noted that "through the ubiquity of advertising, sponsorship, etc. an environment in which tobacco use is seen as familiar and acceptable and the warnings about its health are undermined" (reported in Bates and Rowell 2004 p.41). The arguments of the tobacco industry are being played out again in the twenty-first century as the gambling industry, for example, denies that its advertising in sport has any effect on consumption (Patel 2022), whilst the chief executive of the UK Betting and Gaming Council claims that there is no evidence of any link between gambling advertising and what he calls "problem gambling" (Betting and Gaming Council 2020).

Individual responsibility, public relations and framing

The tobacco industry was able to frame a strategy, developed in the 1950s and 1960s, which it used to lobby and influence behaviour, from government officials to the public (Kessler 2001). The public relations approach of the tobacco industry was to manufacture doubt even when it was clear that smoking causes lung cancer and that second-hand smoke can seriously damage health (Michaels 2020). The industry also focused on personal responsibility, or as Allen describes it, "Social Versus Individual Responsibility for Health" (2021 p.1280). This is core to understanding how harmful industries frame health issues, whereby individual choices and responsible consumption are central values. This is described more fully in Chapter 2. This corporate framing fits the dominant neoliberal economic model in which industries are able to maximise their profits at the expense of consumers' health, arguing that it is industry that should be responsible for any regulation, not government – even if it is the government that is picking up the health bills from the damage caused by this overconsumption.

Brandt's superb dissection of the tobacco industry ('The Cigarette Century', 2007) includes the central role played by Hill & Knowlton, a hugely influential public relations firm in the United States. Hill & Knowlton was engaged by the industry to cast doubt on scientific evidence and to do everything it could to address the looming threat of regulation. We'll meet this company again in the next chapter when the International Olympic Committee was dealing with its own public relations issues.

Case Study: Philip Morris, Virginia Slims and women's tennis

Tobacco companies had used cigarettes to associate themselves with women fighting for equal rights as far back as the 1920s (Frevele 2012), encouraging feminists to smoke so as to challenge patriarchal taboos (Brandt 2007). But the American tobacco companies were quick to see women's new freedoms as an opportunity to cash in. Lucky Strike saw the potential with the slogan, "Reach for a Lucky instead of a sweet", encouraging women to use cigarettes as an alleged mechanism to lose weight (Jacobson 1981). Lower-tar cigarettes – framed as 'safer' than higher-tar brands by the tobacco companies – were aimed mainly at health-conscious women in an approach that other unhealthy commodity industries would copy in later years.

Sport has always been used to target new audiences and the world of women's tennis provided such an opportunity for Philip Morris in 1970. Following the US Surgeon General's Report on Smoking (1964), President Richard Nixon banned cigarette advertising on American television and radio from 1971 (Drucker 2020). In 1970, women players led by Billie Jean King rebelled against the US Lawn Tennis Association because of the wide inequalities in prize money between male and female players to establish a professional women's tennis circuit (King 2021). The initiative was supported by Philip Morris, and the Houston women's invitation tournament in October 1970 was renamed the Virginia Slims Invitational in a promotional move which might arguably be considered the beginning of "event marketing" (Drucker 2020). Philip Morris International had launched its Virginia Slims brand in 1968, with a name suggesting slimness and using aspirational images of confident, jet-setting, independent women. In her autobiography, King described the sponsorship that women's professional tennis received from Philip Morris as "the best business sponsorship in the history of sports" (King 2021 picture caption, pages 216/7). It should be noted that King accepted a place on the board of directors of the tobacco company in 1999 (Pucin 1999).

Philip Morris's sponsorship of the professional women's circuit for 1971 was part of developing a new brand aimed exclusively at women (Dewhirst et al. 2016). During the 1960s about one third of American women smoked, and American tobacco companies wanted to expand this market (Dewhirst *et al.* 2016). Whilst Philip Morris could no longer advertise on television, by sponsoring a sporting event the tobacco company could use the big television audience to target young women and teenage girls (Thomsen 1984). Given women tennis players' attempts to gain pay parity with their male peers, Virginia Slims was positioned as a brand that supported equality, with the campaign line, "You've come a long way, baby" (Dewhirst *et al.* 2016; Vincent 2019). Whilst many of the players were ambivalent about being associated with a tobacco company (King 2021), the offer would have been very tempting when women's tennis was being denied such financial opportunities. During the life of the Virginia Slims tournaments, free cigarettes were given away at stadium entrances, and women players were not allowed to criticise the cigarette brand's sponsorship (O'Keefe and Pollay 1996). In 1977, an additional 400,000 promotional items such as T-shirts and badges featuring the "You've come a long way, baby" slogan were distributed (O'Keefe and Pollay 1996). At this time, both alcohol and tobacco companies referenced the women's liberation movement through aspirations to female emancipation (Hill and Friel 2020). The new women's professional tennis circuit was announced as "You've heard of Women's Lib? This is Women's Lob" (King 2021 p.177).

If there any doubts about whether this type of sponsorship helps to promote smoking, a study examining data from the US National Health Interview Surveys on the age of initiation of smoking concluded that campaigns such as Philip Morris's were associated with a major increase in smoking intake specific to females younger than the legal age for purchasing cigarettes, including a 110 per cent increase in the initiation rate of 12-year-olds between 1967 and about 1973 (Pierce *et al.* 1994). Six years after the launch of Virginia Slims, it was reported that the percentage of teenage women who smoked had nearly doubled (Bates and Rowell 2004 p.26). Tobacco-industry marketing was accompanied by an increase in mortality rates associated with smoking. In 1965, an estimated 30,000 American women died from ten categories of tobacco-related diseases. This figure had risen to 106,000 in 1985 (O'Keefe and Pollay 1996).

Public health advocates criticised the use of tennis stars by cigarette companies in the 1980s, highlighting the Virginia Slims World Championship Series (held in 11 American cities in 1984) and BAT's contract with Martina Navratilova (Thomsen 1984). Billie Jean King herself was strongly challenged both during the Virginia Slims sponsorship and afterwards. King's defence of the sponsorship could have been (and maybe was) written by the tobacco industry direct:

> Look, I know about the dangers of smoking. I understand that and I don't smoke. I'm overweight myself. I eat too much and I eat some of

> the wrong things. It's my own fault. You have to take responsibility for yourself and that's a problem now. Nobody wants to take responsibility. Philip Morris is one of the best corporations I've been associated with. They're starting a campaign now to help keep kids from smoking.
>
> (Pucin 1999)
>
> In 1988, King was quoted as saying, "The freedom of choice is really important … Do you think if you take away cigarette sponsorships people are going to stop smoking? Baloney" (Carr 1988). Dr Rick Richards of Doctors Ought to Care did not mince his words in response and was quoted in the same magazine piece as saying, "Health can be pretty boring when you have the opportunity to line your pockets with millions of dollars". Jensen (1994) noted that the Virginia Slims' slogan, "You've come a long way baby", more accurately described the growing profits of the tobacco companies, which went along with smoking-related diseases becoming the leading cause of premature death amongst women by 1993, than any aspiration towards women's emancipation.

Conclusions

Crompton (1993) argued that the major sponsors of sport were alcohol and tobacco companies which were using an association with healthy lifestyles to promote and normalise their products. The advertising and promotion of tobacco products in sport has largely been stopped following extensive campaigning (Arnott et al. 2007) and effective national and international policies (Shibuya et al. 2003), including the WHO's FCTC (World Health Organization 2003). However, the tactics used by other industries such as 'Big Food', 'Big Soda' or 'Big Alcohol' are very similar to those used by 'Big Tobacco' (Freeman and Sindall 2019). Petticrew et al. (2017) referenced the tobacco industry when examining the tactics of the food, beverage, alcohol and gambling industries in using the concept of complexity to undermine effective public health policies.

The cynical targeting of women smokers by using cigarettes as symbols of freedom and emancipation (O'Keefe and Pollay 1996) is well illustrated in the case study of Virginia Slims. Despite the broadcast ban on American television, cigarettes were the most promoted consumer product in America in the 1970s and 1980s, with the tobacco industry spending heavily in the print media (O'Keefe and Pollay 1996) and in sport sponsorship.

In considering sport sponsorship, there is a strong argument for taking a cohesive systems approach across the unhealthy commodity industries (Knai et al. 2021). It might be argued that a position of "tobacco exceptionalism" (Collin 2012; McCambridge and Morris 2019), in which tobacco has been considered a unique threat to public health, might have inadvertently led to inadequacies in policy coherence in addressing non-communicable diseases by not considering other unhealthy industries such as food and alcohol (to which may be added gambling), which also have global health impacts.

References

Allen, L.N. (2021) 'Commercial determinants of global health' in Kickbusch, I., Ganten, D. and Moeti, M., eds., *Handbook of Global Health*, Cham: Springer International Publishing, 1275–1310.

Alton, R. (2021) 'A lot of bottle', *Spectator*, 2021/06/26/, 346(10061), 61, available: https://link.gale.com/apps/doc/A667265932/LitRC?u=glasuni&sid=googleScholar&xid=4bc789a4 [accessed 2021/11/16/].

Arnott, D., Dockrell, M., Sandford, A. and Willmore, I. (2007) 'Comprehensive smoke-free legislation in England: How advocacy won the day', *Tobacco Control*, 16, 423–428.

Bates, C. and Rowell, A. (2004) *Tobacco Explained… The Truth about the Tobacco Industry… in its Own Words*. Center for Tobacco Control Research and Education, available: https://escholarship.org/uc/item/9fp6566b [accessed 16 August 2022].

Betting and Gaming Council (2020) *BGC Statement on House of Lords Committee Report* [press release], available: https://bettingandgamingcouncil.com/news/bgc-statement-house-of-lords-committee [accessed 30 June 2022].

Brandt, A.M. (2007) *The Cigarette Century*, New York: Basic Books.

Brownell, K.D. and Warner, K.E. (2009) 'The perils of ignoring history: Big tobacco played dirty and millions died. How similar is big food?', *The Millbank Quarterly*, 87(1), 259–294.

Carr, J. (1988) 'Sports junkies are plied with booze and cigarettes as well', *Deseret News*, available: https://www.deseret.com/1988/8/21/18775913/sports-junkies-are-plied-with-booze-and-cigarettes-as-well [accessed 16 November 2021].

Collin, J. (2003) 'Think global, smoke local: Transnational tobacco companies and cognitive globalization' in Lee, K., ed., *Health Impacts of Globalization. Towards Global Governance*, Basingstoke: Palgrave Macmillan.

Collin, J. (2012) 'Tobacco control, global health policy and development: Towards policy coherence in global governance', *Tobacco Control*, 21, 274–280.

Connolly, G.N. (1992) 'Worldwide expansion of transnational tobacco industry', *Journal of the National Cancer Institute. Monographs*, (12), 29–35.

Cornwell, T.B. (1997) 'The use of sponsorship-linked marketing by tobacco firms: International public policy issues', *The Journal of Consumer Affairs*, 31(2), 238–254.

Couch, E.T., Urata, J. and Chaffee, B.W. (2019) 'Limited-edition smokeless tobacco packaging: Behind the camouflage', *Tobacco Induced Diseases*, 17, 58–58, available: http://dx.doi.org/10.18332/tid/110676.

Crompton, J.L. (1993) 'Sponsorship of sport by tobacco and alcohol companies: A review of the issues', *Journal of Sport & Social Issues*, 73, 148–167.

DeParle, J. (1989) 'Warning: Sports stars may be hazardous to your health', *The Washington Monthly*, 21(8), 34–48.

Dewhirst, T. (2004) 'Smoke and ashes: Tobacco sponsorship of sports and regulatory issues in Canada' in Kahle, L.R. and Riley, C., eds., *Sports Marketing and the Psychology of Marketing Communication*, Mahwah: Lawrence Erlbaum.

Dewhirst, T., Lee, W.B., Fong, G.T. and Ling, P.M. (2016) 'Exporting an inherently harmful product: The marketing of Virginia Sims cigarettes in the United States, Japan, and Korea', *Journal of Business Ethics*, 139(1), 161–181.

Drucker, J. (2020) The original nine: The beginning of women's pro tennis, available: https://www.usopen.org/en_US/news/articles/2020-03-09/2020-03-09_2020-03-09_the_original_nine_the_beginning_of_womens_pro_tennis.html [accessed 8 November 2021].

Foer, F. (2004) *How Soccer Explains the World: An Unlikely Theory of Globalization*, New York: HarperCollins.

Freeman, B. and Sindall, C. (2019) 'Countering the commercial determinants of health: Strategic challenges for public health', *Public Health Research & Practice*, 29(3), e2931917.

Frevele, J. (2012) 'That time cigarette manufacturers got women to smoke by equating it with freedom', *Mary Sue*, 27 February 2012, available: https://www.themarysue.com/smoking-suffragettes/ [accessed 17 November 2021].

Gate, R. (1989) *Rugby League. An Illustrated History*, London: Arthur Barker.

Grant-Braham, B. and Britton, J. (2011) 'Motor racing, tobacco company sponsorship, barcodes and alibi marketing', *Tobacco Control*, 21, 529–535.

Griffin, E. (2012) 'Football and smoking: Past and present', *Sportslens*, 20 April 2012, available: https://sportslens.com/smoking-in-football/86928/ [accessed 2 September 2020].

Hansard (1983) *Tobacco Industry (Sports Sponsorship)*, 44, available: https://hansard.parliament.uk/commons/1983-06-30/debates/797d539b-2f05-455a-b2f3-95b25bd32079/TobaccoIndustry [accessed 9 November 2021].

Harris, H. (2018) *Pelé: His Life and Times-Revised & Updated*, London: Kings Road Publishing.

Hill, S.E. and Friel, S. (2020) '"As Long as It Comes off as a Cigarette Ad, Not a Civil Rights Message": Gender, inequality and the commercial determinants of health', *International Journal of Environmental Research and Public Health*, 17, 7902–7920.

Jacobson, B. (1981) *The Ladykillers. Why Smoking Is a Feminist Issue*, London: Pluto Press.

Jensen, P.M. (1994) 'A history of women and smoking', *Canadian Woman Studies*, 14(3), 29.

Kessler, D. (2001) *A Question of Intent: A Great American Battle with a Deadly Industry*, New York: Public Affairs.

King, B.J. (2021) *All In. An Autobiography*, London: Viking.

Knai, C., Petticrew, M., Capewell, S., Cassidy, R., Collin, J., Cummins, S., Eastmure, E., Fafard, P., Fitzgerald, N. and Gilmore, A.B. (2021) 'The case for developing a cohesive systems approach to research across unhealthy commodity industries', *BMJ Global Health*, 6(2), e003543.

MacKenzie, R., Collin, J. and Sriwongcharoen, K. (2007) 'Thailand - lighting up a dark market: British American Tobacco, sports sponsorship and the circumvention of legislation', *Journal of Epidemiology and Community Health*, 61(1), 28–33.

Malik, R. (2010) *Catch Me If You Can: Big Food Using Big Tobacco's Playbook? Applying the Lessons Learned from Big Tobacco to Attack the Obesity Epidemic*, Internal Harvard Library Report, unpublished.

McCambridge, J. and Morris, S. (2019) 'Comparing alcohol with tobacco indicates that it is time to move beyond tobacco exceptionalism', *European Journal of Public Health*, 29(2), 200–201.

Michaels, D. (2020) *The Triumph of Doubt. Dark Money and the Science of Deception*, New York: Oxford University Press.

Mitchell and Kenyon (1902) *First Ever Film of Manchester United (1902)*, London: BFI.

Moodie, R., Stuckler, D., Monteiro, C., Sheron, N., Neal, B., Thamarangsi, T., Lincoln, P. and Casswell, S. (2013) 'Profits and pandemics: Prevention of harmful effects of tobacco, alcohol, and ultra-processed food and drink industries', *Lancet*, 381, 670–679.

O'Keefe, A.M. and Pollay, R.W. (1996) 'Deadly targeting of women in promoting cigarettes', *Journal of the American Medical Women's Association (1972)*, 51(1–2), 67.

O'Malley, N. (2014) 'Pelé reflects on a lifetime of world fame', *The Sydney Morning Herald*, 8 November 2014, available: https://www.smh.com.au/lifestyle/pel-reflects-on-a-lifetime-of-world-fame-20141106-11cdlp.html [accessed 17 November 2021].

Patel, K. (2022) *Gambling and Advertising*, available: https://www.gamblingeducationnetwork.com/post/gambling-and-advertising [accessed 30 June 2022].

Pelé (2007) *Pelé. The Autobiography*, London: Pocket Books.

Petticrew, M., Katikireddi, S.V., Knai, C., Cassidy, R., Hessari, N.M., Thomas, J. and Weishaar, H. (2017) '"Nothing can be done until everything is done": The use of complexity arguments by food, beverage, alcohol and gambling industries', *Journal of Epidemiology and Community Health*, 71, 1078–1083.

Pierce, J.P., Lee, L. and Gilpin, E.A. (1994) 'Smoking initiation by adolescent girls, 1944 through 1988. As association with targeted advertising', *JAMA*, 271(8), 608–611.

Pollay, R.W. (1994) 'Promises, promises: Self-regulation of US cigarette broadcast advertising in the 1960s', *Tobacco Control*, 3(2), 134.

Polley, M. (1998) *Moving the Goalposts. A History of Sport and Society since 1945*, London: Routledge.

Pucin, D. (1999) 'Billie Jean is blowing smoke at her responsibility to youth', *Los Angeles Times*, 22 October, 1999, available: https://www.latimes.com/archives/la-xpm-1999-oct-22-sp-25171-story.html [accessed 8 November 2021].

Royal College of Physicians of London (1962) *Smoking and Health. Summary of a Report of the Royal College of Physicians of London on Smoking in Relation to Cancer of the Lung and Other Diseases*, London, available: https://www.rcplondon.ac.uk/projects/outputs/smoking-and-health-1962 [accessed 17 November 2021].

Shibuya, K., Ciecierski, C., Guindon, E., Bettcher, D.W., Evans, D.B., Murray, C.J.L. and Control, W.H.O.F.C.o.T. (2003) 'WHO framework convention on tobacco control: Development of an evidence based global public health treaty', *BMJ*, 327(7407), 154–157, available: http://dx.doi.org/10.1136/bmj.327.7407.154.

Simkin, J. (2020) 'Football cigarette cards', available: https://spartacus-educational.com/Fcigarette.htm [accessed 14 July 2020].

Sparks, R., Dewhirst, T., Jette, S. and Schweinbenz, A. (2005) 'Historical hangovers or burning possibilities. Regulation and adaption in global tobacco and alcohol sponsorship' in Amis, J. and Cornwell, T. B., eds., *Global Sport Sponsorship*, Oxford: Berg.

Thomsen, R.J. (1984) 'Get the smoke out of tennis', *The Washington Post*, 26 February 1984, available: https://www.washingtonpost.com/archive/opinions/1984/02/26/get-the-smoke-out-of-tennis/14a4a25f-1b31-41ce-af2c-8a205bedc942/ [accessed 9 November 2021].

Vincent, J. (2019) '"You've come a long way baby" but when will you get to deuce? The media (re)presentation of women's tennis in the post Open Era' in Lake, R. J., ed., *Routledge Handbook of Tennis*, London: Routledge, 223–233.

Waxman, H.A. (2002) 'The future of the global tobacco treaty negotiations', *The New England Journal of Medicine*, 346(12), 936–939, available: http://dx.doi.org/10.1056/NEJMsb020030.

Whannel, G. (1986) 'The unholy alliance: Notes on television and the remaking of British sport 1965–85', *Leisure Studies*, 5(2), 129–145, available: http://dx.doi.org/10.1080/02614368600390111.

Whannel, G. (2002) *Fields in Vision. Television Sport and Cultural Transformation*, London: Routledge.

Wilson, N. (1988) *The Sports Business*, London: Piatkus.

World Health Organization (2003) *WHO Framework Convention on Tobacco Control*, Geneva: WHO, available: https://www.who.int/fctc/text_download/en/ [accessed 23 August 2020].

Zoss, J. and Bowman, J. (1989) *Diamonds in the Rough. The Untold History of Baseball*, Lincoln: University of Nebraska.

Chapter 5
Mega-events and sponsorship

Introduction

Unhealthy commodity industries seeking ways to market their brands to as large an audience as possible use mega-sporting events such as the Olympic Games and the FIFA World Cup to reach huge global audiences (Collin and MacKenzie 2006; Morgan et al. 2017). Mega-events demand exclusivity for their brands (Hall 2006). Indeed the International Olympic Committee details how it protects the Olympic brand and monitors broadcasting to identify any messages that might infringe the rights of its commercial partners (International Olympic Committee 2016 p.139). Sponsoring the World Cup and/or the Olympics provides brand exposure across sports venues, broadcasting and digital media (Tomlinson and Young 2006b; Morgan et al. 2017; Bragg et al. 2018; Smart 2018; Semens 2019; Cornwell 2020).

This chapter will explore the relationship between sport and globalisation briefly and describe the characteristics of a mega-event, before considering the sponsorship arrangements at the Summer Olympic Games (the Winter Olympics have not been considered for space reasons) and the World Cup. The chapter will conclude by briefly mentioning the opposition to the commercialisation of these events.

Sport and globalisation

Globalisation might be considered as a system of interconnected communication, transportation and economic networks and markets spread across the planet (Ritzer 2016). It is a contested concept but, in many cases, it is presented by the more affluent countries as a positive process in favour of free and unregulated markets (Robertson and White 2016). The health impacts of globalisation are gradually being explored (Lee 2003) and this was covered in more detail in a previous chapter. However, as was noted earlier, the comparatively new concept of commercial determinants of health (Kickbusch et al. 2016; de Lacy-Vawdon and Livingstone 2020), in which the impacts of the various activities of transnational corporations on population health are investigated, has largely neglected sport (Ireland et al. 2019).

DOI: 10.4324/9781003239734-5

Roche (2006) wrote that sports studies have traditionally taken the nation-state and national identity as a key point of reference in research and that sport is rarely considered as a relevant social phenomenon in studies of globalisation. Tomlinson and Young (2006b) argued that any history of globalisation should include the foundation of the International Olympic Committee (IOC) in 1894 and the Fédération Internationale de Football Association (FIFA) in 1904. They described the cultural and political growth and influence of these organisations, accompanied by the mediated base of their international sports events, which attracted the interest of transnational corporations. Giulianotti and Robertson (2007) saw sport as having a dual role as a motor and metric of globalisation, and Tomlinson and Young (2006b) described sports mega-events as effectively global marketing opportunities for multi-national companies. During the latter part of the twentieth century, sport's popular cultural appeal and "unrivalled aura of authenticity" (Smart 2007 p.7) made it the perfect vehicle for corporate brands and consumerism. With the growth of the broadcasting of televised sport, the marketing of global brands has been described as cultural standardisation or "Coca-Colonization" and "McDonaldization" (Ritzer 2010, 2011), whereby sporting events might be considered new cathedrals of consumption in which fans are lured into consuming at ever higher levels. These transnational fast-food businesses are considered global icons, representing a model of efficient, predictable and controlled consumerism (Ritzer 2011). Coca-Cola and McDonald's are examples of companies that have used sport sponsorship internationally to promote their brands in order to increase consumption and, therefore, contribute to the worldwide burden of obesity (Gokani *et al.* 2021).

Characteristics of a mega-event

Roche described 'mega-events' as "large-scale cultural (including commercial and sporting) events which have a dramatic character, mass popular appeal and international significance" (2000 p.1). Roche saw sport as an essential component of modern studies of globalisation and modern culture, with the Olympics as the most visible and spectacular example of a "dense social eco-system" (2000 p.3), joining the football World Cup in attracting vast global television audiences. These mega-events, mediated through television and the internet, might be considered key elements in the development of global culture and consumerism. Müller (2017) considered the dimensions of mega-events in terms of visitor attractiveness, mediated reach, cost and transformative impact. Using these indicators, the Summer Olympic Games and the men's football World Cup finish at the top of a table based on the value of broadcast rights and tickets sold. But using similar metrics, other events such as the Asian Games and the men's European Football Championships are also highly successful. For the purposes of this chapter, I will consider the Olympics and the men's football World Cup for their unrivalled sporting global reach. In addition, the women's football World Cup will also be briefly considered, as its popularity develops rapidly internationally and attracts the interest of sponsors.

Both the FIFA World Cup and the Olympics might be considered as brands themselves (Tomlinson 2014; Manoli et al. 2022). The events' organisers (FIFA and the IOC) go to great lengths to protect their official logos, names and signage. English Premier League clubs take the same approach, as shown in Chapter 7. The FIFA World Cup and Olympic brands are used to promote positive brand associations and are the cornerstones of their respective sponsorship programmes (Payne 2006; Ferrand et al. 2012; Manoli et al. 2022).

The principal sources of revenue for the Olympics are the sale of television rights and sponsorship, both international and domestic (Zimbalist 2020). Olympic broadcasting revenues grew from US$1.2 million in 1960 to US$4.1 billion for the 2013–2016 Olympiad and the Rio Games (International Olympic Committee 2016). The Olympic Partner (TOPS) worldwide sponsorship programme will be described fully below. Income from sponsorship has risen from US£96 million to over US$1 billion during the last 30 years (International Olympic Committee 2016). FIFA's income is structured similarly, with the World Cup providing its principal commercial vehicle. Its financial statements for 2020 show revenue from the sale of television broadcasting rights for the World Cup held in Russia in 2018 to have been US$343 million (the largest contribution is for rights sold in Asia and North Africa) (FIFA 2021). The second largest source of income in 2019 (US$165 million) was marketing rights, which is income from sponsorship. Revenue from licensing rights is also significant (US$160 million), through which FIFA receives income from brand licensing for video games. Whilst the economics of staging a mega-event become ever more challenging for host cities (Preuss 2004; Zimbalist 2020), it is difficult to see them as anything other than "festivals of consumption" (Smart 2018 p.243).

The FIFA World Cup

Giulianotti and Robertson (2009) presented football as a global game influenced by global processes and flows. They referenced Robertson's earlier work, which defined globalisation as characterised by increasing global connectivity through digital connectiveness and an "intensification of consciousness of the world as a whole" (Robertson 1992 p.8). Giulianotti and Robertson used Robertson's phased historical model of globalisation and applied it to football to enable an understanding of the sport's commercial origins and its global development. The internationalisation of football, combined with the expanding reach of transnational corporations and the development of broadcasting, has made the sport the ideal vehicle for the marketing of brands to a global audience.

In Giulianotti and Robertson's model, the first phase is germinal or pre-history and refers to academic debates relating to the origins of football. The second phase of football's development is from the 1830s to the 1870s when the social elites in England were instrumental in establishing the rules of the game in 1863, following the demand for common rules from teams formed in public schools. The third phase of the football and globalisation model is a take-off phase which covers the 1870s to the mid-1920s. This period was important to football becoming a global sport as this marked the development of the international game, initially across Europe and Latin America, and then into the parts of Africa and Asia most closely linked to Europe. FIFA was formed in 1904. The Confederación Sudamericana de Fútbol (CONMEBOL) was founded in 1916 to represent South American interests and reflected the early global diffusion of the game. The first World Cup was launched by FIFA in 1930 and was won by Uruguay. The 1954 World Cup, held in Switzerland, was televised widely across Europe, building a following and an audience for football (Giulianotti and Robertson 2009). Also in 1954, the Union des Associations Européennes de Football (UEFA) was formed, reflecting the broader range of post-war European alliances (Giulianotti 1999).

Brazil's João Havelange became president of FIFA in 1974 (taking over from Sir Stanley Rous). His election might be considered an event of social and historical significance (Sugden and Tomlinson 1998), marking the transformation of FIFA into a global economic force and brand, which would help influence and effect a similar change in the IOC in 1980 (Burlamaqui 2019). Goldblatt wrote that Havelange's position was "created and sustained by mobilizing the football elites of the global peripheries" (2007 p.527). In turn, "that power was multiplied a thousand times by the global expansion to television" (2007 p.527). International football was transformed through television coverage with the 1970 World Cup, the first finals to be widely televised in colour (Giulianotti and Robertson 2009 p.22). Whannel argued that the growth of television and sponsorship "constituted an economic force that ... in turn generated a cultural transformation" (1986 p.129) between 1965 and 1985. A huge expansion of sports marketing was required to finance the expansion of the World Cup following the election of Havelange.

Modern packages of sponsorship rights, based on the sale of television rights, were first conceived of in the 1970s and developed at the World Cup (Semens 2019). By 1975, FIFA had agreed its first global deal with Coca-Cola. Getting a blue-chip global company such as Coca-Cola associated with football was seen as providing credibility and prestige to the sport and opening the door to the sponsorship of world football (Sugden and Tomlinson 1998). In 1978, Coca-Cola paid FIFA US$8.33 million for exclusive rights to stadium advertising (Tomlinson 2014 p.95). Despite regular corruption scandals involving the world governing body (Conn 2017), FIFA has retained its partnership with Coca-Cola for over 40 years and is still able to attract a string of transnational corporate brands as partners. FIFA's tiered and packaged model has provided a model for all major sports to aspire to and attempt to replicate, including, of course, football in member countries and domestic leagues (Semens 2019). We shall see this described in Chapter 7 in the case study of the English Premier League.

Havelange's election as FIFA president in 1974 was predicated on his commitment to increase the global appeal of football by developing the game in Africa and Asia. This required substantial new funding, and many authors have described how this was developed in a marketing agreement with Horst Dassler, son of the founder of Adidas, and Patrick Nally, marketing and sports sponsorship specialist (Sugden and Tomlinson 1998; Horne and Manzenreiter 2006; Goldblatt 2007; Smart 2007). There were six corporate sponsors for the 1978 World Cup in Argentina which established the basic template. Capitalism's search for new consumer markets, through the process of globalisation, found a happy and willing vehicle in football. And Coca-Cola, following the example of the tobacco industry in its astute marketing and total disregard for any health concerns (Nestle 2015), was the perfect partner for the developing commercialism of the World Cup.

Mexico in 1986 was the second World Cup tournament to feature tobacco company sponsor RJ Reynolds and its Camel brand as one of the four major sponsors. The sponsorship agreement for RJ Reynolds included the placement of 47-metre long Camel signs next to the pitch, ensuring visibility to the 650 million television viewers (Crompton 1993). The broadcasting of the World Cup was supported by many national promotions, including in Malaysia, where competitions were organised in the leading newspapers (Assunta and Chapman 2004). Criticism of the example this was setting to children seemed to have an impact, and FIFA pledged to stop tobacco advertising at its events at this time (Cronin 2018). Between 1982 and 2006, however, unhealthy World Cup sponsors included Anheuser-Busch (Budweiser), Cinzano, Coca-Cola, McDonald's, Snickers (Mars/M&Ms), RJ Reynolds (Camel and Winston cigarettes) and Vini d'Italia (Smart 2007).

In reflecting on France hosting the FIFA World Cup in 1998, French sociologist Pierre Bourdieu described the trend towards commercialisation in sport, and particularly football, in which the key relationship was defined as being between the sport's practitioners and television (1999 pp.15–21). Football is "produced to be commercialised in the form of *televised spectacle*, a *commercial product* which is especially profitable because football is widely practised" (1999 p.16). The factors involved in this commercialisation are the rules of neoliberal economics, as managed by the sport policies of different countries. Bourdieu argued that "sport visible as spectacle hides the reality of a system of actors competing over commercial stakes" (1999 p.17). The actors competing include

> Sports industry managers who control television and sponsoring rights, the managers of television channels competing for national broadcasting rights (or rights covering linguistic areas), the bosses of major industrial companies such as Adidas or Coca-Cola competing with each other for exclusive rights to link their products with the sports event, and finally television producers.
> (Bourdieu 1999 p.18)

The modern-day pattern of sponsorship is illustrated by the FIFA World Cup which was held in Russia in 2018. There were seven FIFA partners as shown in Table 5.1. Each sponsor was reported to be paying 32 million euros to FIFA (Becker 2018).

Table 5.1 FIFA commercial partners at the 2018 World Cup

Sponsor	Country of origin	Industry
Adidas	Germany	Sportswear
Coca-Cola	USA	Soft drinks
Gazprom	Russia	Energy
Hyundai/Kia	South Korea	Automobile
Qatar Airways	Qatar	Airline
Visa	USA	Financial
Wanda	China	Enterprises

In addition, there was a second category of FIFA World Cup sponsors paying between 8 and 20 million euros to advertise at the World Cup and the Confederations Cup (this was held between the winners of the six continental cups, the World Cup winners and the host nation, but was abolished in 2019) (Becker 2018). These were:

- McDonald's (US): fast food;
- Budweiser (US): alcohol;
- Hisense (China): electronics;
- Mengniu Group (China): dairy products and ice cream;
- Vivo (China): smartphones and accessories.

Finally, there was a third tier of 'regional sponsors' including Russian Railways and the Egyptian Tourist Board. The 'energy' drink brand Gatorade used the World Cup to promote its product by featuring international footballers Lionel Messi (Argentina) and Luis Suárez (Uruguay) in its advertising at this time, although Gatorade was not an official World Cup partner (B&T 2018).

As the tobacco industry used sport sponsorship to avoid advertising restrictions on tobacco, so the alcohol industry has demonstrated its corporate power in overruling national regulations regarding the sale of alcohol at the World Cup. In Chapter 2, we saw how FIFA insisted on the sale of beer at the 2014 World Cup in Brazil on behalf of its sponsor, Budweiser (Kickbusch 2012). Similarly, as a condition of being allocated the 2018 World Cup, Russia relaxed advertising restrictions on alcohol in order to accommodate FIFA's sponsors (Moriarty 2018). At the time of writing, it is unclear how alcohol sponsorship will be dealt with at the 2022 World Cup in Qatar, a Muslim country with strict controls on alcohol (Mills 2022).

Case Study: The marketing of unhealthy brands during the 2018 FIFA World Cup

As described above, the World Cup has a huge global audience, with FIFA (2018a) estimating that 3.57 billion people watched at least part of the official broadcast coverage of the 2018 World Cup which was held in Russia. In the United Kingdom, the Broadcasters' Audience Research Board (BARB) (2019) reported that the World Cup reached 53.1 million of the UK's 66.4 million population in 2018. Two million unique viewers watched the Sweden v England quarter-final on the BBC's digital platforms.

A study quantified visual marketing references to unhealthy brands during the UK broadcasting of the World Cup (Ireland et al. 2021). The quarter-finals, semi-finals and final of the competition were selected as broadcast on both the public service provider, the BBC, and the main commercial broadcaster, ITV. References to alcohol, gambling, fast food and sugary drink brands were coded throughout the broadcasts, including the pre- and post-match discussions, half-time and all playing time and any commercial breaks.

The results showed frequent and extensive marketing of unhealthy brands across the eight broadcasts (these included the final as broadcast both on BBC and ITV) totalling 28 hours, 41 minutes and 13 seconds of coverage. With an average of 224 per broadcast and 1.2 per minute, 1,794 unhealthy brand marketing references were recorded. If more than one brand was broadcast at any one time, each separate brand reference was recorded. If, however, the same brand was reproduced many times in the same camera shot (this is very common in perimeter advertising), it was only counted once. Blurred or obscured images were not included.

Hardly surprisingly, 95 per cent of the references were to one of FIFA's official sponsors (the exceptions were in the commercials that aired on ITV during its coverage). McDonald's received 25 per cent of the references, Budweiser 24 per cent, Coca-Cola 22 per cent, Mengniu (a Chinese manufacturing and distribution company of dairy products and ice cream) 17 per cent and Powerade (a brand of Coca-Cola) 9 per cent. The most common location for the branding was the pitch perimeter, as is also the case in similar studies in the United Kingdom that have looked at branding at sports events (Adams et al. 2014; Graham and Adams 2014; Purves et al. 2017). Of the 84 unhealthy marketing references that occurred in the commercial breaks shown by ITV, 38 (45 per cent) were for gambling brands. In-game advertisements using the pitch perimeter are controlled by FIFA, which ensures that their sponsors' logos are easily visible. Thus, FIFA's commercial partnerships are driving exposure to unhealthy brands, allowing transnational corporations to use the rich cultural appeal of the World Cup mega-event to drive up unhealthy consumption globally. Indeed, this is the essential promise of FIFA's marketing rights, which increased FIFA revenue in 2018 to US$1.6 million, with 14 new sponsors, including substantial new investment from China (FIFA 2018b). The contract is explicit in linking event-related media and advertising rights to broadcasting (FIFA 2018b p.76).

The women's World Cup

The commercialisation of women's football has come very late in comparison to men's football (Williams 2021); however, the development of the women's World Cup provides an example of the event packaging and marketing which has brought women's sport into the capitalist consumerist marketplace (Mangan 2004).

Many writers have noted that women's football is lacking in both historical records and research (Hong and Mangan 2004; Dunn 2016; Pope 2017), although the work of Jean Williams (2003; 2007; 2013) should be noted, in particular in exploring the development of women's participation in football in England and globally. Like men's football, many of the early women's teams in England originated in factories, with the most famous, Dick, Kerr Ladies, being established at a Preston engineering works in 1917 whilst many men were fighting in the First World War (Lopez 1997). Despite the success of women's football in attracting crowds of spectators, or perhaps because of this success, the Football Association in England banned women from Football League grounds from 1921 until 1972 (until 1974 in Scotland), which Williams suggested in part represented a "peculiarly English expression of contempt for women who play football" (2003 p.4). During this time, some teams, such as Dick, Kerr Ladies, carried on playing and other teams began to be formed in the 1960s. Finding income in these times must have been very difficult and highlights the problems that some sports, far away from elite professional circles, have in maintaining their leagues and fixtures. Following England's success in the FIFA World Cup in 1966, there was much interest and development in both men's and women's football. As early football pioneer Sue Lopez (1997) recalls, one women's team formed in the Southampton area in 1966 was named Flame United, after the magazine of its parent company, Southern Gas. In a rather unpleasant echo of the future, Flame United obtained sponsorship in 1967/1968 from Charlie Malizia, a Southampton bookmaker, and became known as Inter-Malizia.

The Women's Football Association was formed in 1970 with the objective of establishing an official English women's team (Williams 2007). When the English national team started playing internationals again in 1972, alcohol companies were quick to offer financial support. The only women's home international tournament (involving England, Scotland and Wales) took place in May 1976 and was sponsored by Pony ("the little drink with the big kick"), which gave its name to the competition (Turner 2017). In 1978, Martini & Rossi, now part of Bacardi Ltd, were the sponsors of the Women's Football Association (Williams 2021), and the match programme for England v Belgium, played at The Dell stadium, Southampton, in October, carried the Martini & Rossi logo on the cover together with a full-page advertisement on the back.

This commodification of women's football can also be observed in the development of the women's World Cup, as FIFA saw the growing financial opportunities that could be exploited. This should be viewed in the context of the disparity between sponsorship in men's and women's sports, which has been heavily influenced by the values and beliefs of decision makers and the lack of media representation of women's sport (Shaw and Amis 2001). As women began to attend both women's and men's sports events in larger numbers in the context of their changing leisure lives (Pope 2017), they began to be considered as consumers (Shaw and Amis 2001). In the last chapter, we saw how Philip Morris, a tobacco company, targeted a new market of women smokers through its sponsorship of the Virginia Slims (a cigarette brand) tennis circuit (Dewhirst et al. 2016). Although writers such as Suzanne Wrack (2022) see a more progressive streak in women's football, as women sports fans enter the traditional male domain of the sports stadium (Pope 2017), can we see any differences between men's and women's sport in terms of the companies that wish to associate their brands with these events?

The FIFA women's World Cup was inaugurated in China in 1991, although an unofficial tournament took place in 1988 (Lopez 1997). Williams (2013) argued that as football offered increased profitability, so FIFA ensured it took financial control in finding an additional competition it could market. Strictly speaking, the FIFA women's World Cup is not a mega-event (Williams 2007) by Roche's (2000) previously cited definition, in that it is, arguably, yet to gain mass popular appeal, although that may be changing. However, it is becoming a global event, with 32 nations due to be represented in the 2023 tournament, to be held in Australia and New Zealand. The 2019 women's World Cup, held in France, was the most successful yet in terms of audiences, with FIFA claiming that 1.12 billion people watched the competition, including 82.18 million who watched the final between the United States and the Netherlands (Wagner 2021). This was an increase of 56 per cent from the 2015 final, which in turn had enjoyed a huge rise in television audiences from the previous tournaments (FIFA 2015). It helped that the US team was in the 2019 final, as women's football (soccer) has been very successful for some time in the United States (Roxborough 2019). In England, the home country's Euro 2022 final win over Germany was watched by a British television audience of 17.4 million with 87,192 spectators at Wembley Stadium (BBC 2022). UEFA see the commercial value of women's football increasing sixfold in the next decade with sponsorship being the fastest growing revenue stream (UEFA 2022).

It is difficult to find mention of the financial arrangements of the early women's World Cup, but the professionalisation of women's football provided a growing platform for sponsors (Williams 2013). The first tournament in 1991 was known as the M&M's Cup (Williams 2007 p.142), as confectionery giant Mars (now part of the transnational Mars Wrigley) was the sole sponsor (Glendenning 2019). During the 1999 tournament held in the United States, it was noted that the Canadian captain, Christine Sinclair, was used "as an icon for the tournament, advertising products including the World Cup sponsor, Coca-Cola" (Dunn 2016 p.61). In addition, Mia Hamm, a star of the American football team, made a series of Gatorade commercials with basketball star Michael Jordan (Mullen 1999; Wrack 2022). By the time of the 2019 tournament in France, media commentators were declaring that sponsors were excited about the growing popularity of women's football (Levy 2019). FIFA's global sponsors were almost identical to those at the men's tournament of 2018 (only Gazprom was omitted) and included Coca-Cola once again. The national teams now boasted their own set of sponsors (most had at least five sponsors) including, for example, Australia with a gambling partner (Bet365), Cameroon with a beer (33 Export), England with Budweiser and Lucozade (Lyons 2019), and the United States sponsored by Budweiser, Coca-Cola and Powerade. Coca-Cola sponsored 8 of the 24 teams taking part. Thus, the commodification of the women's game at a global level is beginning to match that of men's football.

It is worth noting, however, as a postscript, that Scottish Women's Football stated in 2016 that it would not accept sponsorship from gambling and alcohol companies (Christie 2019). This position remained in place in the 2021/2022 season (Scottish Women's Football 2021).

The Olympic Games

Unlike the football World Cup, the Olympics has a history dating back to ancient times. The founder of the modern Olympic Games, Baron Pierre de Coubertin, was unafraid to draw on his version of classical civilisation (Kidd 1984; Guttman 1994; Hill 1996) in advocating the revival of the Olympics in Greece in 1894. Despite the mythologising of romantics across the centuries (Gruneau 2017), the ancient Olympics were set within a highly commercialised sporting culture (Goldblatt 2016). The original Olympic Games can be traced back to 776 BCE and continued until at least 261 CE and possibly later; the Roman Emperor Theodosius I banned the games in 392 CE (Hill 1996; Goldblatt 2016). Although there is some disagreement on exactly how the early Olympians were remunerated, it is clear that professionalism was encouraged and that the event winners were richly rewarded by their home cities (Young 2004). Similarly, the Circus Maximus, the principal 'sports' venue of the Roman Empire, with an estimated capacity of 150,000, hosted various activities including chariot racing, for which the winners received substantial sums of money (Gruneau 2017). Young (2004 p.98) noted that festivals such as Thebes and Marathon were described as "money games" in the Hellenistic-Roman period after 500 BCE.

Like the British Victorian elites, de Coubertin saw taking part in sport as an educational and a moral practice (McFee 2012). It suited the upper social classes to formulate rules that debarred mechanics and labourers from competing, based on a concept of amateurism (Young 2004). Kidd argued that de Coubertin's "symbolic return to the past" (1984 p.72) led to the success of today's Olympics, but also distorted history by ignoring the prizes and rewards given to competition victors in the ancient world, whilst propagating the myth that sport somehow stood above politics, despite all evidence to the contrary. These myths have affected how the Olympics are viewed up to the present day. De Coubertin's vision of global sport was rooted in patronage and privilege, depended on elites, and excluded women (Tomlinson 1984). Miller's admirable *Official History of the Olympic Games* (2008) detailed these early years from Athens in 1896, to Paris in 1900, the first games in the United States in St Louis in 1904, and London in 1908.

There was some early commercial involvement in the Games, even at this time. Eastman Kodak, the camera company, advertised in the Book of Official Results in Athens in 1896 (Bramley 2018). At the 1900 Olympics, the French provided prize-money for some events, whilst the Games in St Louis benefited from automobile transport thanks to commercial arrangements (Miller 2008). The 1908 Olympic marathon in London had beef extract manufacturers Oxo as its 'Official Caterers' (Polley 1998). The 1924 Paris Games even had advertising in the stadium for food and alcohol brands such as Ovalmaltine, Cinzano and Dubonnet, whilst the Games Guide featured advertisements for Mercier champagne and Grand Marnier liqueurs. This remains the only time advertising has been allowed in the Olympic stadium (Barney et al. 2002). Tomlinson (2006a) argued that this has been a brilliant piece of marketing. Whilst, at the present-day Olympics, the surrounding streets are "orgies of consumption" (Tomlinson 2006a p.15), the venue itself remains free of commercial signage, providing an illusion of purity and idealism and helping global broadcasters to sell advertising.

Coca-Cola's involvement with the Olympics began in Amsterdam in 1928 but became much more significant at the 1932 Games held in Los Angeles. The company used teenagers to give out its product, billboards promoted the Coca-Cola logo along with the Games, whilst free Coca-Cola merchandise was widely distributed (Keys 2004). These Games were organised by local businessmen who were more interested in the advertising opportunity for the American city than in sport (Keys 2004). The financing of the Olympics had always been a concern and continued to be so in the early part of the twentieth century (Tomlinson 2006a), but, as with all sports and sporting events, it was television that transformed the Games, supported by marketing and sports sponsorship. The Los Angeles Games of 1932 provided a state-of-the-art media operation based around the print media and an early global audience (Tomlinson 2006b; Goldblatt 2016). Whilst there was television at the Berlin Games in 1936, it did not provide any income to the Olympic movement (Polley 1998). However, the Olympics were used to promote Hitler's Nazi regime and supremacist ideology and might be considered the first sporting mega-event (Grix 2016) and "Olympic spectacular" (Goldblatt 2016 p.154). Leni Riefenstahl's pioneering film documentary, *Olympia*, has received numerous interpretations (Guttman 2006; Goldblatt 2016) and is a very early example of the use of sport in film to inspire emotion and passion. It draws on ancient Greek culture and an often-intense focus on the athletes' bodies to promote physical excellence. The film also featured the torch relay, which, whilst an integral part of the imagery of the modern Olympics (and now sponsored by Coca-Cola), was only introduced in 1936 in Berlin to promote the National Socialist government (Goldblatt 2016; Grix 2016).

The German cigarette company Reemsta (a subsidiary of Imperial Brands), still one of the biggest tobacco companies in Europe, issued a set of collectors' cards for the Games (Guttman 2006). It was not the first tobacco company to do so; for example, Godfrey Phillips printed cigarette cards for the 1928 Games in Amsterdam. Advertising at the Games was already driving consumption. For example, Coca-Cola was able to use the Berlin Olympics to develop its European sales (Keys 2004). There were many calls for a boycott of the Berlin Olympics, including from Jewish groups, but they were strongly opposed by the chair of the American Olympic Committee, Avery Brundage (Goldblatt 2016). Brundage went on to become the president of the International Olympic Committee from 1952 to 1972. Famously, he is quoted as saying that 'sport … like music and the other fine arts, transcends politics … We are concerned with sports, not politics and business' (International Olympic Committee 1968, quoted in Grix, 2016). At the Tokyo Games of 1964, the American television network NBC sold commercial time to companies such as Kent cigarettes and Schlitz beer. Brundage resisted corporate sponsorship until the last, and in opposition to this perceived commercialism, a clause was temporarily added to the Olympic Charter in 1966 banning sponsorship by tobacco, brewery and distillery companies (Barney et al. 2002).

Brundage was obsessed with the notion of amateurism (Miller 2008), and it was not until his retirement in 1972 and the election of Lord Killanin, and the subsequent election of Juan Antonio Samaranch in 1980, that the modern successful capitalist trinity of sport, television and sponsorship came to the fore. Simson and Jennings' (1992) coruscating exposé of the rise of Samaranch is a disturbing reminder of the power and money behind modern sport. Samaranch, a former fascist and Spanish parliamentarian under General Francisco Franco, became president of the IOC with the support of João Havelange of FIFA (Sugden and Tomlinson 1998). Havelange's and then Samaranch's elections marked a formal shift away from any semblance of amateurism in both the World Cup and the Olympics, and a direct move towards the commercialisation and commodification of modern sport and sport sponsorship (Simson and Jennings 1992), for the benefit of neoliberal economies and transnational corporations.

Horst Dassler's role in commercialising the World Cup was briefly described in the previous section, as was the importance of FIFA's first sponsorship agreement with Coca-Cola. Simson and Jennings were equally scathing about the relationship between Coca-Cola and the Olympic Games as they were about the politics behind the staging of the Games. As they wrote, "The world's best-loved syrup and the brave new world of international sport were made for each other" (1992 p.43). The formal relationship between Coca-Cola and the IOC was established following the successful example that tobacco companies had provided in developing sports sponsorship in Britain in the late 1970s and early 1980s, as described in the previous chapter. Horst Dassler's father, Adi (Adolf), had already achieved success at the Berlin Olympics by arranging for the black American sprinter Jesse Owens to wear his branded running spikes (Smit 2007). The association between sporting success and brand popularity was already well-made. Horst Dassler approached the British sports marketing company of West Nally, which had persuaded tobacco companies such as Benson & Hedges to invest in sport in the United Kingdom, as traditional advertising was no longer available in many countries (Smit 2007). Horst

Dassler and Patrick Nally were able to develop a template for the commercialisation of sporting mega-events through Dassler's company, International Sports Leisure Marketing (ISL), beginning with the World Cup (Goldblatt 2016). Just as FIFA had begun a process of making the World Cup a mediated spectacular based on income from global broadcasting and sponsorship by transnational corporations, so Samaranch, with the support of Dassler, was able to embark on the same path with the Olympics, which returned to Los Angeles in 1984.

ISL and the IOC established a partnership based on worldwide marketing of the Games which led directly to the beginning of the TOP (The Olympic Programme) marketing model. Coca-Cola, which had been key to Havelange's plans for the World Cup, was equally essential to the Olympics (Simson and Jennings 1992). Barney *et al.* (2002) noted that the 1984 Los Angeles Olympics had 35 commercial partners, 64 suppliers and 65 companies holding licences. Television rights had more than doubled since the Moscow Games in 1980, now being worth just under US$300 million, and 2.5 billion people were said to have followed the action on television or radio. In 1983, the IOC had taken over sole marketing rights for the Games at the same time as forming an agreement with ISL which coordinated commercialising the Olympic logo in a series of exclusive categories, including tobacco and food and drink (Miller 2008). Interestingly, at this same time the UK's Howell inquiry into sponsorship raised ethical issues about the commercialisation of the Olympics, including the financial involvement of Adidas (and hence, Horst Dassler) with the IOC (The Central Council of Physical Recreation 1983). At the 1984 Los Angeles Olympics, Coca-Cola became the official soft drink of the Olympics. Today's IOC website proclaims Coca-Cola's 104-year relationship with the Olympic Games, beginning in 1928 and now announced as continuing through to 2032 (International Olympic Committee 2021). Coca-Cola has also been a sponsor of the Torch Relay for two decades. Coca-Cola's current role in TOP in the exclusive category of 'Non-alcoholic beverages' is shared with Mengniu, the Chinese dairy company, which is also a top-tier sponsor of the FIFA World Cup. This is described as a joint TOP partnership agreement. The IOC stated that the joint TOP agreement also included marketing rights for the International Paralympic Committee (IPC) and the Paralympic Games through the IOC-IPC long-term collaboration agreement as well as for the Youth Olympic Games.

The Los Angeles Games of 1984, based on commodifying and sponsoring as many elements of the Olympics as possible, established a framework for the future financing of the Olympics (Tomlinson 2006b; Tomlinson 2006a). In 1984, along with Coca-Cola's corporate sponsorship, McDonald's became the official food supplier and Anheuser Busch (Budweiser) the Olympic beer supplier (Gruneau 1984). It is no coincidence that these transnational corporations have maintained their interest in mega-events for over 30 years now, as both the Olympics and the World Cup are staged for worldwide media interests that reach global audiences of consumers (although McDonald's terminated its agreement with the IOC in 2017 after 41 years of sponsorship (Guardian Sport 2017)). In turn, it is anticipated that this marketing will encourage consumption.

The hosting of the Olympic Games is now based on finding appropriate settings for modern global consumerism (Roche 2000; Tomlinson 2006a). Goldblatt (2016) argued that the geography of sports mega-events is now shifting towards the Global South and the growing markets of Brazil, Russia, India and China (the BRIC nations), so as to find new sponsors and audiences. The recent IOC hook-up with Coca-Cola and Mengniu demonstrates these new alignments very clearly.

Increasing consumption

It is difficult to measure the effectiveness of the sponsorship of global sports events (Nufer and Bühler 2010). Whilst companies are notoriously reticent to share their commercial secrets, after the 1996 Atlanta Olympics, commonly called the "Coca-Cola Olympics" (Tomlinson and Young 2006a p.10), as Atlanta is the home of the sugary drink, Coca-Cola claimed to have increased its sales in Eastern Europe by 41 per cent and in China by 40 per cent (Preuss 2004 p.159).

An article in *Beverage Daily* (Arthur 2018) illustrates the value of the World Cup to the former Anheuser Busch, now AB InBev (and SABMiller, which it took over in 2016), and its global brands, Budweiser, Stella Artois and Corona. The company is quoted as saying, "Football is a passion point in the new markets we've expanded into". Revenues were driven up by over 10 per cent following the brand's activation as the global sponsor of the 2018 World Cup, with "strong growth" in Brazil, China and the United Kingdom. Budweiser's 'Light Up the FIFA World Cup' campaign ran in 50 countries, using television, digital and social media channels. This brand activation used Red Light Cups which light up with increased frequency as the cheering gets louder. Budweiser has now been the official beer sponsor of the World Cup for 30 years and sees the World Cup as "a unique opportunity to engage with 3.2 billion football fans … around the world and drive awareness" (Arthur 2018 p.3).

The resistance

Opposition is, however, growing to the "capitalist mega-sports" of the Olympics (Lenskyj 2012; Boykoff 2020) and the World Cup (Conn 2017). Some of the causes of this opposition, including those concerned with sponsorship, are discussed below. Chapter 9 will cover the regulation of sport, and many of the concerns raised are discussed in more detail there.

Legacy

In bidding for sports mega-events, the leaders in the host cities always promise financial windfalls. However, it is FIFA and the IOC that take by far the largest share of income from their events, which, as we have seen, rely on broadcasting rights and commercial revenue from sponsorship. The local infrastructure costs, including building and refurbishing stadiums and constructing the necessary transport links, have to be met by the hosts. Zimbalist's 'Circus Maximus' (2020) dissected the figures behind the rhetoric and examined previous host cities, London, Rio and Barcelona, to explore the reality. Brazil hosted the 2014 World Cup whilst Rio de Janeiro was the site of the 2016 Olympics. As Zimbalist described, the events resulted in displacement for many of the cities' most disadvantaged as they were forced to move to accommodate new stadiums and their parking lots; building works resulted in the poor treatment of migrant construction workers, huge environmental costs and stadiums paid for by public not private money. Zimbalist concluded that, contrary to claims made in advance of these events, the Olympics and World Cups leave massive debts and often disused or underutilised stadiums.

There are also environmental and sustainability concerns over mega-events (Orr et al. 2022). As these events change location, they raise new environmental issues for each location. The largest contributors to the environmental footprint are travel and the consumption behaviours of the athletes, staff, fans and various event workforces (Collins et al. 2009). FIFA has signed the UN Sports for Climate Action Framework, however, which shows that the climate crisis is at least on its agenda (United Nations Climate Change 2018).

Governance/ethics

Both FIFA and the IOC have endured corruption scandals in recent years. Conn (2017) detailed the corruption in football's governing body, which continued throughout the tenure of João Havelange and his successor, Sepp Blatter (Blatter was the president of FIFA from 1998 to 2015). Boykoff, a former US soccer player, saw the Olympics as a "capitalist behemoth" (2020 p.15) and quoted the IOC itself, in describing the mega-event as one of the most effective marketing platforms in the world. Arguably, the Olympics has the greatest benefits to its transnational sponsors such as Coca-Cola and Mengniu in reaching global audiences and, of course, to the IOC officials themselves. Gruneau correctly ascribed the first use of the phrase "bread and circuses" to the Roman commentator Juvenal in 31 CE (2017 p.43). At the time of an attempted coup, it was easy to distract the mob from more serious underlying issues by providing them with food and sporting distractions. Boykoff argued eloquently that the Olympics might be considered "celebratory capitalism" (2020 p.17), helping to disguise crises in capitalism.

As a sidenote, it is fascinating to note that when Samaranch faced a public relations disaster in 1998 which threatened the withdrawal of the IOC's corporate sponsors, it was Hill and Knowlton that the IOC turned to – the same public relations firm that had assisted Big Tobacco in the years it had spent arguing that the tobacco industry's first priority was to public health, whilst claiming that there was no link between smoking and cancer (Jennings 2000 p. 81–100; Brandt 2007).

Promoting health

Frawley et al. (2013) examined the evidence around the assertion that international sports events encourage participation, focusing on the Sydney 2000 Olympic Games. They concluded that there is little evidence to support this claim. Indeed, only significant resources spent on sports development after a mega sport event are likely to have any impact. A study of sports participation following the London Olympics in 2012 showed that whilst some participation increased, it varied according to socio-economic group. As Wagg wrote about the London Games, the Olympics only generally benefit elite performance (Wagg 2015). It is telling that Zimbalist (2020 p. 113–114) referred to a leading Brazilian sports commentator, Juca Kfouri, who said that the Olympic Games justified themselves through the World Health Organization's claim that every dollar invested in mass sport was rewarded by a saving in public health. Kfouri was quoted as arguing that there was ten times more public money spent on the Games than was anticipated, and that they provided no positive legacy for the city of Rio de Janeiro.

Hastings noted the corporate takeover of the Olympics – "an event that should be a beacon of healthy activity not another shopping opportunity" (Hastings 2012 e5124). Whilst mega-sports events should be promoting health, the constant messaging by unhealthy sponsors is likely to have had a negative impact on public health. The London Olympic Games was criticised for its 'junk food' sponsors including Coca-Cola, McDonald's and Cadbury at a time of growing global obesity rates (Garde and Rigby 2012). Piggin (2019) has written similarly about the food and drink provided at the 2016 Rio Olympics.

Conclusions

The scale of the commodification and commercialisation of both the Olympics and the FIFA World Cup in the last 50 years has been staggering. These are both globally mediated spectaculars which generate millions of dollars for the organisers and help to drive consumption across the world. As we saw in the previous chapter, the tobacco industry was an early innovator in sport sponsorship. The lesson was quickly learned that sport enables access to global audiences, with transnational corporations including Coca-Cola, AB InBev (Anheuser Busch) and McDonald's benefiting most. The next chapter will consider how the commodification of sports mega-events is reproduced in sports across the world, and how this commodification might be bad for our health.

References

Adams, J., Coleman, J. and White, M. (2014) 'Alcohol marketing in televised international football: Frequency analysis', *BMC Public Health*, 14, 473.

Arthur, R. (2018) 'World Cup boost for Budweiser: 'Football is a passion point in the new markets we've expanded in'', *Beverage Daily*, 26 July 2018, available: https://www.

beveragedaily.com/Article/2018/07/26/World-Cup-boost-for-Budweiser-and-AB-InBev [accessed 8 July 2022].

Assunta, M. and Chapman, S. (2004) 'The tobacco industry's accounts of refining indirect tobacco advertising in Malaysia', *Tobacco Control*, 13(Suppl 2), ii63-ii70, available: http://dx.doi.org/10.1136/tc.2004.008987.

B&T (2018) 'Footballing Royalty Messi & Suárez Star in New Global Gatorade Campaign', *B&T Magazine*.

BARB (2019) *Universes*, available: https://www.barb.co.uk/resources/universes/ [accessed 8 July 2019].

Barney, R.K., Wenn, S.R. and Martyn, S.G. (2002) *Selling the Five Rings. The IOC and the Rise of Olympic Commercialism*, Salt Lake City: The University of Utah Press.

BBC (2022) *Euro 2022: England Win Over Germany Watched by Record Television Audience of 17.4m*, available: https://www.bbc.co.uk/sport/football/62375750 [accessed 16 August 2022].

Becker, L. (2018) 'These are the official sponsors at the World Cup', 16 May 2019, available: https://www.ispo.com/en/trends/2018-world-cup-overview-fifa-sponsors [accessed

Bourdieu, P. (1999) 'The state, economics and sport' in Dauncey, H. and Hare, G., eds., *France and the 1998 World Cup. The National Impact of a World Sporting Event*, London: Frank Cass, 15–21.

Boykoff, J. (2020) *Nolympians. Inside the Fight against Capitalist Mega-Sports in Los Angeles, Tokyo & Beyond*, Winnipeg: Fernwood Publishing.

Bragg, M.A., Miller, A.N., Roberto, C.A., Sam, R., Sarda, V., Harris, J.L. and Brownell, K.D. (2018) 'Sports sponsorships of food and nonalcoholic beverages', *Pediatrics*, 141(4), e20172822.

Bramley, E. (2018) *Kodak & the Olympic Games, 1896–2008*, available: https://collections.museumsvictoria.com.au/articles/16566 [accessed 22 December 2021].

Brandt, A.M. (2007) *The Cigarette Century*, New York: Basic Books.

Burlamaqui, L.G. (2019) 'The 'invention' of FIFA history: João Havelange's election to FIFA presidency as a historic event', *Soccer and Society*, 20(7–8), 1056–1070, available: http://dx.doi.org/10.1080/14660970.2019.1680503.

Christie, K. (2019) 'Scottish Women's Football announces sponsorship with alcohol action group', *The Scotsman*, 7 March 2019, available: https://www.scotsman.com/sport/football/scottish-womens-football-announces-sponsorship-alcohol-action-group-86322 [accessed 14 December 2021].

Collin, J. and MacKenzie, R. (2006) 'The World Cup, sport sponsorship, and health', *The Lancet*, 367, 1964–1966.

Collins, A., Jones, C. and Munday, M. (2009) 'Assessing the environmental impacts of mega sporting events: Two options?', *Tourism Management*, 30(6), 828–837, available: http://dx.doi.org/10.1016/j.tourman.2008.12.006.

Conn, D. (2017) *The Fall of the House of FIFA*, London: Yellow Jersey Press.

Cornwell, T.B. (2020) *Sponsorship in Marketing. Effective Partnerships in Sports, Arts and Events*, Second ed., Abingdon: Routledge.

Crompton, J.L. (1993) 'Sponsorship of sport by tobacco and alcohol companies: A review of the issues', *Journal of Sport & Social Issues*, 73, 148–167.

Cronin, B. (2018) '1950–2014: A history of sponsorship at the FIFA World Cup', *Sport-Business*, 1 June 2018, available: https://www.sportbusiness.com/2018/06/1950-2014-the-history-of-world-cup-sponsorship/ [accessed 14 July 2020].

de Lacy-Vawdon, C. and Livingstone, C. (2020) 'Defining the commercial determinants of health: A systematic review', *BMC Public Health*, 20(1), 1022, available: http://dx.doi.org/10.1186/s12889-020-09126-1.

Dewhirst, T., Lee, W.B., Fong, G.T. and Ling, P.M. (2016) 'Exporting an inherently harmful product: The marketing of Virginia Slims cigarettes in the United States, Japan, and Korea', *Journal of Business Ethics*, 139(1), 161–181.
Dunn, C. (2016) *Football and the Women's World Cup*, Basingstoke: Palgrave Macmillan.
Ferrand, A., Chappelet, J.-L. and Séguin, B. (2012) *Olympic Marketing*. Abingdon: Routledge.
FIFA (2015) *Key Figures from the FIFA Women's World Cup Canada 2015* [press release], available: http://www.fifa.com/womensworldcup/news/y=2015/m=7/news=key-figures-from-the-fifa-women-s-world-cup-canada-2015tm-2661648.html [accessed 2 December 2021].
FIFA (2018a) *2018 FIFA World Cup Russia*, available: https://resources.fifa.com/image/upload/njqsntrvdvqv8ho1dag5.pdf [accessed 9 November 2020].
FIFA (2018b) *FIFA Financial Report 2018*, Zurich, available: https://digitalhub.fifa.com/m/337fab75839abc76/original/xzshsoe2ayttyquuxhq0-pdf.pdf [accessed 16 December 2021].
FIFA (2021) *FIFA Annual Report 2020*, Zurich, available: https://publications.fifa.com/en/annual-report-2020/2020-at-a-glance/ [accessed 15 December 2021].
Frawley, S., Toohey, K., & Veal, A. J. (2013) 'Managing sport participation legacy at the olympic games' in Frawley, S. and Adair, D., eds., *Managing the Olympics*, Basingstoke: Palgrave Macmillan, 66–83.
Garde, A. and Rigby, N. (2012) 'Going for gold – should responsible governments raise the bar on sponsorship of the Olympic Games and other sporting events by food and beverage companies?', *Communications Law*, 17(2), 42–49.
Giulianotti, R. (1999) *Football. A Sociology of the Global Game*, Cambridge: Polity Press.
Giulianotti, R. and Robertson, R. eds. (2007) *Globalization and Sport*, Oxford: Blackwell Publishing.
Giulianotti, R. and Robertson, R. (2009) *Globalization & Football*, London: Sage.
Glendenning, B. (2019) 'Women's World Cup game-changing moments No 3: China in 1991', *The Guardian*, available: https://www.theguardian.com/football/2019/jun/18/womens-world-cup-game-changing-moments-no-3-china-in-1991 [accessed 8 December 2021].
Gokani, N., Garde, A., Philpott, M., Ireland, R., Owens, R. and Boyland, E. (2021) 'UK Nutrition Research Partnership 'Hot Topic' workshop report: A 'game changer' for dietary health – addressing the implications of sport sponsorship by food businesses through an innovative interdisciplinary collaboration', *Nutrition Bulletin*, available: http://dx.doi.org/10.1111/nbu.12535.
Goldblatt, D. (2007) *The Ball Is Round: A Global History of Football*, Harmondsworth: Penguin Viking.
Goldblatt, D. (2016) *The Games. A Global History of the Olympics*, London: W.W. Norton.
Graham, A. and Adams, J. (2014) 'Alcohol marketing in televised English professional football: A frequency analysis', *Alcohol and Alcoholism*, 49(3), 343–348.
Grix, J. (2016) *Sports Politics. An Introduction*, London: Palgrave Macmillan.
Gruneau, R. (1984) 'Commercialism and the modern Olympics' in Tomlinson, A. and Whannel, G., eds., *Five-ring Circus. Money, Power and Politics at the Olympic Games*, London: Pluto Press, 1–15.
Gruneau, R. (2017) *Sport & Modernity*, Cambridge: Polity.
Guardian Sport (2017) 'McDonald's pulls out of Olympics contract to end 41-year sponsorship', *The Guardian*, 16 June 2017, available: https://www.theguardian.com/sport/2017/jun/16/mcdonalds-pulls-out-olympics-contract-end-41-year-sponsorship [accessed 24 December 2021].

Guttman, A. (1994) *Games and Empires. Modern Sports and Cultural Imperialism*, New York: Columbia University Press.
Guttman, A. (2006) 'Berlin 1936: The most controversial Olympics' in Tomlinson, A. and Young, C., eds., *National Identity and Global Sports Events. Culture, Politics and Spectacle in the Olympics and the Football World Cup*, Albany: State University of New York, 65–82.
Hall, C.M. (2006) 'Urban entrepreneurship, corporate interests and sports mega-events: The thin policies of competitiveness within the hard outcomes of neoliberalism', *The Sociological Review*, 54(2 (Suppl.)), 59–70.
Hastings, G. (2012) 'Why corporate power is a public health priority', *British Medical Journal*, 345(7871), 26–29.
Hill, C.R. (1996) *Olympic Politics. Athens to Atlanta 1896–1996*, Second ed., Manchester: Manchester University Press.
Hong, F. and Mangan, J.A. eds. (2004) *Soccer, Women, Sexual Liberation. Kicking Off a New Era*, London: Frank Cass.
Horne, J. and Manzenreiter, W. (2006) 'An introduction to the sociology of sports mega-events' in Horne, J. and Manzenreiter, W., eds., *Sports Mega-Events. Social Scientific Analyses of a Global Phenomenon*, Oxford: Blackwell, 1–24.
International Olympic Committee (1968) *The Speeches of President Avery Brundage*, Lausanne: International Olympic Committee.
International Olympic Committee (2016) *International Olympic Committee Marketing Report Rio 2016*, Lausanne, available: https://stillmed.olympics.com/media/Document%20Library/OlympicOrg/Games/Summer-Games/Games-Rio-2016-Olympic-Games/Media-Guide-for-Rio-2016/IOC-Marketing-Report-Rio-2016.pdf?_ga=2.155397115.1187065074.1639555488-329404714.1639555488 [accessed 15 December 2021].
International Olympic Committee (2021) *Coca-Cola and Mengnui*, available: https://olympics.com/ioc/partners/coca-cola-mengniu [accessed 22 December 2021].
Ireland, R., Bunn, C., Reith, G., Philpott, M., Capewell, S., Boyland, E. and Chambers, S. (2019) 'Commercial determinants of health: Advertising of alcohol and unhealthy foods during sporting events', *Bulletin of the World Health Organization*, 97, 290–295.
Ireland, R., Muc, M., Bunn, C. and Boyland, E. (2021) 'Marketing of unhealthy brands during the 2018 Fédération Internationale de Football Association (FIFA) World Cup UK broadcasts–a frequency analysis', *Journal of Strategic Marketing*, 1–16. Ahead of print.
Jennings, A. (2000) *The Great Olympic Swindle. When the World Wanted its Games Back*, London: Simon and Schuster.
Keys, B. (2004) 'Spreading Peace, Democracy, and Coca-Cola®: Sport and American Cultural Expansion in the 1930s', *Diplomatic History*, 28(2), 165–196.
Kickbusch, I. (2012) 'Addressing the interface of the political and commercial determinants of health', *Health Promotion International*, 27(4), 427–428.
Kickbusch, I., Allen, L. and Franz, C. (2016) 'The commercial determinants of health', *The Lancet*, 4, 895–896.
Kidd, B. (1984) 'The myth of the ancient games' in Tomlinson, A. and Whannel, G., eds., *Five Ring Circus. Money, Power and Politics at the Olympic Games*, London: Pluto Press, 71–83.
Lee, K. ed. (2003) *Health Impacts of Globalization. Towards Global Governance*, Basingstoke: Palgrave Macmillan.
Lenskyj, H.J. (2012) 'The case against the Olympic games: The buck stops with the IOC' in Lenskyj, H. J. and Wagg, S., eds., *The Palgrave Handbook of Olympic Studies*, Basingstoke: Palgrave Macmillan, 570–579.

Levy, J. (2019) 'Women's World Cup 2019 commercial guide: Every country, every sponsor, every broadcaster', *SportsProMedia*, 6 June 2019, available: https://www.sportspromedia.com/analysis/womens-world-cup-france-2019-sponsors-broadcasters/ [accessed 9 December 2021].

Lopez, S. (1997) *Women on the Ball. A Guide to Women's' Football*, London: Scarlet Press.

Lyons, E. (2019) 'Women's World Cup: How brands are leveraging a "culturally relevant" moment', *Marketing Week*, 30 May 2019, available: https://www.marketingweek.com/womens-world-cup-sponsorship/ [accessed 9 December 2021].

Mangan, J.A. (2004) 'Managing monsters' in Hong, F. and Mangan, J. A., eds., *Soccer, Women, Sexual Liberation. Kicking Off a New Era*, London: Frank Cass, 1–5.

Manoli, A.E., Anagnostou, M. and Liu, L. (2022) 'Marketing, sponsorship and merchandising at FIFA World Cups' in Chadwick, S., Widdop, P., Anagnostopoulos, C. and Parnell, D., eds., *The Business of the FIFA World Cup*, Abingdon: Routledge, 190–202.

McFee, G. (2012) 'The promise of Olympism' in Sugden, J. and Tomlinson, A., eds., *Watching the Olympics. Politics, Power and Representation*, Abingdon: Routledge, 36–54.

Miller, D. (2008) *The Official History of the Olympic Games and the IOC. Athens to Beijing, 1894–2008*, Edinburgh: Mainstream.

Mills, A. (2022) 'EXCLUSIVE World Cup stadium stands will be alcohol free under Qatari curbs - source', *Reuters*, 8 July 2022, available: https://www.reuters.com/lifestyle/sports/exclusive-world-cup-stadiums-will-be-alcohol-free-under-qatari-curbs-source-2022-07-07/ [accessed 8 July 2022].

Morgan, A., Frawley, S., Fujak, H. and Cobourn, S. (2017) 'Sponsorship and sport mega-events' in Frawley, S., ed., *Managing Sport Mega-Events*, Abingdon: Routledge.

Moriarty, K. (2018) 'Football – the boozy-ful game', 13 July 2018, available: https://ahauk.org/news/football-the-boozy-ful-game/ [accessed 8 July 2022].

Mullen, L. (1999) 'Women's World Cup readies $21 million advertising blitz', *Sports Business Journal*, 5 October 1999, available: https://www.sportsbusinessjournal.com/Journal/Issues/1999/05/10/No-Topic-Name/Womens-World-Cup-Readies-$21-Million-Advertising-Blitz.aspx [accessed 8 December 2021].

Müller, M. (2017) 'What makes an event a mega-event? Definitions and sizes' in Frawley, S., ed., *Managing Sport Mega-Events*, Abingdon: Routledge.

Nestle, M. (2015) *Soda Politics. Taking On Big Soda (And Winning)*. Oxford: Oxford University Press.

Nufer, G. and Bühler, A. (2010) 'How effective is the sponsorship of global sports events? A comparison of the FIFA World Cups in 2006 and 1998', *International Journal of Sports Marketing and Sponsorship*, 11(4), 33–49, available: http://dx.doi.org/10.1108/IJSMS-11-04-2010-B004.

Orr, M., Murfree, J.R., Anahory, A. and Edwabne, R.E. (2022) 'Environment and sustainability in FIFA World Cups' in Chadwick, S., Widdop, P., Anagnostopoulos, C. and Parnell, D., eds., *The Business of the FIFA World Cup*, Abingdon: Routledge, 106–118.

Payne, M. (2006) *Olympic Turnaround: How the Olympic Games Stepped Back from the Brink of Extinction to Become the World's Best Known Brand*, Greenwood Publishing Group.

Piggin, J. (2019) *The Politics of Physical Activity*, Abingdon: Routledge.

Polley, M. (1998) *Moving the Goalposts. A History of Sport and Society since 1945*, London: Routledge.

Pope, S. (2017) *The Feminization of Sports Fandom. A Sociological Study*, Abingdon: Routledge.

Preuss, H. (2004) *The Economics of Staging the Olympics. A Comparison of the Games. 1972–2008*, Cheltenham: Edward Elgar.

Purves, R.I., Critchlow, N., Stead, M., Adams, J. and Brown, K. (2017) 'Alcohol marketing during the UEFA EURO 2016 football tournament: A frequency analysis', *International Journal of Environmental Research and Public Health*, 14(704), available: http://dx.doi.org/10.3390/ijerph14070704.

Ritzer, G. (2010) *Enchanting a Disenchanted World: Continuity and Change in the Cathedrals of Consumption*, Thousand Oaks, CA: Pine Forge.

Ritzer, G. (2011) *The McDonaldization of Society*, Thousand Oaks, CA: Pine Forge.

Ritzer, G. ed. (2016) *The Blackwell Companion to Globalization*, Chichester: John Wiley.

Robertson, R. (1992) *Globalization: Social Theory and Global Culture*, London: Sage.

Robertson, R. and White, K.E. (2016) 'What Is Globalization?' in Ritzer, G., ed., *The Blackwell Companion to Globalization*, Oxford: John Wiley.

Roche, M. (2000) *Mega-events and Modernity*, London: Routledge.

Roche, M. (2006) 'Mega-events and modernity revisited: Globalization and the case of the Olympics', *The Sociological Review*, 54(2 (Suppl)), 27–40.

Roxborough, S. (2019) 'Women's World Cup smashes global ratings records', *The Hollywood Reporter*, 1 July 2019, available: https://www.hollywoodreporter.com/news/general-news/womens-2019-soccer-world-cup-smashes-global-ratings-records-1221957/ [accessed 2 December 2021].

Scottish Women's Football (2021) *SHAAP and Scottish Women's Football Announce Renewed Partnership during Awareness Week on Alcohol Related Harms* [press release], 18 November 2021, available: https://scotwomensfootball.com/shaap-and-scottish-womens-football-announce-renewed-partnership-during-awareness-week-on-alcohol-related-harm/ [accessed 14 December 2021].

Semens, A. (2019) 'Football Sponsorship' in Hughson, J., Moore, K., Spaaij, R. and Maguire, J., eds., *Routledge Handbook of Football Studies*, Paperback ed., Abingdon: Routledge, 111–123.

Shaw, S. and Amis, J. (2001) 'Image and investment: Sponsorship and women's sport', *Journal of Sport Management*, 15(3), 219–246.

Simson, V. and Jennings, A. (1992) *The Lords of the Rings. Power, Money and Drugs in the Modern Olympics*, Toronto: Stoddart.

Smart, B. (2007) 'Not playing around: Global capitalism, modern sport and consumer culture' in Giulianotti, R. and Robertson, R., eds., *Globalization and Sport*, Oxford: Blackwell Publishing, 6–27.

Smart, B. (2018) 'Consuming Olympism: Consumer culture, sport star sponsorship and the commercialisation of the Olympics', *Journal of Consumer Culture*, 18(2), 241–260, available: http://dx.doi.org/10.1177/1469540517747146.

Smit, B. (2007) *Pitch Invasion. Adidas, Puma and the Making of Modern Sport*, London: Penguin Books.

Sugden, J. and Tomlinson, A. (1998) *FIFA and the Contest for World Football. Who Rules the Peoples' Game?* Cambridge: Polity Press.

The Central Council of Physical Recreation (1983) *Committee of Enquiry Into Sports Sponsorship. "The Howell Report"*, London: The Central Council of Physical Recreation.

Tomlinson, A. (1984) 'De Coubertin and the modern Olympics' in Tomlinson, A. and Whannel, G., eds., *Five Ring Circus. Money, Power and Politics at the Olympic Games*, London: Pluto Press, 84–97.

Tomlinson, A. (2006a) *The Commercialization of the Olympics: Cities, Corporations and the Olympic Commodity*, Internal University of Brighton Report, unpublished.

Tomlinson, A. (2006b) 'Los Angeles 1984 and 1932: Commercializing the American dream' in Tomlinson, A. and Young, C., eds., *National Identity and Global Sports Events. Culture, Politics, and Spectacle in the Olympics and the Football World Cup*, Albany: State University of New York Press, 163–176.

Tomlinson, A. (2014) *FIFA (Fédération Internationale de Football Association). The Men, the Myths and the Money*, Abingdon: Routledge.

Tomlinson, A. and Young, C. (2006a) 'Culture, politics in the global sports event - An introduction' in Tomlinson, A. and Young, C., eds., *National Identity and Global Sports Events. Culture, Politics, and Spectacle in the Olympics and the Football World Cup*, Albany: State University of New York, 1–14.

Tomlinson, A. and Young, C. eds. (2006b) *National Identity and Global Sports Events. Culture, Politics, and Spectacle in the Olympics and the Football World Cup*, Albany: State University of New York Press.

Turner, K. (2017) 'Pony, the little drink with the big (W.F.A.) kick', *Unlocking the Hidden History of Women's Football*, available: https://unlockingthehiddenhistory.wordpress.com/2018/04/03/pony-the-little-drink-with-the-big-w-f-a-kick/amp/ [accessed 8 December, 2021].

UEFA (2022) *The Business Case for Women's Football*, Nyon, available: https://editorial.uefa.com/resources/0278-15e121074702-c9be7dcd0a29-1000/business_case_for_women_s_football-_external_report_1_.pdf [accessed 18 August 2022].

United Nations Climate Change (2018) *Sports for Climate Action*, available: https://unfccc.int/climate-action/sectoral-engagement/sports-for-climate-action [accessed 8 July 2022].

Wagg, S. (2015) *The London Olympics of 2012: Politics, Promises and Legacy*, Basingstoke: Palgrave Macmillan.

Wagner, A. (2021) 'Women's football in numbers: 147,000 players, 80,000 referees and 1.12bn viewers. With you all the way', *Verve Times*, 20 April 2021, available: https://vervetimes.com/womens-football-in-numbers-147000-players-80000-referees-and-1-12bn-viewers-with-you-all-the-way/ [accessed 2 December 2021].

Williams, J. (2003) *A Game for Rough Girls? A History of Women's Football in Britain*, Abingdon: Routledge.

Williams, J. (2007) *A Beautiful Game. International Perspectives on Women's Football*, Oxford: Berg.

Williams, J. (2013) *Globalising Women's Football. Europe, Migration and Professionalization*, Bern: Peter Lang.

Williams, J. (2021) *The History of Women's Football*, Barnsley: Pen & Sword.

Wrack, S. (2022) *A Woman's Game. The Rise, Fall, and Rise Again of Women's Football*, London: Guardian Faber.

Young, D.C. (2004) *A Brief History of the Olympic Games*, Hoboken, NJ: Wiley-Blackwell.

Zimbalist, A. (2020) *Circus Maximus. The Economic Gamble behind Hosting the Olympics and the World Cup*, Third ed., Washington, DC: The Brookings Institution.

Tobacco Sponsorship

1 Badge for Virginia Slims Circuit (women's professional tennis). "You've come a long way, baby". 1972. *Source: R. Ireland.*

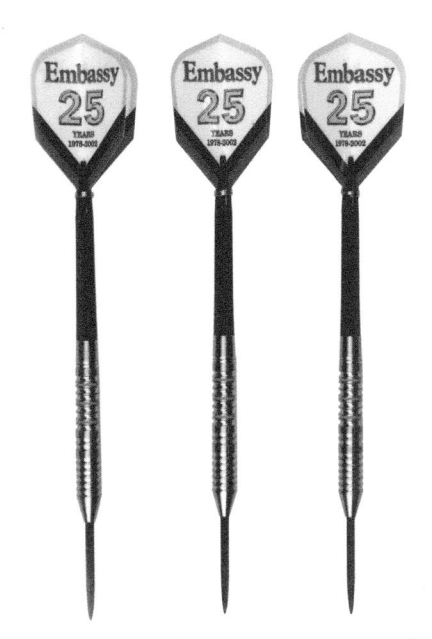

2 Embassy World Professional Darts Championship 25th Anniversary (1978–2002) dart flights. 2002. *Source: R. Ireland.*

3 WD & HO Wills Scissors Cigarette Cards (Sporting Girls series). 1913. *Source: R. Ireland.*

4 John Player Special League Official Programme and Scorecard. Essex v Kent. 1985. *Source: R. Ireland.*

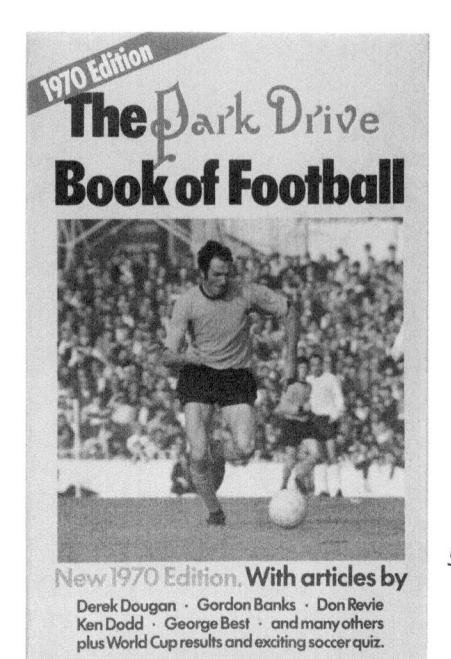

5 The Park Drive Book of Football. 1970. Source: R. Ireland.

6 Honus Wagner, Pittsburgh Pirates. Reproduction of T206 Piedmont cigarette card. Originally issued in 1909. *Source: R. Ireland.*

7 G.L. Garnsey, New South Wales. Capstan cigarette card (Prominent Australian and English Cricketers series). 1907. *Source: R. Ireland.*

8 B.L. Osler, South Africa. United Tobacco Cos. cigarette card (Springbok Rugby and Cricket Teams series). 1931. *Source: R. Ireland.*

9 FC Bayern Snuff. 2022. *Source: R. Ireland.*

Mega-Events Sponsorship

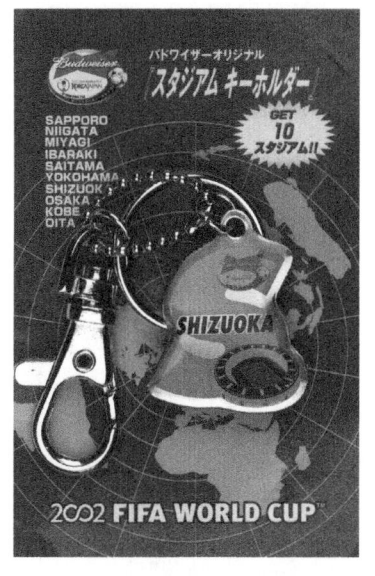

1 Budweiser 2002 FIFA World Cup Keyring, Japan and South Korea. Source: R. Ireland.

4 Torch Relay Coca-Cola Towel, Tokyo 2020 Olympics (postponed). Source: R. Ireland.

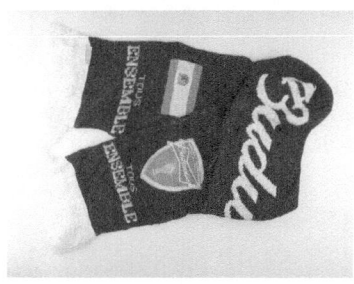

2 Budweiser 2014 FIFA World Cup Scarf 'Tous Ensemble' Spain, Brazil. Source: R. Ireland.

3 Budweiser 2018 'Light Up the FIFA World Cup' glass, Russia. Source: R. Ireland.

5 Romania v Albania Coca-Cola cup, UEFA EUROs, 19 June 2016. Source: R. Ireland.

6 Coca-Cola Commemorative Badge, Los Angeles Olympics, 1932. *Source: R. Ireland.*

8 Reemsta Olympia #194 Television Recording Equipment and #103 Torch Ceremony, Berlin 1936 Olympics. *Source: R. Ireland.*

7 Coca-Cola Cricket World Cup Cards, India, 1996. *Source: R. Ireland.*

Alcohol Sponsorship

1 Huddersfield Town FC, The John Smith's Stadium, 2017/2018. *Source: R. Ireland.*

2 Guinness Six Nations Official Rugby Cap, 2022. *Source: R. Ireland.*

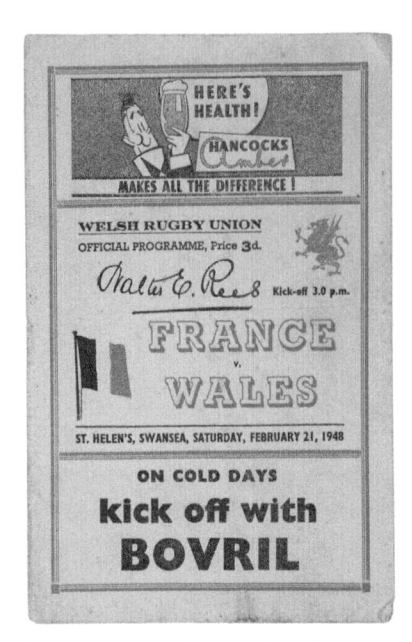

3 France v Wales (Rugby Union) Official Programme, 1948. Source: R. Ireland.

4 England v Belgium (Women's International Football) Official Programme, 1978. Source: R. Ireland.

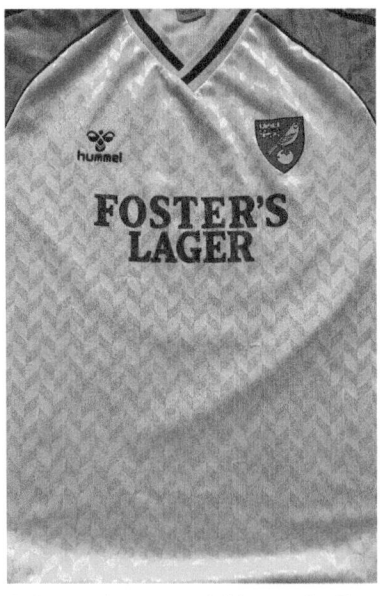

5 Reproduction of Norwich City FC shirt, 1986/1987. *Original image with kind permission of G. Parry.*

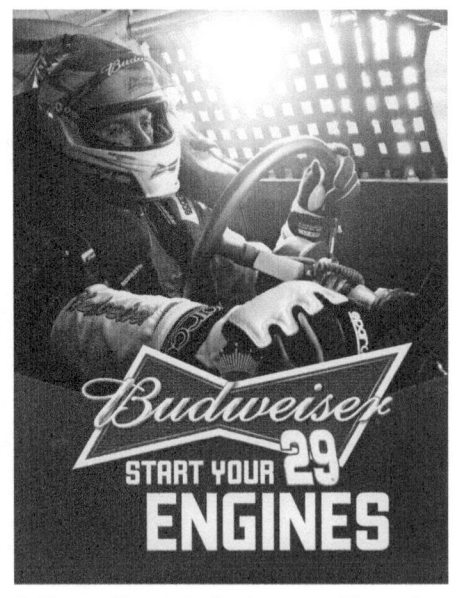

6 Kevin Harvick, Budweiser Chevrolet, NASCAR Sprint Cup Series, 2013. Source: R. Ireland.

Junk Food and Drink Sponsorship

1 Jeff Astle, West Bromwich Albion FC, A & BC Gum (Footballers Series), 1969. *Source: R. Ireland.*

2 Michael Owen, Cadbury Legend Sticker, Panini Premier League 2020 Collection. *Source: R. Ireland.*

Ian Wright, Cadbury Legend Sticker, Panini Premier League 2020 Collection. *Source: R. Ireland.*

4 Cadbury Dairy Milk Limited Club Edition, 360 grams, Official Partner of Liverpool FC, 2021/2022. *Source: R. Ireland.*

5 Tom Westerman (aged six years), Milo cricket, Australia, 2013. *Original image with kind permission of L. and T. Westerman.*

6 Kellogg's swimming badges, 2002. *Source: R. Ireland.*

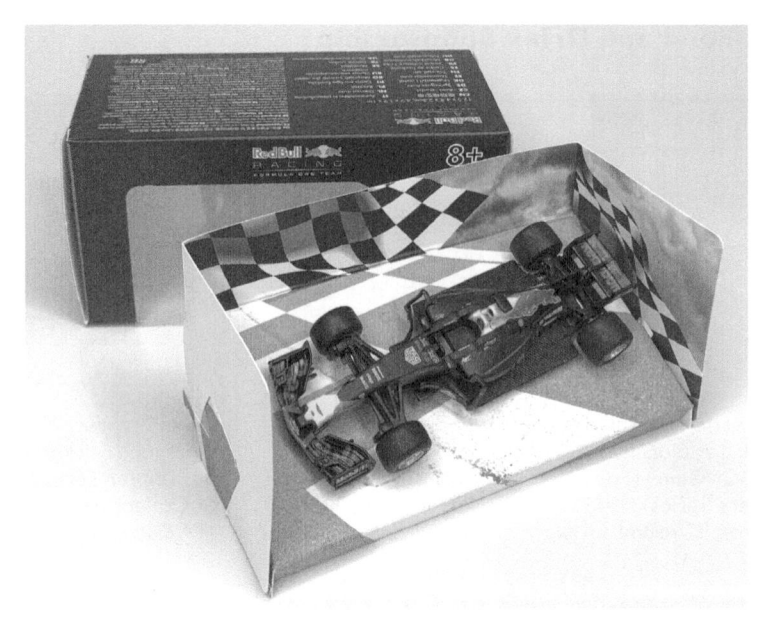

7 Red Bull Racing Formula One Team – 1:43 Scale Model, 2017. *Source: R. Ireland.*

8 Coca-Cola English Premier League Trophy Tour, Liverpool, 23 March 2019. *Original image with kind permission of E. Boyland.*

9 Scoreboard, FC Valur, Reykjavik, 1998. *Original image with kind permission of B. Sweeney.*

10 Dyson Heppell, Essendon, AFL Team Coach, 2021. *Source: R. Ireland.*

Gambling Sponsorship

1 Littlewoods' Football Pools Coupon, 30 January 1932. Source: R. Ireland.

2 Ashley Barnes, Burnley FC. English Premier League Panini Trading Card, 2019/2020. Source: R. Ireland.

3 Fulham FC shirt (Betfair), 2002/2003. Original image with kind permission of P. Terry.

4 St. Andrews Trillion Trophy Stadium, Birmingham City FC, 2021/2022. Original image with kind permission of The Big Step.

5 Bet365 Stadium, Stoke City FC, 2018/2019. *Source: R. Ireland.*

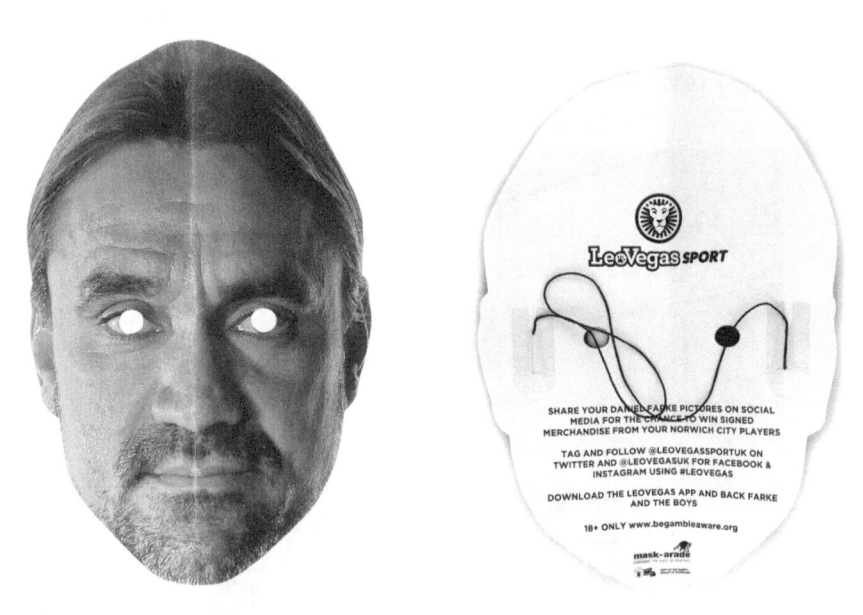

6 Front and back of Daniel Farke mask (Manager, Norwich City FC). Circulated at Arsenal v Norwich City Carabao Cup, 25 October 2017. *Source: R. Ireland.*

Chapter 6

The commodification of modern sport

Sociology, culture and sport

Sport only began to attract the attention of social theorists towards the second half of the twentieth century. Much of this writing came after the Second World War when sociologists sought to explain the rise of fascism in Germany and the failure of the working class to exercise its predicted revolutionary role (Morgan 1988). One of the most prominent theorists, Theodor Adorno, presented culture as the organisation of free time in which the masses were permitted the gratification of their desires whilst their subjugation under capitalism was maintained (Bernstein, 2001). Adorno considered sport as part of mass culture but as a parody of freedom: "Sport itself is not play but ritual in which the subjected celebrate their subjection" and indeed are actively complicit in their own subjugation to the system (Adorno 2001 [1991]). Lash and Lury (2007) argued that Adorno was writing at a time when the growth of capitalism depended on the development of consumerism and the creation of new markets, and he saw the cultural industry as comprising products whose representation would lead to capital accumulation. Following Lash and Lury's position, it can be suggested that today's global culture industry works through brands generated across a range of products, which use football to secure symbolic recognition. Although Adorno's view of essentially passive consumerism is still relevant in today's mass-produced representations of popular culture (Jeffries 2016), it excludes the role of the agency of individuals.

Like Adorno, Norbert Elias was another who sought exile from Nazi Germany. Elias had already written *The Civilizing Process* in German in 1939 but it was not translated into English until 1978 and 1982 in two volumes (Elias 1978, 1982). Giulianotti (2004) wrote that Elias's status in the sociological analysis of sport is secured by his recognition that sport and leisure are important social activities, an analysis that was still comparatively rare at this time. Elias described the civilising process as developments in socially accepted codes of conduct and sentiment. These had begun to change from the sixteenth century onwards and were part of the process of state formation (Elias 1986). Elias collaborated with Eric Dunning to build on these ideas of a civilising process to develop a theory of leisure incorporating sociological perspectives on sport from medieval ball games to the

DOI: 10.4324/9781003239734-6

crowd violence which marred English football in the 1970s and 1980s (Elias and Dunning 1986).

Elias described the "pleasurable excitement" (Elias and Dunning 1986 p.63) of sport in his explanation of its role in providing an emotional outlet in today's routine and constrained societies. Whilst Elias's descriptions of the thrill of the struggle of football and the accompanying raising of the emotions and passions of football fans remain relevant, his civilising process theory can be criticised. For example, Giulianotti argued that it is difficult not to be sceptical in the face of arguments that express faith in any civilising aspects of modernity and that Elias's approach fails to consider the power relations of sport (Giulianotti 2004).

Pierre Bourdieu and sport

Like Elias, Pierre Bourdieu wrote extensively about sport, and sociologists have used Bourdieu's understanding of social processes to apply his approach (Jarvie and Maguire 1994; Tomlinson 2004; Giulianotti 2016; Roberts 2016; Grenfell 2018). Bourdieu used the concepts of *habitus*, *capital* and *field* to inform his analysis. For Bourdieu, a *habitus* is a series of dispositions which reflect a social actor's education, upbringing and circumstances. Bourdieu used the term *capital* to describe a system of exchanges linked with the values and beliefs of social groups (*doxa*). Various capitals are placed and valued by particular groups, with a dominant *habitus* often determining that value. According to Bourdieu, there is *economic* and *symbolic capital*. In sport, economic capital is clear and may be measured in terms of commercial income from a sponsorship agreement for example. Symbolic capital is the intrinsic value attached to a football club, for example, including its badge, its stadium and indeed its history of playing success (or failure), its *cultural capital*. In order to understand interactions between social actors, Bourdieu argued, it is necessary to examine the space in which these interactions or transactions take place. He called this social space a *field*.

In 'Sport and Social Class', Bourdieu considered the historical and social conditions of modern sport, describing it as a "system of agents and institutions" functioning as a "field of competition" and the "site of confrontations between agents with specific interests linked to their position within the field" (1978 p.821). As with other practices, Bourdieu viewed sport as shaped by a struggle between members of the dominant classes and also between the social classes. This struggle was determined by the position of dominant power within the field of competition and struggle. Bourdieu considered the opposition between participation in sport and purely consuming sport, via television for example, as something which emerged in the shift towards "sport as a spectacle produced by professionals for consumption by the masses" (1978 p.830). Bourdieu was clear that "sport is an object of political struggle" (1978 p.832).

In this description of the struggles of competition within the sporting field, Bourdieu describes the various agents as reflecting their system of tastes and references (*habiti*). Bourdieu provides an explanatory model concerning the distribution of sporting practices (in this sense he is describing participation), which takes account of access to economic and cultural capital. In 'Programme for a Sociology of Sport', Bourdieu positioned sport as "inserted into a universe of practices and consumptions that are themselves structured and constituted in a system" (1988 p.155). Thus, the site of sporting struggle represents "socially constituted dispositions" (1988 p.158) which are imported into the field. Bourdieu's perspective is well demonstrated in Collins' masterly history of rugby football (Collins 2012), which illustrated a sport in which social, cultural and economic divisions led to the development of the two codes: rugby union and rugby league.

Bourdieu (1999) published a paper to coincide with France hosting the FIFA World Cup in 1998, 'The State, Economics and Sport'. He wrote of the trend towards commercialisation in sport, and particularly football, in which they defined the key relationship as that existing between the sport's practitioners and television. Football is "produced to be commercialised in the form of *televised spectacle, a commercial product* which is especially profitable because football is widely practised" (1999 p.16). The factors involved in this commercialisation are those of the rules of neoliberal economics, as managed by the sporting policies of different countries. Bourdieu argued that "sport visible as spectacle hides the reality of a system of actors competing over commercial stakes" (1999 p.17). The actors competing include:

> Sports industry managers who control television and sponsoring rights, the managers of television channels competing for national broadcasting rights (or rights covering linguistic areas), the bosses of major industrial companies such as Adidas or Coca-Cola competing with each other for exclusive rights to link their products with the sports event, and finally television producers.
> (Bourdieu 1999 p.18)

The ability of sport to deliver major audiences to advertisers and sponsors brings with it increases in subscriptions to television channels and lucrative broadcasting rights (Rowe 2009). From this have followed both battles to control the 'media sports complex' and, further, the cultural commodification of sport (Wenner 1989, 1998; Hutchins and Rowe 2009; Evens *et al.* 2013; Serazio 2019). Bourdieu's analysis enables us to recognise that sporting practice is embedded in, and profoundly shaped by, these struggles within the wider field of power.

To take a Bourdieusian theoretical perspective, within the football 'field' of competition, *habitus* represents a system of dispositions or a 'way of being', and there is a struggle between those who hold economic capital (sports' club owners), and the fans, who perceive themselves as the rightful owners of the cultural capital which is associated with their clubs. Bourdieu's writing helps both in addressing the commercial determinants of health in sport, and the dominant neoliberal capitalist ideology demonstrated in twenty-first-century globalised sport. As briefly discussed in the next chapter concerning the English Premier League, whilst English football supporters can and do challenge this economic model (Numerato 2018), many also accept the commercialisation and commodification of their sport (Dixon 2013).

Whilst Adorno saw passive, subjugated consumption under capitalism, Bourdieu used the concept of *symbolic violence* to describe the suffering resulting from the reproduction of the social order, particularly in education and art (Bourdieu 1993), where underlying power relations reproduce the legitimacy of existing structures. In accepting the economic model of the Premier League, through which sponsorship and television have transformed sport (Whannel 2002; Boyle and Haynes 2009), fans can be argued to be acquiescing in the symbolic domination to which they are subject. Bourdieu was also very critical of neoliberal capitalism and, rather than accepting a passive role in his engagement with contemporary society, he called for social scientists to help shape the future (see *Acts of Resistance* (Bourdieu 1998)) and intervene politically (Bourdieu 2010). Whilst arguing that Bourdieu's work remains relevant, Lash stated that he was essentially pessimistic in his view of social transformation (Lash 1993). Fan movements might offer alternative views of sport whilst remaining as consumers, although digital media practices often simply offer more ways for commercialised sport to mediate and control fan practices (Hutchins *et al.* 2022).

Sport as a mediated spectacle for consumption

Rupert Murdoch based the development of BSkyB, a British broadcaster but part of Murdoch's global media conglomerate News Corporation, around winning the broadcasting rights in 1992 to live coverage of English Premier League football and its potential worldwide audience through satellite television (Falcous 2005). This is described more fully in the next chapter. Collins described the approach by News Corporation as "acknowledging the historical importance of sport to media companies of all technologies since the eighteenth century" (2013 p.119).

Castells (2000) has documented the transformation of economic power through the integration of economic, cultural and political interests in a networked society. This has been described as a process of "Murdochization" (David *et al.* 2017) in which News Corporation has built digital media networks around sport. News Corporation has used sport as an instrument to penetrate national television markets in the United States, the United Kingdom and Australia (Andrews 2003). Murdoch was very explicit about this and has been widely quoted as saying "we intend to … use sports as a 'battering ram' and a lead offering in all our pay television operations" (Andrews 2003 p.239).

Since 1992, there has been a migration of free-to-air broadcasting to digital pay-to-view subscription services, which has allowed football in England to provide a key source of globalised media power (Lawrence and Crawford 2019). Like other transnational corporations, however, News Corporation was careful to recognise the local within its global strategising in order to make its sport product relevant to its local audience. Thus, it showed Premier League football on BSkyB (now Sky) in the United Kingdom and National Rugby League on Foxtel in Australia (Andrews and Grainger 2016). Robertson discussed concepts of authenticity of experience in introducing the term 'glocalization' in relation to marketing, where "micro-marketing takes place within the contexts of increasingly-global economic practices" (1992 p.173). Thus, transnational sponsors such as Budweiser and Coca-Cola use local cultural contexts to promote their global products from the FIFA World Cup to the Indian Premier League (cricket). As well as being shown in 212 territories, the English Premier League is broadcast in a wide range of languages from Malay to Mongolian, Mandarin to Montenegrin (Dickson and Malaia Santos 2017).

Themes of sporting tradition and authenticity are reinterpreted through the medium of television and commercial media. Hill wrote:

> The traditional experience has been replaced with something manufactured in a television studio, not for a 'spectator' but for a 'viewer' and, ultimately in many cases, for a 'consumer' of advertising.
>
> (2002 p.51)

Other writers (Horne et al. 1999; Sandvoss 2003) have described how television provides an interpretation of reality and has reshaped football consumption and fandom. Technology overcomes geography so that fans can watch matches from almost anywhere in the world, with access limited only through cost, legislation and equipment. The digitisation of football coverage has enabled fans to follow their club through livestreaming and through social media (Petersen-Wagner 2019). These later digital technologies provide opportunities for even wider connections of fans (and consumers).

Beck and Bosshart wrote:

> The very 'symbiotic relationship' between the media and sports has profoundly affected both participants. And the advertising industry forms an important part of the relationship. Both sports and mass media keep trying to reach people as spectators, fans, and consumers.
>
> (2003 p.3)

Understanding this relationship is critical to an understanding of how commercial interests interact with football and potentially help to damage our health. The presentation of sport via television is through the medium of the camera in which close-ups and the view of the action are determined by the camera operator or the director rather than the consumer (Sandvoss 2003). Thus, interview positions may be determined by advertising boards, and a focus on key players is likely to use images provided by their club, with sponsors highlighted such as on the front of club uniforms.

The new technology of the twenty-first century is likely to advance consumption through increasing social media networking and making sports events even more interactive (Jarvie *et al.* 2018). Lawrence and Crawford (2019) used the term "hyperdigitalization" to describe these digital technologies and the social, cultural and economic transformations resulting to theorise how football cultures are affected by the various ways in which football-related content is produced, accessed and consumed in digital sports broadcasting. Digital communication has enabled sports-related content on various media social platforms such as Twitter, YouTube and Facebook, which fans, clubs and commercial sponsors make use of (Hutchins and Rowe 2012; Lawrence and Crawford 2019; Hutchins *et al.* 2022). This will be explored further in Chapter 8.

Sociologists such as Walsh and Giulianotti (2001) have discussed the commodification of sport in terms of the introduction of market-centred processes. Commodification might be considered simply in terms of a system of production and exchange (such as a club charging entry to a stadium in order to watch a match), but Walsh and Giulianotti used "hyper-commodification" to describe the intensive commodification of non-playing aspects of the game such as the huge increase in club merchandising (described further below). They argued that elite sports clubs such as Manchester United are organised as transnational corporations, with profit prioritised over historical and community-based origins.

Returning to the sociological theories presented at the beginning of this chapter, it might be argued that Adorno's claims about sport and capitalism have been substantiated given the increased commodification of the game, and the many-layered identification of the sports fan as a consumer under capitalism. However, Bourdieu's perspective is also useful in appreciating how the distribution of economic power has determined the growth of the English Premier League, for example. This is explored further in the following chapter.

The sports fan as consumer

Serazio (2019) drew on Émile Durkheim and his concept of "totemic principle" (Durkheim 1912) which describes how cultures seek religious bonds of identity, in accounting for the totemic fandom that Serazio argued thrives in contemporary American culture for supporters of teams such as the Boston Red Sox (baseball), the Green Bay Packers (American football) and the Los Angeles Lakers (basketball). Hutchins and Rowe quoted Donald Horne in describing how sport was life to many Australians and that to many "it is considered a sign of degeneracy not to be interested in it" (2009 p.358). Whilst the word fan is derived from 'fanatic', there are many typologies of fans (and many discussions in forums as to what constitutes an 'authentic' fan); but from a sports business perspective, all fans share the common characteristic of being consumers (Crawford 2004; Sandvoss 2005). It is the role of the marketeers of transnational corporations to encourage them to consume more and to use sport for this purpose. Virtually every form of sport sponsorship is intended to service revenue streams (Schaaf 2004) and companies will explore all aspects of the affective, behavioural and cognitive reactions of fans (Wann and James 2019) to promote consumption.

The broadcasting of most sport is perceived to attract high concentrations of 18–34-year-old male consumers, which is very attractive to corporate advertisers (Andrews 2003) as these consumers are considered to have disposable income. Holt described football as a "celebration of intensely male values" (Holt 1992 p.173) which he defined in terms of the characteristics of the men who followed it. Football articulated male identity with its own language and initiation rites in which friendships and communities were built. Giulianotti and Armstrong (1997) wrote that both playing football and spectating provided a collective source of male imagery and ideals which allowed men to play out their emotions. A shared language of football terms, expressions and indeed history provided "access to male credibility" (1997 p.7) or what Archetti calls "a privileged male participation" (1994 p.236). Football settings, as with other sports, are therefore tied to constructions of masculinity (Connell and Messerschmidt 2005; Bunn et al. 2016).

This description of football is reproduced in other sports settings. Burstyn (1999) analysed sport and concluded that it promoted an aggressive ideal of manhood which is then used to harness sport as a sales agent. Sports are intertwined with male culture (Serazio 2019) and this representation is then drawn on to sell tobacco, alcohol, junk food and gambling. NASCAR (the National Association for Stock Car Auto Racing in the United States) has received considerable attention in both sociological and marketing literature because of its significant television audience in the United States and its fans' loyalty to the motorsport's sponsoring brands (Levin et al. 2004; Hugenberg and Hugenberg 2008; Shank and Lyberger 2014). Vavrus drew a compelling picture of "NASCAR dads" as a "population of citizen consumers" (2007 p.248). NASCAR dads are seen as Southern, working-class and white, and Vavrus's paper describes their specific masculine identity, which is then drawn on to market brands targeted at a masculine audience, including beer and formerly tobacco. The NASCAR Winston Cup Championship (Winston cigarettes is a subsidiary of RJ Reynolds) took place from 1970 to 2003 (Hugenberg and Hugenberg 2008). NASCAR's minor league circuit was sponsored by the alcohol company Anheuser-Busch from 1982 to 2007 (the latest manifestation being the NASCAR Busch Series). NASCAR racing enables an emotional connection between its customer-fans, the sport and its sponsors (Hagstrom 2001). Anheuser-Busch's long-term sponsorship seemed to pay dividends, as a study published in 2004 showed a high loyalty to and consumption of its leading brand, Budweiser (Levin et al.).

The alcohol industry has teamed up with other sports to promote a hyper-masculinised version of sport as a vehicle to promote consumption. In New Zealand, the All Black rugby team's sponsorship by Steinlager resulted in a commercial featuring the haka (a ceremonial dance in Māori culture often performed before New Zealand's sports teams' international matches) and an "eroticized masculinity" (Hope 2002 p.244) designed to appeal across a wide range of demographic groups. As Hope (2002 p.245) concluded, "All Black rugby was now a televisual product designed for mass consumption". The commercial invoked beer and team bonding (the soundtrack was John Lennon's 'Stand By Me') and linked watching rugby and drinking beer, at a time when television's advertising rules did not permit the showing of the Steinlager product itself (Perry 2013).

However, the identification of sports fans as consumers may be contested, particularly by the fans themselves (Numerato 2018). For example, "there remains a stubborn denial that 'real fans' of football can be labelled as consumers at all" (Dixon 2013 p.2). The rejection of consumerism (Hamil 2008) was at least one of the reasons behind the actions of one group of Manchester United supporters in establishing FC United in 2005 following the takeover of the club by the Glazer family, and this links to the opposition to "the development of the club as a global leisure brand" (Brown 2008 p.347). FC United was seen as a counterpoint to corporate, consumer-driven football culture and incorporated an opposition to 'plastic' (inauthentic) fans (Brown 2008). The rejection of what some football supporters consider the commercialisation of football has been accompanied by some resistance across Europe (Kennedy and Kennedy 2013). Numerato described activism by football supporters based on a "nostalgia for old times" (2018 p.59) as highlighting what they saw as authenticity and a rejection of the hyper-commodified football culture promoted by club owners who are often disconnected from local communities.

In sum, the relationships between sports, clubs and fans are contested. It might be an oversimplification to describe the process of commercialisation and globalisation as a "conversion of a pure working-class activity into some form of mass-produced and mass-consumed culture" (Critcher 2007 p.183). However, the literature reviewed and presented here demonstrates a shift from sports and clubs viewing fans as community members at the end of the nineteenth and the beginning of the twentieth centuries in Britain especially, to treating fans as a community of consumers in modern-day sport. Following the sociological theories described earlier, the intensification of the modern commodification of sport makes Elias's 'civilising process' seem dated. I will revisit Bourdieu's theory in the following chapter, but next I will explore a case study from a sport, cricket, which above all else has been completely transformed by the relationship between television and commercial sponsorship, to become a sport intended for consumption by the masses, in Bourdieu's words.

Case Study: The commodification of cricket

In Chapter 3, we saw that the first example of modern sponsorship is sometimes considered to be the Australian catering company Spiers and Pond, which supported the first England cricket tour of Australia in 1861/1862 (The Central Council of Physical Recreation 1983). The view of cricket as a purely commercial enterprise might be considered slow to have emerged, however, partly because of its development on class lines. Birley (2013 [1999]) noted the considerable relationship with the brewery industry and gambling in the first days of cricket in the seventeenth and eighteenth centuries in England. The MCC (Marylebone Cricket Club), the first governing body of the sport, was formed in 1787 and further established the rules of the game following the patronage of gamblers who needed clarity for their betting (Vamplew 2021). Collins saw the birth of the MCC as reflecting the "interplay between commercialism, gambling and aristocratic patronage" (Collins 2013 p.10) being led by the Earl of Winchilsea and the Duke of Richmond. The club was already charging for admission to its ground (which became known as Lord's after its founder, Thomas Lord).

Cricket spanned social classes in a deeply hierarchical way, and professional cricketers were evident even in the eighteenth century when aristocrats were happy to pay working men to play for their teams. However, many amateurs, including the renowned W.G. Grace, received considerable payment through 'expenses' (Birley 2013). Social segregation in English cricket lasted until 1962, and amateurs and professionals used different dressing rooms and entrances to the field of play. As cricket spread globally, the Imperial Cricket Conference, comprising the MCC, Australia and South Africa, first met in 1909 (Arlott 1975), and the Conference was joined by other countries from the British Commonwealth (India, New Zealand, the West Indies and Pakistan), following the path of the former British Empire (Guttman 1994). The Conference was renamed the International Cricket Conference (ICC) in 1965 (Arlott 1975).

As in other sports, the first steps towards the thoroughgoing commodification of the modern game in England came with the arrival of television, which provided an opportunity for exposure for advertisers and increased income for the sport (Whannel 2002). Even in the 1950s, the BBC was working with cricket administrators to ensure that all aspects of a match could be covered to improve its entertainment value (Boyle and Haynes 2009). The relaxation of Sunday observance laws in the United Kingdom in 1961 provided an opportunity for Sunday cricket (Birley 2013) and its further commercialisation. As described in Chapter 4, the tobacco companies were never slow to seize a new opportunity for the exposure of their products. In 1966, the tobacco company Rothman's launched the International Cavaliers series of 40-over televised matches (Birley 2013). The cricket authorities, concerned about this challenge to their control of players, swiftly responded by finding another tobacco company to sponsor their own made-for-television Sunday League, the John Player League (Schofield 1982; Milne 2016). Attendances for the new league doubled between 1969 and 1976 and the broadcaster BBC2's viewing figures also quadrupled

(Wagg 2018). Following this success, the MCC set up another one-day tournament in 1971, again sponsored by a tobacco brand, Benson and Hedges (owned by the Gallaher Group). The deal was brokered by West Nally, a sports marketing group, which would go on to work with Horst Dassler and establish the sponsorship model for the World Cup in the 1970s (see the previous chapter).

> The historic English rite of cricket was now a lucrative brand, but could only remain so as long as it was not *seen* as a brand ... the sponsors were buying not cricket, but an *idea* – the idea being of a civilised, gentlemanly English pursuit which had always placed itself above the tumult of politics and naked commerce.
>
> (Wagg 2018, pages 193,194)

Part of the power of sport for commercial organisations is precisely this sense that it represents a sphere of activities or values which are in some sense not commercialised and therefore more authentic. This is an essential point that will be returned through throughout this book. Unhealthy commodity industries are able to use the symbolic and cultural capital of sport to promote consumption.

Effectively cricket, having allowed sponsorship into the game, now allowed the needs of television and sponsors to determine the modification of its laws. Limited-over cricket was ideal for television with its shorter format, speed of play (Boyle and Haynes 2009) and newer, bigger audiences, and it spread quickly to Australia, the Caribbean, India and South Africa (where Benson and Hedges sponsored a competition in 1981) (Wagg 2018).

The first cricket World Cup, following the one-day format, was organised by the ICC in 1975. The event was designed to draw an international audience and, like the FIFA World Cup and the Olympics, illustrates sport's contribution to globalisation (Gratton *et al.* 2012). The new television audience attracted the interest of Australian television magnate Kerry Packer, who sought a monopoly of cricket broadcasting. When he was unable to achieve this, Packer set up an alternative competition, World Series Cricket (WSC), which ran for two years in 1977 and 1978 (Cashman 1994). Packer had previous form in that he had televised the Australian Open golf tournament in 1975, working with the tobacco company W.D. & H.O. Wills on the following year's event (Haigh 2007 [1993]). Packer's Channel Nine transformed the televisual spectacle of cricket using multiple camera angles and frequent action replays (Whannel 2002). WSC became a game-changer for a new form of cricket and showed its potential as a "premium media franchise" (Haigh 2007 [1993] p.ix). Sports rights became a further battleground for pay-TV in Australia, when Packer's telecommunications consortia (Optus) came up against Rupert Murdoch's New Limited (along with Telstra) in their attempts to exploit the broadcasting of the Australian Football League and National Rugby League in the 1990s (Evens *et al.* 2013).

Following India's triumph in the 1983 limited-over World Cup, it was demonstrated that there was a market for short-form cricket in the Indian subcontinent. In 1996, when the Cricket World Cup was held in India, Pakistan and Sri Lanka, it had become a showpiece for its multinational corporate sponsors, with Coca-Cola one of those represented. The title sponsorship was with ITC's (originally the Imperial Tobacco Company of India) Wills brand and was the biggest individual sponsorship deal of its time in the subcontinent (Marqusee 1996).

One-day cricket was now inextricably linked to television and to sponsorship, and in countries which offered the biggest audiences not only for insurance and mobile phones, but also for tobacco companies and fast food and fizzy drinks (Wagg 2018). Making cricket more television friendly turned it into a spectacle based on mass consumption (Harriss 1990). The introduction of Twenty20 (T20) cricket in England in 2001 was strongly supported by Sky television (Wagg 2018). The new format consisted of two innings of 20 overs allowing matches to be completed in three and a half hours. It was soon popular across the cricket world, with fast food companies keen to provide sponsorship. In Australasia, Georgie Pie (a New Zealand fast food company), McDonald's and Kentucky Fried Chicken (KFC) were early sponsors (Wagg 2018). Following Packer's innovation in introducing coloured uniforms in cricket, the new T20 format featured lurid outfits for its teams, providing the opportunity for spectators to purchase replica shirts (Boyle and Haynes 2009) but also space for a sponsor's brand.

The Australian T20 league has been called the KFC Big Bash League since its inception in 2011. It uses an array of televisual technologies to encourage viewer engagement (Sturm 2015) and this enables the main sponsor's logo to be shown on the players' uniforms (shirt, cap and trousers), umpires' shirts, the playing surface, on the stumps, on telecast graphics (such as the match statistics and player line-ups) and on the fence signage behind the wicket. The game has been 'colonialised', with brands penetrating on to the field of play itself. An Australian academic study (Sherriff *et al.* 2009) of one Big Bash match in 2008 showed that the KFC logo was visible for 61 per cent of the time during the game. The Big Bash is certainly appealing to young cricketers (Hinds 2017).

Since its establishment in 2008, the Indian Premier League (IPL) has become the most spectacular and richest T20 competition. It was initially opposed by international cricket boards in the same way that Packer's WSC initiative had been opposed 30 years earlier (Wagg 2018). Gupta sees the success of the IPL as signifying the transformation of India to a free-market economy, as the IPL was entirely focused on commercial promotion and turning cricket into a "twenty-first century sport" (Gupta 2011 p.1317). Elite sport has evidently become an important form of representation in the postcolonial world (Bale and Cronin 2020 (2003)). With a huge support base, the sport thinks globally but acts locally in its blend of Bollywood and cricket. Like the English Premier League, the IPL has international stars playing for it but maintains its local identity. "Infused with Indian money, motifs, and meanings, a new spectacle of consumption is on offer" (Khondker and Robertson 2018 p.280).

The original founder of the IPL, Lalit Modi, was the president of the International Tobacco Company from 1987 to 1991 and an executive director at Godfrey Phillips India, one of India's largest tobacco companies (part of a venture with Philip Morris International) between 1992 and 2010. Modi's model of privately owned franchises for the eight teams in the IPL was modelled on Major League basketball in the United States (Wagg 2018). The Bangalore Royal Challengers are owned by Vijay Mallya (India Fantasy 2021), who made his fortune through alcohol (United Breweries). In 2013, Modi was found guilty on a series of charges including bribery, insider trading, money laundering and tax evasion and banned for life from cricket by the Board of Control for Cricket in India (BCCI) (Marqusee 2010). Marqusee saw Modi's demise as a demonstration of how neoliberalism has failed sport. The modernisation of cricket was seen only as a matter of maximising profits, with the welfare of the sport, the teams or the fans a secondary consideration (Marqusee 2010). As Rumford argued:

> The rapid development of the IPL, and its massive impact on the global sporting consciousness, demonstrates that the key actors in cricket are no longer the traditional elites in metropolitan centres but the businessmen of India and the media entrepreneurs worldwide who seek to shape new audiences for the game and create new marketing opportunities on a global scale.
>
> (Rumford 2013 p.1)

The IPL's sponsors have included alcohol companies. However, the BCCI has refused gambling and alcohol sponsorship in the past, and British cricketer Moeen Ali, who played in the IPL for Chennai Super Kings, refused to have the team sponsor's alcohol brand SNJ 10,000 (owned by the Chennai-based SNJ Distilleries) displayed on his shirt in 2021 because of his religious beliefs (India TV 2021).

Whilst limited-overs cricket began in India in 1951 (RediffNews 2010), the first competitive league was the John Player League in England. It was in this country that the latest made-for-television cricket initiative was launched by the England and Wales Cricket Board (ECB) in 2021. The Hundred (based on 100 balls to be faced by each team) was modelled on the IPL and was aimed at children and families (Humphries and Ammon 2019), with the main sponsor being KP Snacks, whose brands were displayed prominently on the players' shirts, "another stark reminder of the incongruent relationship between unhealthy products and sports" (Chambers and Sassi 2019 p.1). A complaint to the UK advertising watchdog, the Advertising Standards Authority, from Sustain's Children's Food Campaign and Food Active, resulted in a ruling in 2022, that found a promotional campaign for the Hundred broke rules established by the industry self-regulator, the Committee for Advertising Practices, to prevent targeting advertising HFSS food or drink at children (Rudling 2022). The campaign used a paid-for Instagram advertisement, illustrating the growing use of social media platforms to promote unhealthy commodities through sport.

Holden discussed international cricket in a piece which compared commercial imperatives with the principles of morality and ethics. Whilst he was not addressing unhealthy sponsorship, his conclusion that "As governmental authority declines in comparison to that of a small number of multi-national conglomerates, the development of cricket appears to be driven by the ever-more powerful forces of commodification in preference to anxieties regarding morality" (2009 p.643) seems very sound.

Conclusions

This chapter has used sociological theories to discuss the commodification of modern sport. As in previous chapters, it has drawn on a case study, in this instance cricket, to illustrate how a sport has been transformed by television and sponsorship, its rules and presentation redesigned for mass consumption. Limited-over cricket has proved a willing vehicle for the promotion of tobacco, alcohol and junk food brands. The centre of cricket may now be considered to be India, the home of the richest and most glamorous T20 competition. The IPL's mix of a global product with a local identity has many similarities with the English Premier League, considered in the next chapter. This will also draw on Bourdieusian theory to examine how economic and social capital are represented in English elite football.

References

Adorno, T. (2001) *The Culture Industry*, Abingdon: Routledge.
Andrews, D.L. (2003) 'Sport and the transnationalizing media corporation', *The Journal of Media Economics*, 16(4), 235–251.
Andrews, DL. and Grainger, A.D. (2016) 'Sport and globalization' in Ritzer, G., ed., *The Blackwell Companion to Globalization*, Chichester: John Wiley & Sons.
Archetti, E.P. (1994) 'Masculinity and football: the formation of national identity in Argentina' in Giulianotti, R. and Williams, J., eds., *Game Without Frontiers. Football, Identity and Modernity*, Aldershot: Arena, 225–243.
Arlott, J. ed. (1975) *The Oxford Companion to Sports & Games*, London: Oxford University Press.
Bale, J. and Cronin, M. (2020) *Sport and Postcolonialism*, Abingdon: Routledge.
Beck, D. and Bosshart, L. (2003) 'Sports and media', *Communications Research Trends*, 22(4), 1–44.
Bernstein, J.M. (2001) 'Introduction to the 'The Culture Industry' by Theodor Adorno' in *The Culture Industry*, Abingdon: Routledge.
Birley, D. (2013) *A Social History of English Cricket*, London: Aurum.
Bourdieu, P. (1978) 'Sport and social class'. *Social Science Information*, 17(6), 819–840.
Bourdieu, P. (1993) *The Field of Cultural Production*, Cambridge: Polity Press.
Bourdieu, P. (1998) *Acts of Resistance. Against the Tyranny of the Market*, New York: The New Press.
Bourdieu, P. (1999) 'The state, economics and sport' in Dauncey, H. and Hare, G., eds., *France and the 1998 World Cup. The National Impact of a World Sporting Event*, London: Frank Cass, 15–21.
Bourdieu, P. (2010) *Sociology Is a Martial Art*, New York: New Press.
Boyle, R. and Haynes, R. (2009) *Power Play. Sport, the Media and Popular Culture*, Second ed., Edinburgh: Edinburgh University Press.
Brown, A. (2008) '"Our club, our rules": Fan communities at FC United of Manchester', *Soccer and Society*, 9(3), 346–358.
Bunn, C., Wyke, S., Gray, C.M., Maclean, A. and Hunt, K. (2016) '"Coz football is what we all have": Masculinities, practice, performance and effervescence in a gender-sensitised weight-loss and healthy living programme for men', *Sociology of Health & Illness*, 38(5), 812–828.
Burstyn, V. (1999) *The Rites of Men: Manhood, Politics and the Culture of Sport*, Toronto: University of Toronto Press.
Cashman, R. (1994) 'Cricket' in Vamplew, W. and Stoddart, B., eds., *Sport in Australia. A Social History*, Cambridge: Cambridge University Press.
Castells, M. (2000) *The Rise of the Network Society*, Oxford: Blackwell.
Chambers, T. and Sassi, F. (2019) 'Unhealthy sponsorship of sport', *BMJ*, 367, l6718, available: http://dx.doi.org/10.1136/bmj.l6718.
Collins, T. (2012) *Rugby's Great Split: Class, Culture and the Origins of Rugby League Football*, Abingdon: Routledge.
Collins, T. (2013) *Sport in Capitalist Society. A Short History*, Abingdon: Routledge.
Connell, R.W. and Messerschmidt, J.W. (2005) 'Hegemonic masculinity: Rethinking the concept', *Gender and Society*, 19(6), 829–859.
Crawford, G. (2004) *Consuming Sport. Fans, Sport and Culture*, Abingdon: Routledge.
Critcher, C. (2007) 'Football since the war' in Clarke, J., Critcher, C. and Johnson, R., eds., *Working-Class Culture*, Abingdon: Routledge.

David, M., Kirton, A. and Millward, P. (2017) 'Castells, 'Murdochization', economic counterpower and livestreaming', *Convergence*, 23(5), 497–511.

Dickson, G. and Malaia Santos, J.M.C. (2017) 'Globalisation and professional sport' in Schulenkorf, N. and Frawley, S., eds., *Critical Issues in Global Sports Management*, Abingdon: Routledge.

Dixon, K. (2013) *Consuming Football in Late Modern Life*, Farnham: Ashgate.

Durkheim, E. (1912) *The Elementary Forms of the Religious Life*, London: George Allen & Unwin Ltd.

Elias, N. (1978) *The Civilizing Process*, Oxford: Blackwell.

Elias, N. (1982) *State Formation and Civilization*, Oxford: Blackwell.

Elias, N. (1986) 'Introduction to "Quest for Excitement. Sport and Leisure in the Civilizing Process"' in *Quest for Excitement. Sport and Leisure in the Civilizing Process*, Oxford: Basil Blackwell.

Elias, N. and Dunning, E. (1986) *Quest for Excitement. Sport and Leisure in the Civilizing Process*, Oxford: Basil Blackwell.

Evens, T., Iosifidis, P. and Smith, P. (2013) *The Political Economy of Television Sports Rights*, Basingstoke: Palgrave Macmillan.

Falcous, M. (2005) 'Global struggles, local impacts' in Nauright, J. and Schimmel, K. S., eds., *The Political Economy of Sport*, London: Palgrave Macmillan.

Giulianotti, R. (2004) 'Norbert Elias and the sociology of sport' in Giulianotti, R., ed., *Sport and Modern Social Theorists*, Basingstoke: Palgrave Macmillan.

Giulianotti, R. (2016) *Sport. A Critical Sociology*, Cambridge: Polity.

Giulianotti, R. and Armstrong, G. (1997) 'Introduction: Reclaiming the game - an introduction to the anthropology of football' in Armstrong, G. and Giulianotti, R., eds., *Entering the Field. New Perspectives on World Football*, Oxford: Berg.

Gratton, C., Liu, D., Ramchandani, G. and Wilson, D. (2012) *The Global Economics of Sport*, Abingdon: Routledge.

Grenfell, M. (2018) 'Pierre Bourdieu on sport' in Giulianotti, R., ed., *Routledge Handbook on the Sociology of Sport*, Abingdon: Routledge.

Gupta, A. (2011) 'The IPL and the Indian domination of global cricket', *Sport in Society*, 14(10), 1316–1325, available: http://dx.doi.org/10.1080/17430437.2011.620373.

Guttman, A. (1994) *Games and Empires. Modern Sports and Cultural Imperialism*, New York: Columbia University Press.

Hagstrom, R.G. (2001) *The NASCAR Way: The Business that Drives the Sport*, New York: John Wiley & Sons.

Haigh, G. (2007 [1993]) *The Cricket War. The Inside Story of Kerry Packer's World Series Cricket*, Second ed., Carlton: Melbourne University Press.

Hamil, S. (2008) 'Manchester United: The commercial development of a global football brand' in Chadwick, S. and Arthur, D., eds., *International Cases in the Business of Sport*, Oxford: Butterworth-Heinemann.

Harriss, I. (1990) 'Packer, cricket and postmodernism' in Rowe, D. and Lawrence, G., eds., *Sport and Leisure: Trends in Australian Popular Culture*, Sydney: Harcourt Brace Jovanovich.

Hill, J. (2002) *Sport, Leisure & Culture in Twentieth-Century Britain*. Basingstoke: Palgrave.

Hinds, R. (2017) 'Big Bash League winning over Test cricket purists as kids embrace the game', 21 December, 2017, available: https://www.abc.net.au/news/2017-12-22/hinds:-even-test-purists-must-see-the-bright-side-of-the-bbl/9278950 [accessed 31 January 2022].

Holden, R. (2009) 'International cricket–the hegemony of commerce, the decline of government interest and the end of morality'? *Sport in Society*, 12(4–5), 643–656.

Holt, R. (1992) *Sport and the British. A Modern History*, Oxford: Clarendon Press.

Hope, W. (2002) 'Whose all blacks?', *Media, Culture & Society*, 24(2), 235–253.

Horne, J., Tomlinson, A. and Whannel, G. (1999) *Understanding Sport. An Introduction to the Sociological and Cultural Analysis of Sport*, London: Spon Press.

Hugenberg, L.W. and Hugenberg, B. (2008) 'NASCAR fans in their own words' in Hugenberg, L. W., Haridakis, P.M. and Earnheardt, A. C., eds., *Sports Mania: Essays on Fandom and the Media in the 21st Century*, Jefferson: McFarland & Company, 172–186.

Humphries, W. and Ammon, E. (2019) 'Family cricket series The hundred criticised for choosing snack sponsor', *The Times*, 3 October 2019, available: https://www.thetimes.co.uk/article/family-cricket-series-the-hundred-criticised-for-choosing-snack-sponsor-z3dwdmtmt [accessed 1 February 2022].

Hutchins, B. and Rowe, D. (2009) 'From broadcast scarcity to digital plenitude: The changing dynamics of the media sport content economy', *Television & New Media*, 10(4), 354–370.

Hutchins, B. and Rowe, D. (2012) *Sport Beyond Television. The Internet, Digital Media and the Rise of Networked Media Sport*, Abingdon: Routledge.

Hutchins, B., Rowe, D. and Ruddock, A. (2022) 'Commodification and mediatization of fandom. Creating executive fandom' in Coombs, D.S. and Osborne, A.C., eds., *Routledge Handbook of Sports Fans and Fandom*, Abingdon: Routledge, 365–376.

India Fantasy (2021) *IPL Team Owner Name List, Net Worth, Profession*, available: https://www.indiafantasy.com/cricket/cricket-news/ipl-team-owners-list-and-their-net-worth/ [accessed 31 January 2022].

India TV (2021) *IPL 2021: CSK Allow Moeen Ali to Drop Liquor Brand Logo*, available: https://www.indiatvnews.com/amp/sports/cricket/ipl-2021-csk-allow-moeen-ali-to-drop-liquor-brand-logo-695544 [accessed 1 February 2022].

Jarvie, G. and Maguire, J. (1994) *Sport and Leisure in Social Thought*, London: Routledge.

Jarvie, G., Thornton, J. and Mackie, H. (2018) *Sport, Culture and Society. An Introduction*, Third ed., Abingdon: Routledge.

Jeffries, S. (2016) *Grand Hotel Abyss. The Lives of the Frankfurt School*, London: Verso.

Kennedy, P. and Kennedy, D. (2013) *Football Supporters and the Commercialisation of Football. Comparative Responses across Europe*, Abingdon: Routledge.

Khondker, H.H. and Robertson, R. (2018) 'Glocalization, consumption, and cricket: The Indian Premier League', *Journal of Consumer Culture*, 18(2), 279–297.

Lash, S. (1993) 'Pierre Bourdieu: Cultural economy and social change' in Calhoun, C., LiPuma, E. and Postone, M., eds., *Bourdieu: Critical Perspectives*, Cambridge: Polity Press.

Lash, S. and Lury, C. (2007) *Global Culture Industry*, Cambridge: Polity.

Lawrence, S. and Crawford, G. (2019) 'The hyperdigitalization of football cultures' in Lawrence, S. and Crawford, G., eds., *Digital Football Cultures. Fandom, Identities and Resistance*, Abingdon: Routledge.

Levin, A.M., Beasley, F. and Gamble, T. (2004) 'Brand loyalty of NASCAR fans towards sponsors: the impact of fan identification', *International Journal of Sports Marketing and Sponsorship*, 6(1), 7–17, available: http://dx.doi.org/10.1108/IJSMS-06-01-2004-B004.

Marqusee, M. (1996) *War Minus the Shooting: A Journey through South Asia during Cricket's World Cup*, Random House (UK).

Marqusee, M. (2010) 'IPL's dark side of neoliberal dream', *The Guardian*, 9 May 2010, available: https://www.theguardian.com/commentisfree/2010/may/09/india-cricket-ipl [accessed 31 January 2022].

Milne, M. (2016) *The Transformation of Television Sport. New Methods, New Rules*, Basingstoke: Palgrave Macmillan.

Morgan, W.J. (1988) 'Adorno on sport. The case of the fractured dialectic', *Theory and Society*, 17, 813–838.

Numerato, D. (2018) *Football Fans, Activism and Social Change*, Abingdon: Routledge.

Perry, N. (2013) *The Dominion of Signs: Television, Advertising and Other New Zealand Fictions*, Auckland: Auckland University Press.

Petersen-Wagner, R. (2019) 'Between old and new traditions. Transnational solidarities and the love for Liverpool FC' in Lawrence, S. and Crawford, G., eds., *Digital Football Cultures. Fandom, Identities and Resistance*, Abingdon: Routledge.

Rediff News (2010) *World's First Limited Over Tournament Turns 60*, available: https://www.rediff.com/cricket/report/world-first-limited-overs-pooja-cricket-tournament-turns-60/20100727.htm [accessed 1 February 2022].

Roberts, K. (2016) *Social Theory, Sport, Leisure*, Abingdon: Routledge.

Robertson, R. (1992) *Globalization: Social Theory and Global Culture*. London: Sage.

Rowe, D. (2009) 'Media and sport: The cultural dynamics of global games', *Sociology Compass*, 3(4), 543–558.

Rudling, M. (2022) 'Promotion for the hundred pulled up by ASA after junk food campaign targeted children', *The Cricketer*, available: https://www.thecricketer.com/Topics/thehundred/promotion_the_hundred_banned_junk_food_campaign_children_.html [accessed 10 July 2022].

Rumford, C. (2013) 'Introduction: Twenty20 and the future of cricket' in Rumford, C., ed., *Twenty20 and the Future of Cricket*, Abingdon: Routledge, 13–17.

Sandvoss, C. (2003) *A Game of Two Halves. Football, Television and Globalization*, Abingdon: Routledge.

Sandvoss, C. (2005) *Fans. The Mirror of Consumption*, Cambridge: Polity Press.

Schaaf, P. (2004) *Sport, Inc. 100 Years of Sports Business*, New York: Prometheus Books.

Schofield, J.A. (1982) 'The development of first-class cricket in England: An economic analysis', *The Journal of Industrial Economics*, 30(4), 337–360, available: http://dx.doi.org/10.2307/2097922.

Serazio, M. (2019) *The Power of Sports. Media and Spectacle in American Culture*, New York: New York University Press.

Shank, M.D. and Lyberger, M.R. (2014) *Sports Marketing: A Strategic Perspective*, Abingdon: Routledge.

Sherriff, J., Griffiths, D. and Daube, M. (2009) 'Cricket: Notching up runs for food and alcohol companies?', *Australian and New Zealand Journal of Public Health*, 34(1), 19–23.

Sturm, D. (2015) 'Smash and bash cricket? Affective technological innovations in the big bash', *Media International Australia*, 155(1), 80–88, available: http://dx.doi.org/10.1177/1329878X1515500110.

The Central Council of Physical Recreation (1983) *Committee of Enquiry into Sports Sponsorship. "The Howell Report"*, London.

Tomlinson, A. (2004) 'Pierre Bourdieu and the sociological study of sport: Habitus, capital and field' in Giulianotti, R., ed., *Sport and Modern Social Theorists*, Basingstoke: Palgrave Macmillan.

Vamplew, W. (2021) *Games People Played. A Global History of Sport*, London: Reaktion Books.

Vavrus, M.D. (2007) 'The politics of NASCAR dads: Branded media paternity'. *Critical Studies in Media Communication*, 24(3), 245-261. doi:10.1080/07393180701520942

Wagg, S. (2018) *Cricket: A Political History of the Global Game, 1945–2017*, Abingdon: Routledge.

Walsh, A.J., & Giulianotti, R. (2001) 'This sporting mammon: A normative critique of the commodification of sport', *Journal of the Philosophy of Sport*, 28(1), 53–77.

Wann, D.L. and James, J.D. (2019) *Sports Fans. The Psychology and Social Impact of Fandom*, Second ed., Abingdon: Routledge.

Wenner, L.A. ed. (1989) *Media, Sports & Society*, London: SAGE Publications.

Wenner, L.A. ed. (1998) *MediaSport*, London: Routledge.

Whannel, G. (2002) *Fields in Vision. Television Sport and Cultural Transformation*, London: Routledge.

Chapter 7

The commercialisation and globalisation of football in England

The media and the transformation of English football

Newspapers and the sporting press played a major part in the development of Victorian sport, and television has had a similarly profound effect on how contemporary elite football is presented to the public (Domeneghetti 2017). As early as 1938, the FA Cup final in England drew around 10,000 television viewers (Giulianotti and Robertson 2009). By 1950 about 350,000 TV licences had been issued when Liverpool and Arsenal played in the FA Cup final (Domeneghetti 2017). The 1953 final featuring Stanley Matthews had 10 million viewers according to Domeneghetti. As Mason (1980) wrote, whereas only 10 per cent of people had a television in Britain in the early 1950s, by the late 1960s only 10 per cent did not. The arrival of television in homes made football a significant "advertising platform" (Chanavat et al. 2017 p.111).

The post-war phase of British football's development was marked by the growing commercial success of Manchester United and the development of its iconic brand. Following the austerity and damage caused by the war, Manchester United was the club with the largest number of spectators (45,000 on average) between 1946 and 1960 (Boli 2017), and it won First Division (the precursor to the Premier League) titles in 1952, 1956 and 1957. In 1957, Manchester United was the first English team to compete in the European Cup (established by UEFA in 1955 for the champions of the top divisions in Europe, this was rebranded as the Champions League in 1992 and broadened its qualifications to include more clubs). In 1958, a plane bringing the Manchester United team back from a European Cup match crashed in Munich, killing 23 people, including eight players, and injuring several more. Boli (2017) argued that the Munich crash shaped the mythology of the club.

Jimmy Hill, the chairman of the Professional Footballers' Association (PFA) at this time, saw a new position for the footballer in English culture. Hill framed football as part of the entertainment business and, as entertainers, footballers were producing commodities which should be valued in the same way as television, cinema and theatre (Hill 1961). By the late 1950s, many players were paid by companies to advertise their goods. The tobacco industry was an early innovator,

DOI: 10.4324/9781003239734-7

with Everton star Dixie Dean promoting Carreras Clubs cigarettes in the 1930s, and Craven A capitalising on the fame of England footballer Stanley Matthews (Matthews was not even a smoker) two decades later (Griffin 2012). The celebrity is an important part of contemporary football culture, centred on the encouragement of consumption (Smart 2005; Cashmore 2006; Harris 2017). Matthews was a representative of his age and class and earned more from his royalties from advertising and writing a newspaper column (and two autobiographies) than he did from playing football (Hopcraft 2006). Following the Munich plane crash, the Manchester United team was rebuilt in the 1960s and the club brand developed around the success of players such as Bobby Charlton, Denis Law and George Best. Best might be considered the first football celebrity in an era when football players were transformed from "local heroes to global stars" (Turner 2014 p.751).

In the early 1960s, football saw significant drops in attendances and thus losses in matchday income. The expansion of television provided a great attraction for potential sponsors (Whannel 1986). The banning of cigarette advertising on British television in 1965 led to major tobacco company brands such as Benson and Hedges and Rothmans ploughing large sums into televised sports (Whannel 1986, 2002) such as cricket, darts, tennis and motor racing to maintain exposure for their brands (see Chapter 4 for more detail). As the commercial potential of sport on television grew, there was increasing pressure on the "traditional amateur, benevolent paternalism of sports organization" by entrepreneurial interests (Whannel 1986 p.130).

The 1970s and 1980s brought attention both to fan behaviour and the decaying and unsuitable stadiums of British football. Taylor wrote that Prime Minister Margaret Thatcher's government argued that the disasters that were to occur in football grounds were linked with hooliganism, and also "by the characteristically unregulated and inefficiently organized condition of a working-class mass sport" (1987 p.172). The Hillsborough disaster of 1989, when 97 Liverpool fans lost their lives due to the devastatingly inadequate crowd-control measures employed by South Yorkshire Police at Sheffield Wednesday's Hillsborough Stadium, proved a turning point both in how football was viewed and how it was governed (Tempany 2016). Lord Justice Taylor's reports (1989, 1990) into the Hillsborough tragedy led to a review of stadium safety. The resulting changes led to the refurbishment or reconstruction of stadiums, including the introduction of all-seater facilities (Rookwood and Hughson 2017). This has also been described as a deliberate move to change the fan demographic to marginalise crowd disorder, with increased ticket prices contributing both to rebuilding costs and to changing football culture (Inglis 2002).

The launch of the English Premier League

Football's administrators and its leading clubs had already been seeking ways of making more money from the game, which had originally been established by the Football League on a system of shared gate money (Conn 2005). The FA had established restrictions against unlimited dividends in 1892 to prevent what it saw as "the dangers of commercialism" (Conn 2005 p.42), and these rules had stayed in place until the 1980s. In 1983, seeking new sources of income, the directors of Tottenham Hotspur floated their club on the stock market, thus avoiding the FA's restrictions on dividends and enabling the club to become a profit-making vehicle for investors (Conn 2005). In 1991, the FA's *Blueprint for the Future of Football* recommended the establishment of a Premier League based around the "realisation of full commercial revenue" (Football Association 1991 p.55). There were three major areas of commercial activity which were highlighted: television rights (in 1991, the sale of television rights was lower in England than in Italy, Spain, Germany and France), sponsorship, and licensing and merchandising (Football Association 1991).

The establishment of the FA Premier League (now known as the English Premier League or EPL) in the 1992/1993 football season established a new business model and took professional football to new levels of exposure and scrutiny. It provided opportunities to commodify all aspects of the game from the players themselves to the stadiums in which they played. Many writers have described the decision by the Football Association in September 1991 to allow the top 22 clubs to break away from the other 70 clubs as a power-grab for the elite clubs. Conn (2005 p.102) quotes the chief executive of the PFA, Gordon Taylor, as describing it as "a way for the leading clubs to seize virtually all the money". Once there was an agreement that the top clubs would form their own league, they were able to negotiate their own broadcasting rights package.

With the launch of the Premier League, the top tier of English football became a "highly developed and globally marketed commodity for worldwide media audiences" (Tomlinson 2013 p.6). Walsh and Giulianotti (2001) used the term "hyper-commodification" in their description of football as a truly global sport at the beginning of the twenty-first century. They described the market-centred processes in football as entailing

> the greater professionalization and global migration of players, the corporatization of clubs, the proliferation of merchandising, rule-changes to draw in new customers, and a general redefinition of the competitive structures and *ethos* of the sport.
>
> (2001 p.53)

The launch of the Premier League helped to fully commercialise the top tier of the English game, bombarding fans with new, more targeted messaging from every possible angle (Dittmore and McCarthy 2016), and making it a key marketing platform for unhealthy commodity industries. As noted in the previous chapter, Rupert Murdoch based the development of BSkyB on securing the broadcasting rights to live coverage of Premier League football in 1992. Baimbridge *et al.* (1996) detailed the value of the BSkyB bid in 1992, which gave it exclusive rights to the live matches of the newly established Premier League. The live broadcasting deal was worth £305 million over five years. Within the new Premier League, TV and sponsorship revenue was split three ways. Half was shared equally between the clubs, a quarter was related to the games selected for live coverage and the final quarter was paid out in decreasing slices according to a club's final league position. Following this key acquisition, BSkyB's sports channel, Sky Sports, was encrypted and its new subscriber base enabled it to secure rights to other sports events including Ryder Cup golf and international one-day cricket (Evens *et al.* 2013). This transformation of the televising of English football did not happen in isolation and mirrors the rapid growth of televised global sports events, including the Olympics and the World Cup (as described in Chapter 5) (Milne 2016).

Robertson discussed concepts of authenticity of experience in introducing the term 'glocalization' in relation to marketing, where "micro-marketing takes place within the contexts of increasingly-global economic practices" (1992 p.173). Thus, multi-national corporations and football sponsors such as Budweiser and Coca-Cola use local cultural contexts to promote their global products from the FIFA World Cup to the EPL. Notions of football tradition and authenticity are now reinterpreted through the medium of television and commercial media. Hill wrote that:

> The traditional experience has been replaced with something manufactured in a television studio, not for a 'spectator' but for a 'viewer' and, ultimately in many cases, for a 'consumer' of advertising.
>
> (2002 p.51)

Turner provided a brief conceptualisation of "traditional football fandom" and "the imaginary constructions of authenticity" (2017 p.113) as he examined the changes to English football since the launch of the Premier League. The broadcast revolution transformed spectator identity away from simply attending in person. Dixon (2016) noted that concepts of tradition and authenticity are malleable and fluid. For example, since the emergence of regular live broadcasting of football, the pub (whether an alehouse in Manchester or a bar in Nigeria) could be viewed as a modern locus of authentic fandom where football supporters gather to watch the game (Brown 2008; Dixon 2014). However, referencing Anderson (1983), modern fandoms may be characterised as "imagined communities fostered by technologies that enable geographically dispersed people to overcome time and distance in forging virtual communities of affect" (Morimoto and Chin 2017 p.174).

The launch of regular televised football brought a new and seemingly inexhaustible global market to the cultural-media industries (Williams 1994) and a transformation in the finances of the game, at least at elite level. Morrow restated the ongoing debate as football "being conceptualized as economic in basis, but social in nature" (2003 p.43). King argued that English football responded to the findings of the Taylor Report (Rt Hon Lord Justice Taylor 1990) through the "unfettered application of free market principles" (King 1997 p.225). This was enabled by BskyB's winning of the broadcasting rights to the new English Premier

League. This transformed the political economy of football from the "traditional spectator-based model" (Evens et al. 2013 p.17) to one based on the exploitation of media rights, merchandising and sponsorship.

The revenue of an English Premier League club

Modern EPL clubs generate income from three sources: matchday receipts, broadcasting rights and commercial transactions (Maguire 2020). However, there are big differences between the revenues of a global brand such as Manchester United or Liverpool and, say, Norwich City. In the season 2019/2020, which was temporarily halted because of the coronavirus pandemic, Liverpool finished as champions whilst Norwich City finished last. This was a very successful time for Liverpool on the pitch and its financial accounts posted on 31 May 2020 reflected this (The Liverpool Football Club and Athletic Grounds Limited 2020). During the reporting period, Liverpool won the Champions League in 2019, the FIFA Club World Cup and the UEFA Super Cup. Matchday receipts were £71 million, a little down on 2019 figures as some matches took place without supporters in the stadium because of the pandemic. Broadcasting income was £202 million, and commercial income was £217 million. In total Liverpool FC posted revenue of £489.9 million. In contrast, Norwich City's respective figures were £8 million (matchday receipts), £90 million (broadcasting) and £21 million (commercial), producing a total revenue of £119.4 million (Norwich City Football Club PLC 2020). Because of the global reach of the Premier League, income from broadcasting is still substantial even to the less well-supported teams and represents their most important source of revenue. Similarly one of the 'big six' clubs (generally taken to mean Arsenal, Chelsea, Liverpool, Manchester United, Manchester City and Tottenham Hotspur (Potts 2020)) in the Premier League is able to use its reach in terms of followers to generate huge sums of commercial income from sponsorship and merchandising.

For all clubs, commercial income, typically described as sponsorship arrangements, provides revenue. These commercial arrangements are often agreed over a long timeframe, with shirt sponsorship deals commonly in place for a period of years (PwC 2018). As these agreements are commercially sensitive, clubs do not generally divulge their financial details, although the amounts are frequently speculated about in the press. Manchester United's seven-year (2014–2021) sponsorship deal with Chevrolet was described in detail in Chapter 3.

Marketeers describe the leading clubs, such as Manchester United, as major brands which may be compared to Pepsi or Toyota, whilst having a loyal global fanbase far in excess of that achieved by almost every major brand (Carling 2020). The Premier League itself also achieves global recognition. In 2018, Populus published research on the global popularity of leading British brands (Populus 2018); their results showed the Premier League finishing first in an online survey of 20,882 adults in 20 'international markets', in front of Rolls Royce and Jaguar Land Rover. Whilst the research was commissioned by the EPL itself, it is still noteworthy given the Premier League's good showing in East and South-East Asia and Africa, finishing first in South Korea, Thailand, Kenya and Morocco. The building of the Premier League brand duplicates the process of development of the Olympic and World Cup brands (described in Chapter 5).

Football is now the subject of detailed economic analysis and comment from leading auditing and financial services companies, and these in turn focus on the financial opportunities being provided through new technology. The Deloitte Sports Business Group commented that "consumers' desire for anytime, anywhere access to content" (2017 p.23) is enabling the growth of streaming platforms and goes hand-in-hand with social media networks. Powerful teams and leagues are also establishing their own televisual networks (Miller 2013; Boli 2017). The Deloitte's financial lists show that the English Premier League continues to be the richest in Europe, driven by the value of its broadcast rights revenue (Deloitte Sports Business Group 2020). Castells (2000) described a network society based on interactions between global actors where flows enter the most lucrative space. Millward (2011) drew on this work to describe the most successful English teams as nodes in a European network that have been able to generate even further income through their participation in European tournaments and through the sale of overseas television rights (Williams 2013).

Club shirt sponsorships by unhealthy commodity industries

Shirt (also referred to as 'jersey') sponsorship is considered the principal marketing outlet in football (Chanavat *et al.* 2017). Revenues from shirt sponsorship have grown consistently (Unlucan 2015), which may indicate that sponsoring brands better understand its impact (Chanavat *et al.* 2017). As with Chevrolet and Manchester United, sponsors pay large sums to be associated with the popularity of football so as to improve their brand image and to reach large audiences globally through television coverage (Jensen *et al.* 2013). With their brand on the front of the shirt, as well as benefiting from the extensive media coverage that accompanies all clubs in the EPL, sponsors also gain further exposure from the strong market for replica kits amongst teenagers and adults (Rosson 2001).

Bunn *et al.* (2018) tracked shirt sponsorship in the English and Scottish Premier Leagues to ascertain the level of sponsorship by gambling companies. They consulted the websites of the EPL and identified every club that had participated in the league since its establishment in 1992/1993. The first shirt sponsorship by a gambling company in the EPL was Fulham FC's sponsorship by Betfair in 2002/2003. As Bunn *et al.* showed, there was a pronounced increase in gambling companies sponsoring EPL teams following the Gambling Act 2005, which liberalised the marketing of gambling. This study used the same method of examining an online football shirt archive site, www.historicalfootballkits.com, to track the shirt sponsors of the 41 clubs that have participated in the EPL from the league's inaugural season up to 2019/2020. Rather than solely looking at gambling sponsors, all sponsorship from UCIs (defined as alcohol, food and beverages and gambling) was considered. The results are shown in Figure 7.1.

There has been a clear and pronounced increase of shirt sponsorship by gambling brands even since the 2016/2017 football season when Bunn et al.'s study was undertaken. By 2019/2020, 25 of the 41 clubs (61 per cent) had their shirts sponsored by gambling companies. Bunn et al.'s study only considered shirt sponsorship and omitted other types of advertising, including pitch perimeter advertising, in-programme adverts, social media and app-driven content. The study, however, provided sufficient evidence of the exposure of gambling in football for the authors to argue that the football authorities should consider the ethical issues relating to this type of advertising, and the impact this type of sponsorship might have on gambling-related harms.

It is notable that whilst shirt sponsorship by gambling companies has increased, sponsorship by other UCIs has decreased. Whilst the sponsorship of the club shirt is generally the most valuable (Bűhler and Nufer 2013), there are a wide variety of other commercial partners, as demonstrated on the official club websites. The sponsorship of football clubs involves a suite of commercial partners with category exclusivity (e.g., official beer partner) at various levels of financial commitment (Semens 2019). The details of sponsorship packages are kept commercially confidential and are related to the requirements of the brand. The value of sponsorship is directly related to the potential television audience, and thus Manchester United's kit arrangement with Adidas would have been negatively affected if the

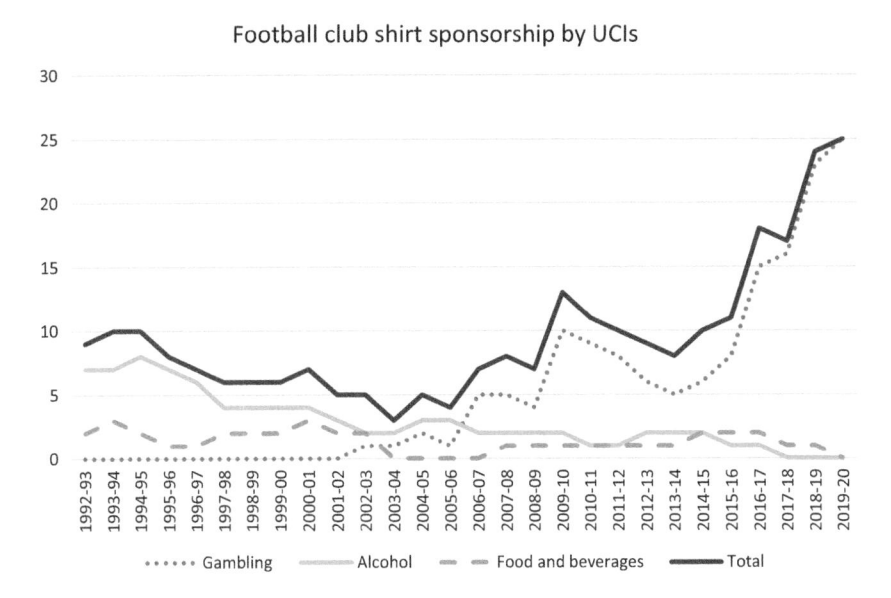

Figure 7.1 Shirt sponsorship of clubs that have participated in the English Premier League.

club had failed to qualify for the Champions' League in 2019/2020 (Blitz 2020). Television audiences who watch the Premier League in the United Kingdom are exposed to marketing primarily through the live action, where brands are advertised on the front and sleeves of players' shirts, on pitchside LED digital boards and in static advertising on available surfaces such as the stands and on the coaches' and players' dugouts (the shelters provided by the side of the pitch for non-playing staff and substitutes). The commercial breaks that divide up the match and the punditry before and after the live action also provide opportunities for advertisers. The broadcasters, Sky, BT Sport and Amazon Prime, take their income from subscriptions to their services and from the advertising they sell, which features in the commercial breaks.

Sport sponsorship has grown exponentially in the last 40 years (Cornwell 2020), as demonstrated by the increased commercial value of broadcast rights for both the EPL and the Australian Football League (Fujak and Frawley 2016). Corporate brands need to find a way to stand out in an overcrowded marketplace (Goldman and Papson 2006), and sport offers an opportunity to transnational corporations to raise global awareness of their brands whilst promoting commodity consumption (Smart 2007). Gambling sponsorship is most prominent in the Premier League and commentators have argued that football plays a problematic role in the promotion and normalisation of gambling (Jones *et al.* 2020). UEFA's Benchmarking Report (2022) confirmed the English Premier League as having the highest total revenue across the European football leagues, with the highest broadcasting and sponsorship incomes, and five of the top ten richest clubs in Europe. Sports betting and gambling companies were the most common shirt sponsors, accounting for 19 per cent of shirt sponsorship in Europe despite restrictions on gambling sponsorship in Italy, France, Denmark and Spain.

A global television audience

The development of television has made sport a mass phenomenon, and watching sport has become part of global culture (Whannel 2002). As the development of digital platforms has enabled a worldwide audience, football clubs such as Manchester United and Liverpool may be considered global brands (Millward 2011; Carling 2020). Much as with other successful brands, supporters identify with the team and consume match tickets, broadcasting subscriptions and merchandise on which the team logo appears. Similarly, transnational corporations use sport to develop their own brands. In an era of high media visibility, brands strain to be seen amongst an increasing flow of mediated communication (Thompson 2005; Goldman and Papson 2006). A football jersey, with the brand of the club's leading sponsor on the front, is considered as a key sign value in consumption, helping to develop both the club's and sponsor's client base (Millward 2011).

European football clubs and their sponsors seek to penetrate the huge audiences of the United States, China and India (Miller 2013). The importance of this global audience is demonstrated by the broadcast rights packages with their different kick-off times. For example, the match on 30 December 2018 between Crystal Palace and Chelsea, two clubs based in London, kicked off on a Sunday at 12 noon, UK time. Whilst noon on a Sunday is certainly not a very convenient time for English fans more used to mid-afternoon and evening kick-offs, it enabled global viewing, with this match beginning at 7 p.m. in Jakarta (Western Indonesia Time), and in Bangkok and Hanoi (Indochina Time), all representing important Asian markets. Maguire (2020) wrote that live football is the most popular team sport in the world judged on the number of global television viewers. Football has a long season and is popular amongst young males in particular (aged 15–34 years), which in turn makes the sport attractive to advertisers, who can target this audience who often have a high disposable income (Maguire 2020). Global Web Index's audience report on Premier League fans in 2015 (Global Web Index 2015) showed television as the main way in which fans view matches, with large audiences in Indonesia, Vietnam and Thailand, including approximately twice as many male as female viewers, and with the greater proportion of the audiences aged under 45 years.

Gambling brands and Premier League club sponsors, such as ManBetX and Dafabet, target large betting markets in Asia (Hancock and Ahmed 2019). Variable EPL kick-off times support this approach, and many gambling brands are based in Asia, such as Crystal Palace FC's shirt sponsor from 2017 to 2020, ManBetX, based in Thailand. Football has a dual role in generating revenue for the gambling industry in that it provides gambling opportunities through live matches as well as unlimited opportunities to bet in games from the next scorer to the next yellow card (Jones *et al.* 2020). There has been an explosion of gambling marketing in Britain since the Gambling Act 2005 (Bunn *et al.* 2018) with sport playing a key role. The British Code of Advertising Practice (BCAP) rules that gambling adverts must not feature in programmes aimed specifically at children, but of course many children watch football (Jones *et al.* 2020).

The final section of this chapter includes two case studies of how global brands use the Premier League, and its clubs, to promote unhealthy consumption.

Case Study 1: Coca-Cola, an official soft drink of the English Premier League

Coca-Cola is "the most recognised brand in the world" (Williams 2000 p.14). In Chapter 5, it was shown how Coca-Cola was key to the commercial development of both the Olympics and the FIFA World Cup. Whilst commercial organisations are very careful not to share too much information about their marketing campaigns, the objective is almost always to increase consumption. A large-scale consumer packaged producer such as Coca-Cola is able to assess the value of its sport sponsorship, and its return on investment, through increased retail sales (Jensen and White 2018).

Coca-Cola used the 1936 Olympics in Berlin to drive up sales in Germany (Keys 2004); its marketing at the World Cup in South Africa in 2010 had a similar objective on the African continent (Choueke 2010); and Coca-Cola has been increasing marketing expenditure in North American sport in its ongoing battle for consumers with PepsiCo (McKelvey 2006).

As previously described, Coca-Cola's activities have attracted criticism from public health advocates. The London Olympic Games was criticised for its 'junk food' sponsors including Coca-Cola, McDonald's and Cadbury at a time of growing global obesity rates (Garde and Rigby 2012). Freudenberg (2016) observed that companies use corporate social responsibility as a public relations tool to distract from criticism of their products, citing PepsiCo and Coca-Cola's 'philanthropic' contributions to physical activity programmes which they claim is their corporate response to addressing obesity (which their products directly contribute to).

Coca-Cola was unveiled as an English Premier League partner and 'Official Soft Drink' in September 2018, with Coca-Cola itself launching the partnership in February 2019, when it took care that the sponsorship campaign featured both fans and Manchester United and England star Jesse Lingard (Coca-Cola GB 2019a). A study of its partnership with the Premier League was conducted using Twitter (Ireland et al. 2022). The company's overall marketing approach is well summarised by its use of a 90-second film, using the strapline "Where Everyone Plays" (Coca-Cola GB 2019b). This film, together with shortened edited versions, featuring fans from all 20 clubs that were members of the Premier League that season, was used to draw attention throughout the two seasons (2019/2020 and 2020/2021) to the fact that Coca-Cola was an official Premier League partner. The video explicitly connected fans' emotions and passion with the brand and its products and attracted millions of viewers (Ireland et al. 2022). In addition, Coca-Cola was able to leverage its sponsorship to engage a global audience, such as through a targeted campaign in Nigeria (LBB Online 2020). The campaign used another 60-second film made for this African market and featured fans wearing the shirts of six Premier League clubs, including five of the biggest brands (Arsenal, Chelsea, Liverpool, Manchester City and Manchester United) and Everton, which was sponsored by SportPesa, a Kenyan-based betting concern.

Transnational corporations are taking increasing steps to present themselves as good corporate citizens, with sports sponsorship sometimes considered part of a global corporate social responsibility programme (Amis and Cornwell 2005). This might be seen as companies trying to demonstrate that they provide a social return on investment as well as seeking greater profits (Doane 2005). As Cornwell (2020) has noted, though, unhealthy industries have been criticised for their sport sponsorship programmes, often because these address youth audiences. Nestle (2015) provided a devastating analysis of the tactics adopted by the soda companies in promoting their brands.

Whilst Coca-Cola sponsored the English Premier League, it also promoted its corporate social responsibility relationship with a registered charity, Street Games UK. In July 2019, Coca-Cola tweeted a message including a 1-minute 20-second film promoting the company's relationship with Street Games. The text of the film included the phrase "we're helping communities to access pitches", and a notice referencing young people's hatred of signs which forbade them from playing games, at the same time as linking to the drink brand. The film's text stated that Coca-Cola would donate £200,000 to Street Games. The film received 28.4K views. This would be considered very significant exposure for a charity that promotes sport and physical activity in local communities where such opportunities may be limited. This message explicitly endorsed Coca-Cola, a sugary, calorie-laden drink, in areas of the English Midlands where levels of obesity are directly linked to poverty (Bann et al. 2018). A second tweet on the same day from Coca-Cola featured another 1-minute 10-second film promoting the relationship with Street Games and the training of football coaches.

Case Study 2: Cadbury, football's chocolate habit

Cadbury has a long history, having been established by John Cadbury as a tea, coffee and confectionery company at Bourneville in Birmingham, England, in 1824. His son George did much to build the sporting ethos within the Cadbury firm (Bromhead 2000), whose modern grand image still evokes its traditions and its reconstructed history (Rowlinson and Hassard 1993). The company has, however, been owned by Mondelez International (originally Kraft Foods) since 2010 and is a transnational company. Cadbury used extensive advertising and innovative marketing throughout the twentieth century (Fitzgerald 2005; Bailey and Alexander 2019) to become Britain's most successful chocolate brand, with its strapline of "A Glass and a Half of Full Cream Milk" and its purple and gold wrapper suggesting "the richness, healthiness and freshness of the product" (Williams 2000 p.36). Cadbury has a track record of sponsoring sport including both the Olympics in Sydney in 2000 and the London Olympics in 2012 (Sweney 2008). It has also previously attracted criticism for promoting a Get Active! campaign in which children were encouraged to eat chocolate so as to collect vouchers which could be redeemed for school sports equipment (Elliot 2003), whilst reinforcing the values of consumer culture in schools (Wilkinson 2016).

In 2017, at the beginning of its three-year partnership with the Premier League, Cadbury was described as the nation's favourite chocolate and, having built on its sponsorship of the London Olympics in 2012, it promised "to bring moments of joy to millions of people" (Premier League 2017). Brand activation was clear, with the purchase of products necessary for the chance to win matchday tickets and meet Premier League stars past and present. "Cadbury wants to bring the Premier League to consumers for them to share in the moments of excitement that football brings" (Premier League 2017). The sponsorship deal with Cadbury met with negative comments from campaigners from the start, with critics questioning how a snack brand could promote healthy lifestyles (Connelly 2017). Cadbury products in UK supermarkets carried the Premier League brand with a 'Match and Win' logo, offering a chance to link to a code on the wrapper to win matchday experiences and other prizes.

In Chapter 4, I described the concept of collectors' cards, which were introduced by the tobacco industry at the end of the nineteenth century to promote cigarette consumption. As with many other marketing innovations, the tobacco industry developed "important incentives for smoking in the cultural rituals of youth" (Brandt 2007 p.32). Collectors' cards featuring sports stars and events have been used since then in every major sport, including Australian Rules football, NASCAR, baseball, cricket, rugby and of course football, encouraging consumption by children and young adults, particularly males (Martin and Baker 1996; Brandt 2007). Cadbury has followed this approach and promoted its relationship with the Premier League through its partnership with Panini, an Italian company that produces trading cards and other collectibles. The cards used a series of images of former and current players featuring the Cadbury logo together with that of the Premier League to encourage consumers to 'treat' themselves.

Mondelez International and Cadbury draw on the Premier League brand to promote their own brand and their products internationally. The project 'Joy Schools' was established in 2011 by Mondelez International (Malaysia), "which empowers people to snack right" (by promoting Oreo, Cadbury's Dairy Milk and other brands) (Mondelez International (Malaysia) 2019). Mondelez International's press release featured a former Premier League and England player, Michael Owen, taking part in a football school in Malaysia whilst promoting the chocolate brand. Other former players were in Dublin in 2018 with Mondelez and Cadbury (O'Brien 2018) and, once again, in Malaysia in 2020 (Ryan Raj 2020). Cadbury described its project in Malaysia as a "community investment initiative".

In 2021, during the coronavirus pandemic, Mondelez/Cadbury moved its sponsorship of the Premier League to financially partner 20 football clubs across Britain, including all of the top six Premier League clubs. In

Mondelez's press release, it described its corporate social responsibility programme organised with the charity Age UK, to raise awareness of loneliness in older people, as "bringing to life the brand's generous ethos" (Mondelez International 2021). This campaign capitalised on the pandemic, using the company's "glass and a half" slogan to suggest "generosity and kindness". Mondelez's press release also referenced the Cadbury strategy to "inspire mindful snacking". However, promoting foods with high levels of sugar when data was already showing that people with obesity were more susceptible to complications and death from COVID-19 might be argued to have been of more benefit to Mondelez than its consumers (Global Health Advocacy Incubator 2020). The senior brand manager at Cadbury Sponsorships described the campaign in this way:

> We do not see ourselves as a sponsor, we are a partner. Because of this we've worked extremely closely with football clubs ... to ensure Cadbury plays its part in supporting and bringing together communities and local people ... The beautiful game is only beautiful when we are all in it together.
>
> (Mondelez International 2021 p.3)

To reference Bourdieu from the last chapter, "sport visible as spectacle hides the reality of a system of actors competing over commercial stakes" (Bourdieu 1999 p.14). One lesson from the pandemic was that we certainly were not "all in it *together*" (Bambra et al. 2020) and the same can be said about the different economic interests of fans, clubs and the Premier League. During the public health emergency, companies moved swiftly to portray themselves in a positive light (van Schalkwyk et al. 2021) turning the health crisis into a marketing opportunity for brands such as Cadbury and its football club 'partners'. Finally, in this same period, there was also a chance to market the Cadbury and football club brands together in a 'limited-edition' 360-gram bar aimed squarely at collectors (and dads) and happily promoted by local media through its own commercial arrangements (Browne 2021).

Conclusion

In Britain, after the Hillsborough disaster in 1989, the prevailing neoliberal economic conditions enabled a structural change in football, with the new Premier League reinforcing the further development of the fan as customer. The economic and crowd-control crises of the 1980s enabled the representatives of the elite clubs to transform the nature of the 'consumption' of the game by fans. The old, uncomfortable (and unsafe) football grounds with their open terraces and limited catering facilities were replaced by homogenised all-seater modern stadia offering club shops with branded merchandise supported by websites where purchases can be made without any need to visit the home of the club. As television has broadcast the English Premier League globally, gambling, alcohol and food and beverage brands, such as Cadbury and Coca-Cola, have used the passion, excitement and cultural traditions of what is often called the 'home of football' to drive consumption of sugar-laden products to audiences in London, Lagos, Sydney and Kuala Lumpur alike.

References

Amis, J. and Cornwell, T.B. (2005) 'Sport sponsorship in a global age' in Amis, J. and Cornwell, T. B., eds., *Global Sports Sponsorship*, Oxford: Berg.

Anderson, B. (1983) *Imagined Communities. Reflections on the Origin and Spread of Nationalism*, London: Verso.

Bailey, A.R. and Alexander, A. (2019) 'Cadbury and the rise of the supermarket: Innovation in marketing 1953–1975', *Business History*, 61(4), 659–680.

Baimbridge, M., Cameron, S. and Dawson, P. (1996) 'Satellite television and the demand for football: A whole new ball game?', *Scottish Journal of Political Economy*, 43(3), 317–333.

Bambra, C., Riordan, R., Ford, J. and Matthews, F. (2020) 'The COVID-19 pandemic and health inequalities', *Journal of Epidemiology and Community Health*, 74(11), 964–968.

Bann, D., Johnson, W., Li, L., Kuh, D. and Hardy, R. (2018) 'Socioeconomic inequalities in childhood and adolescent body-mass index, weight, and height from 1953 to 2015: An analysis of four longitudinal, observational, British birth cohort studies', *The Lancet*, 3(4), e194–e203.

Blitz, S. (2020) 'Manchester United keep money-spinning £75m Adidas sponsorship deal intact after qualifying for Champions League', *Daily Mail*, 27 July 2020, available: https://www.dailymail.co.uk/sport/football/article-8562877/Manchester-United-75m-year-adidas-sponsorship-deal-reaching-Champions-League.html [accessed 31 July 2020].

Boli, C. (2017) 'Manchester United: The capitalized history, from the 1960s to today' in Chanavat, N., Desbordes, M. and Lorgnier, N., eds., *Routledge Handbook of Football Marketing*, Abingdon: Routledge.

Bourdieu, P. (1999) 'The state, economics and sport' in Dauncey, H. and Hare, G., eds., *France and the 1998 World Cup. The National Impact of a World Sporting Event*, London: Frank Cass, 15–21.

Brandt, A.M. (2007) *The Cigarette Century*, New York: Basic Books.

Bromhead, J. (2000) 'George Cadbury's contribution to sport', *Sports Historian*, 20(1), 97–117.

Brown, A. (2008) "Our club, our rules': Fan communities at FC United of Manchester', *Soccer and Society*, 9(3).

Browne, A. (2021) 'Cadbury has launched a new limited edition chocolate bar and some will be excited to try it', *Liverpool Echo*, 15 June 2021, available: https://www.liverpoolecho.co.uk/whats-on/shopping/cadbury-launched-new-limited-edition-20818019 [accessed 10 February 2022].

Bühler, A. and Nufer, G. (2013) *Relationship Marketing in Sport*, Abingdon: Routledge.

Bunn, C., Ireland, R., Minton, J., Holman, D., Philpott, M. and Chambers, S. (2018) 'Shirt sponsorship by gambling companies in the English and Scottish Premier Leagues: Global reach and public health concerns', *Soccer and Society*, 17 Jan 2018, available: http://dx.doi.org/17 Jan 2018.

Carling, P. (2020) 'The rise of Liverpool – From super club to super brand', *Sportbusiness*, 27 July 2020, available: http://www.sportbusiness.com/2020/07/phil-carling-the-rise-of-liverpool-from-super-club-to-super-brand/ [accessed 3 September 2020].
Cashmore, E. (2006) *Celebrity/Culture*, London: Routledge.
Castells, M. (2000) *The Rise of the Network Society*, Oxford: Blackwell.
Chanavat, N., Desbordes, M. and Lorgnier, N. (2017) 'Sports sponsorship and professional football' in Chanavat, N., Desbordes, M. and Lorgnier, N., eds., *Routledge Handbook of Football Marketing*, Abingdon: Routledge.
Choueke, M. (2010) 'Putting some fizz into drinks marketing', *Strategic Direction*, 26(4), available: http://dx.doi.org/10.1108/sd.2010.05626dad.007.
Coca-Cola GB (2019a) *Welcome to 'Where Everyone Plays'* [press release], available: https://www.coca-cola.co.uk/marketing/sponsorships-and-partnerships/premier-league/coca-cola-and-the-premier-league-welcome-to-where-everyone-plays [accessed 15 July 2020].
Coca-Cola GB (2019b) *Where Everyone Plays*, available: https://www.youtube.com/watch?v=WWzujkwoRNE [accessed
Conn, D. (2005) *The Beautiful Game? Searching for the Soul of Football*, London: Yellow Jersey Press.
Connelly, T. (2017) *Cadbury: 'We're Sponsoring the Premier League to Stay Relevant with Future Generations'*, available: https://www.thedrum.com/news/2017/01/26/cadbury-were-sponsoring-the-premier-league-stay-relevant-with-future-generations [accessed 31 January 2020].
Cornwell, T.B. (2020) *Sponsorship in Marketing. Effective Partnerships in Sports, Arts and Events*, Second ed., Abingdon: Routledge.
Deloitte Sports Business Group (2017) *Eye on the Prize. Football Money League*, available: file:///C:/Users/Rob/Downloads/deloitte-uk-deloitte-football-money-league-2020%20(1).pdf [accessed 8 June 2020].
Dittmore, S.W. and McCarthy, S.T. (2016) 'Sports marketing and new media' in Billings, A. C. and Hardin, M., eds., *Routledge Handbook of Sport and New Media*, Abingdon: Routledge.
Dixon, K. (2014) 'The football fan and the pub: An enduring relationship', *International Review for the Sociology of Sport*, 49, 382–399.
Dixon, K. (2016) 'Fandom' in Cashmore, E. and Dixon, K., eds., *Studying Football*, Abingdon: Routledge.
Doane, D. (2005) 'Beyond corporate social responsibility: Minnows, mammoths and markets', *Futures*, 37(2–3), 215–229.
Domeneghetti, R. (2017) *From the Back Page to the Front Room: Football's Journey through the English Media*, Second ed., Glasgow: Ockley Books.
Elliot, A. (2003) 'Sports expert defends "chocolate for equipment" scheme', *BMJ: British Medical Journal*, 327(7424), 1125.
Evens, T., Iosifidis, P. and Smith, P. (2013) *The Political Economy of Television Sports Rights*, Basingstoke: Palgrave Macmillan.
Fitzgerald, R. (2005) 'Products, firms and consumption: Cadbury and the development of marketing, 1900–1939', *Business History*, 47(4), 511–531, available: http://dx.doi.org/10.1080/00076790500132977.
Football Association (1991) *The Blueprint for the Future of Football*, London: Football Association.
Freudenberg, N. (2016) *Lethal but Legal. Corporations, Consumption, and Protecting Public Health*, New York: Oxford University Press.

Fujak, H. and Frawley, S. (2016) 'The relationship between television viewership and advertising content in Australian Football Broadcasts', *Communication & Sport*, 4(1), 82–101.

Garde, A. and Rigby, N. (2012) 'Going for gold - Should responsible governments raise the bar on sponsorship of the Olympic Games and other sporting events by food and beverage companies?', *Communications Law*, 17(2), 42–49.

Giulianotti, R. and Robertson, R. (2009) *Globalization & Football*, London: SAGE.

Global Health Advocacy Incubator (2020) *Facing Two Pandemics. How Big Food Undermined Public Health in the Era of COVID-19*, available: https://advocacyincubator.org/wp-content/uploads/2020/11/GHAI-Facing-Two-Pandemics-Report-November-2020.pdf [accessed 10 February 2022].

Global Web Index (2015) *Premier League Fans Summary. Analyzing the Digital Behaviors and Attitudes of Premier League Fans*, available: https://insight.globalwebindex.net/hs-fs/hub/304927/file-2593818997- [accessed 8 April 2020].

Goldman, R. and Papson, S. (2006) 'Capital's Brandscapes', *Journal of Consumer Culture*, 6(3), 327–353.

Griffin, E. (2012) 'Football and smoking: Past and present', *Sportslens*, 20 April 2012, available: https://sportslens.com/smoking-in-football/86928/ [accessed 2 September 2020].

Hancock, A. and Ahmed, M. (2019) 'Gambling and football: A relationship under scrutiny. Shirt sponsorship deals reignite debate over close ties between betting groups and clubs', *Financial Times*, 23 August 2019, available: https://www.ft.com/content/e46afb14-c36a-11e9-a8e9-296ca66511c9 [accessed 26 July 2020].

Harris, J. (2017) 'The football star. Celebrity, culture and consumption in the English Premier League' in Elliott, R., ed., *The English Premier League. A Socio-Cultural Analysis*, Abingdon: Routledge.

Hill, J. (1961) *Striking for Soccer*, Kingswood: Peter Davies.

Hill, J. (2002) *Sport, Leisure & Culture in Twentieth-Century Britain*. Basingstoke: Palgrave.

Hopcraft, A. (2006) *The Football Man*, London: Aurum.

Inglis, S. (2002) 'All gone quiet over there' in Perryman, M., ed., *Hooligan Wars: Causes and Effects of Football Violence*, London: Mainstream.

Ireland, R., Bunn, C., Chambers, S., Reith, G., & Viggars, M. (2022) 'How unhealthy commodity industries find a global audience in the English Premier League: Three case studies of brand engagement', *Soccer & Society*, 23(4–5), 334–348.

Jensen, J.A. and White, D.W. (2018) 'Trends in sport sponsorship evaluation and measurement: Insights from the industry', *International Journal of Sports Marketing and Sponsorship*, 19(1), 2–10, available: http://dx.doi.org/10.1108/IJSMS-07-2017-0057.

Jensen, R.W., Bowman, N.D., Larson, B.V. and Wang, Y. (2013) 'Looking at shirt sponsorships from both sides of the pond: Comparing global trends versus America's Major League Soccer', *Soccer & Society*, 14(4), 515–524.

Jones, C., Pinder, R. and Robinson, G. (2020) 'Gambling sponsorship and advertising in British Football: A critical account', *Sport, Ethics and Philosophy*, 14(2), 163–175.

Keys, B. (2004) 'Spreading peace, democracy, and Coca-Cola®: Sport and American cultural expansion in the 1930s', *Diplomatic History*, 28(2), 165–196.

King, A. (1997) 'New directors, customers, and fans: The transformation of English football in the 1990s', *Sociology of Sport Journal*, 14.

LBB Online (2020) *Coca-Cola Ups the Football Banter Level for English Premier League Sponsorship*, available: https://www.lbbonline.com/news/coca-cola-ups-the-football-banter-level-for-english-premier-league-sponsorship [accessed 9 February 2022].

Maguire, K. (2020) *The Price of Football. Understanding Football Club Finance*, Newcastle upon Tyne: Agenda

Martin, M.C. and Baker, S.M. (1996) 'An ethnography of Mick's sports card show: Preliminary findings from the field' in Corfman, K. P. and Lynch, J. G., eds., *North American Advances in Consumer Research*, Provo: Association for Consumer Research, 329–336.

Mason, T. (1980) *Association Football and English Society, 1863-1915*, Brighton: The Harvester Press.

McKelvey, S.M. (2006) 'Coca-Cola vs. PepsiCo-A" Super" battleground for the cola wars?', *Sport Marketing Quarterly*, 15(2), 114.

Miller, T. (2013) 'Where next? Football's new frontiers' in Steen, R., Novick, J. and Richards, H., eds., *The Cambridge Companion to Football*, Cambridge: Cambridge University Press.

Millward, P. (2011) *The Global Football League. Transnational Networks, Social Movements and Sport in the New Media Age*, Basingstoke: Palgrave Macmillan.

Milne, M. (2016) *The Transformation of Television Sport. New Methods, New Rules*, Basingstoke: Palgrave Macmillan.

Mondelez International (2021) *Cadbury Redefines Football Sponsorship to Support Local Communities* [press release], 25 March 2021, available: https://www.mynewsdesk.com/uk/mondelez-uk/pressreleases/cadbury-redefines-football-sponsorship-to-support-local-communities-3085349 [accessed 10 February 2022].

Mondelez International (Malaysia) (2019) *Young Aspiring Footballers Treated to Cadbury's Football Clinic with Michael Owen* [press release], available: http://redzoommedia.blogspot.com/2019/03/young-aspiring-footballers-treated-to.html [accessed 2 February 2020].

Morimoto, L.H. and Chin, B. (2017) 'Reimagining the imagined community' in Gray, J., Sandvoss, C. and Harrington, C. L., eds., *Fandom. Identities and Communities in a Mediated World*, Second ed., New York: New York University Press.

Morrow, S. (2003) *The People's Game? Football, Finance and Society*, Basingstoke: Palgrave Macmillan.

Nestle, M. (2015) *Soda Politics. Taking On Big Soda (and Winning)*. Oxford: Oxford University Press.

Norwich City Football Club PLC (2020) *Annual Report*, Norwich, available: https://files.canaries.co.uk/canaries/ARG2020.pdf [accessed 7 February 2022].

O'Brien, B. (2018) 'Neville misses local dimension to Premier League mix', *Irish Examiner*, 10 August 2018, available: https://www.irishexaminer.com/breakingnews/sport/soccer/neville-misses-local-dimension-to-premier-league-mix-861255.html [accessed 6 February 2020].

Populus (2018) *British Icon Index II. How Home-Grown Brands, Industries and Institutions Carry the Story of Modern Britain to the World*, available: https://www.populus.co.uk/wp-content/uploads/2018/07/The-British-Icon-Index-II-Online.pdf [accessed 12 June 2020].

Potts, M. (2020) 'Who are the big six in the Premier League? Project big picture explained', *Radio Times*, October 2020, available: https://www.radiotimes.com/news/sport/football/2020-10-13/premier-league-big-6/amp/ [accessed 23 November 2020].

Premier League (2017) *The Premier League and Cadbury Kicked Off their Exciting Partnership in the 2017/18 Season*, available: https://www.premierleague.com/partners/cadbury [accessed 31 January 2020].

PwC (2018) *Accounting for Typical Transactions in the Football Industry. Issues and Solutions under IFRS*, available: https://www.pwc.com/gx/en/audit-services/ifrs/publications/ifrs-9/accounting-for-typical-transactions-in-the-football-industry.pdf [accessed 8 July 2020].

Robertson, R. (1992) *Globalization: Social Theory and Global Culture*. London: Sage.
Rookwood, J. and Hughson, J. (2017) 'A history of the English Premier League. Cultures, consumption and commerce' in Elliott, R., ed., *The English Premier League. A Socio-Cultural Analysis*, Abingdon: Routledge.
Rosson, P. (2001) 'Football shirt sponsorships: SEGA Europe and Arsenal FC', *International Journal of Sports Marketing & Sponsorship*, 3(2), 28–54.
Rowlinson, M. and Hassard, J. (1993) 'The invention of corporate culture: A history of the histories of Cadbury', *Human Relations*, 46(3), 299–326.
Rt Hon Lord Justice Taylor (1989) *The Hillsborough Stadium Disaster: Interim Report*, London.
Rt Hon Lord Justice Taylor (1990) *The Hillsborough Stadium Disaster: Final Report*, London.
Ryan Raj, M. (2020) 'Reliving sweet memories: Jamie Redknapp teams up with Cadbury FC to help Malaysians experience the EPL', *Malay Mail*, 5 February 2020, available: https://www.malaymail.com/news/life/2020/02/05/reliving-sweet-memories-jamie-redknapp-teams-up-with-cadbury-fc-to-help-mal/1834717 [accessed 6 February 2020].
Semens, A. (2019) 'Football sponsorship' in Hughson, J., Moore, K., Spaaij, R. and Maguire, J., eds., *Routledge Handbook of Football Studies*, Paperback ed., Abingdon: Routledge.
Smart, B. (2005) *The Sport Star. Modern Sport and the Cultural Economy of Sporting Celebrity*, London: SAGE.
Smart, B. (2007) 'Not playing around: Global capitalism, modern sport and consumer culture' in Giulianotti, R. and Robertson, R., eds., *Globalization and Sport*, Oxford: Blackwell Publishing.
Sweney, M. (2008) 'Olympic 2012 chief insists Cadbury is appropriate sponsor', *The Guardian*, available: https://www.theguardian.com/media/2008/oct/20/olympicsandthemedia-advertising [accessed 8 February 2022].
Taylor, I. (1987) 'Putting the boot into a working-class sport: British soccer after Bradford and Brussels', *Sociology of Sport Journal*, 4, 171–191.
Tempany, A. (2016) *And the Sun Shines Now. How Hillsborough and the Premier League Changed Britain*, London: Faber & Faber.
The Liverpool Football Club and Athletic Grounds Limited (2020) *Annual Report and Consolidated Financial Statements*, Liverpool, available: https://d3j2s6hdd6a7rg.cloudfront.net/images/misc/Liverpool-Football-Club-Annual-Report-and-Consolidated-Financial-Statements.pdf [accessed 7 February 2022].
Thompson, J.B. (2005) 'The new visibility', *Theory, Culture & Society*, 22(6), 31–51.
Tomlinson, A. (2013) 'Introduction to The Cambridge companion to football' in Steen, R., Novick, J. and Richards, H., eds., *The Cambridge Companion to Football*, Cambridge: Cambridge University Press.
Turner, M. (2014) 'From local heroism to global celebrity stardom: A critical reflection of the social cultural and political changes in British football culture from the 1950s to the formation of the premier league', *Soccer and Society*, 15(5), 751–760.
Turner, M. (2017). '"Football without fans is nothing". Contemporary fan protests and resistance communities in the English Premier League era' in Elliott, R., ed., *The English Premier League. A Socio-Cultural Analysis*. Abingdon: Routledge, 112–132.
UEFA (2022) *The European Club Footballing Landscape. Club Licensing Benchmarking Report. Living with the Pandemic*, Nyon, available: https://editorial.uefa.com/resources/0272-145d8b8c8c5f-2d817c2474af-1000/master_bm_repor_midres_20220204170044.pdf [accessed 8 February 2022].

Unlucan, D. (2015) 'Jersey sponsors in football/soccer: The industry classification of main jersey sponsors of 1147 football/soccer clubs in top leagues of 79 countries', *Soccer and Society*, 16(1), 42–62.

van Schalkwyk, M.C., Maani, N. and McKee, M. (2021) 'Public health emergency or opportunity to profit? The two faces of the COVID-19 pandemic', *The Lancet Diabetes & Endocrinology*, 9(2), 61–63.

Walsh, A.J. and Giulianotti, R. (2001) 'This sporting mammon: A normative critique of the commodification of sport', *Journal of the Philosophy of Sport*, 28(1), 53–77.

Whannel, G. (1986) 'The unholy alliance: Notes on television and the remaking of British sport 1965–85', *Leisure Studies*, 5(2), 129–145, available: http://dx.doi.org/10.1080/02614368600390111.

Whannel, G. (2002) *Fields in Vision. Television Sport and Cultural Transformation*, London: Routledge.

Wilkinson, G. (2016) 'Marketing in schools, commercialization and sustainability: Policy disjunctures surrounding the commercialization of childhood and education for sustainable lifestyles in England', *Educational Review*, 68(1), 56–70, available: http://dx.doi.org/10.1080/00131911.2015.1058750.

Williams, G. (2000) *Branded?*, London: V&A Publications.

Williams, J. (1994) 'The local and global in English soccer and the rise of satellite television', *Sociology of Sport Journal*, 11(4), 376–397.

Williams, J. (2013) 'Fans: Consumers, hooligans and activists' in Steen, R., Novick, J. and Richards, H., eds., *The Cambridge Companion to Football*, Cambridge: Cambridge University Press.

Chapter 8

Sport and brand engagement

Introduction

As has been shown throughout this book, sponsorship is much more than advertising and can take many forms (Cornwell 2019). In its earliest forms, sponsorship was seen as a form of patronage, as a means of increasing community standing (Carrigan and Carrigan 1997) or even as a type of philanthropy (Chanavat et al. 2017). At its simplest level, sponsorship is a form of communication which pursues a business objective through a commercial transaction between concerned parties (Chanavat et al. 2017). The marketing of brands aims not only to increase consumption but also to influence attitudes and social norms (Petticrew et al. 2017). Sponsorship is associated with improving images of a brand as well as consumers' attitudes towards buying a sponsor's products (Madrigal 2004).

This book has provided a series of examples of sport's unique ability to engage its fans through emotion and passion. NASCAR (the National Association for Stock Car Auto Racing in the United States) was mentioned in Chapter 6 in terms of the relationship between the sport and its fans. As with other sports, NASCAR was transformed by television and its ability to draw in commercial sponsors. Hagstrom's description of the NASCAR business model provides an in-depth view of the power of sponsorship and its ability to provide "a lasting bond between consumers and the company" (2001 p.49). In 1998, the sport's leading sponsors were Philip Morris, Anheuser-Busch and Coca-Cola. The sponsoring companies knew that the value of their investment came not only from the multiple exposures and impressions that their brands received from television coverage but also "from the emotions the impressions generate" (Hagstrom 2001 p.57). Sport sponsorship has become a sophisticated means of communicating a business's advertising messages (Chanavat et al. 2017). Sponsorship is more successful than traditional advertising in its potential to influence consumer engagement. Engagement, in this sense, directly involves the consumer in a relationship with a brand, which can be a form of emotional bonding (Cornwell 2019). Sports fans are therefore the objects of sophisticated approaches to encourage them to consume not only products from their club but also the products of the brands that sponsor the club or are associated with it.

As described in Chapter 4, the tobacco industry looked for ways to promote its products when traditional advertising routes (such as in the broadcast and print media) were being closed to it. Whilst millions of people were dying from tobacco-related diseases, the transnational tobacco companies continued to promote their brands globally (Collin 2003). Transnational corporations used conventional advertising as well as product placement in the film industry to develop their market (Collin 2003). Sport also offered an opportunity to develop awareness of tobacco brands in popular culture, with the industry's move to sponsor motor racing being used as a means to achieve a global presence at the same time that cigarette advertising was banned on American television (Collin 2003). Whilst sponsorship is designed to encourage consumption (Cornwell 1997), tobacco sponsorship of sport was particularly problematic as it reached a youth market and enabled an association with a healthy activity, whilst its international promotion could allow exemption from national regulations (Cornwell 1997).

Brand activation

Brand activation is the term used for the means by which sponsors seek to interact and engage with fans (Cornwell 2020). It describes a process of building a popular perception of a brand through consumer engagement and participation strategies. Activations aim to "give the consumer an experience that will make them feel a real personal connection to the company" (Broadbent 2015 p.1). The definition of brand activation overlaps with that of brand engagement, in which companies seek customer engagement to create loyalty and drive consumption and profitability (Hollebeek 2011). Activation and engagement are critical for brands if they wish to stand out and receive positive responses from consumers whilst building confidence and trust in their brands (Gambetti and Graffigna 2010). Corporate sponsors, including unhealthy commodity industries, use their commercial agreements with sports organisations to activate their brands and secure engagement with sports fans and viewers, their intended consumers.

If companies pay millions of pounds for shirt sponsorship, greater emphasis is placed on raising awareness of the sponsorship with fans (O'Keefe *et al.* 2009). Meenaghan (2001) provided a model for understanding the effects of commercial sponsorship on consumers, and there is an entire psychology and marketing literature around sponsorship and the recall of sponsors (Lardinoit and Derbaix 2001). Sponsorship communications are received in a "halo of goodwill" (Meenaghan 2001, p.101) generated by a perception of benefit which has been noted elsewhere in a study of junior sport in Australia (Kelly *et al.* 2011). This effect means that if fans are aware of companies sponsoring their team, they are more likely to feel favourable towards them. The commercial content of the communication may also be disguised if the message is subtle enough (Meenaghan 2001). Meenaghan argued that the concept of fan involvement is key to an understanding of how sponsorship works. He defined this as the extent to which consumers identify with, and are motivated by, their engagement and affiliation with their chosen activity (such as sport). Pracejus (2004) used the term "affect transfer" to describe how positive feelings towards a sporting event or team may be transferred to the sponsoring brand through association. He argued that even without conscious awareness of an association, one might expect that the more a consumer enjoys a sponsored event, the more positive feelings will be generated regarding the sponsoring brand.

There is an additional literature around the interactive relationship between the consumer and the brand (Leckie *et al.* 2016). Consumers are more likely to exhibit intensified levels of engagement when they have fulfilling experiences with brands (Vivek *et al.* 2012; Dwivedi 2015). Further, a recent study (Tonietto and Barasch 2020) described how corporations encourage sports fans to communicate about their events and experiences using branded hashtags and rewards posted on social media to enhance their experience and potentially encourage consumption.

Engaging with young consumers

Academics have described how social media has been used by corporate brands to target and engage with young audiences to market unhealthy products (Dunlop *et al.* 2016). As described in Chapter 4, the tobacco industry was (and still is) always looking to recruit new consumers, given the high death rate of its regular consumers, using advertising that appeals to the young, such as the cartoon character Joe Camel (Brandt 2007). Whilst this book is principally about how television and the internet have enabled transnational corporations to use advertising and sponsorship at high-profile sporting events to promote consumption to a global audience, including high numbers of young people, it should be noted that many corporations also promote their brands direct to children through junior sport. Whilst advertising regulations generally prevent overt marketing to children by the alcohol, tobacco and gambling industries, this is not the case with the food and drink industry. As already indicated, there is clear evidence that such marketing affects both the food preferences and consumption of children (Smith *et al.* 2019).

Kellogg's promoted its high-sugar cereals to children who were learning to swim in the United Kingdom for 20 years between 1997 and 2007. Its brand appeared on certificates and badges and was often then displayed on swimming costumes and sportswear. Its Frosties brand even appeared on a 'Duckling Award' as part of the programme to help toddlers learn to swim (Ireland and Boyland 2019). In 2017, Cricket Australia and Nestlé's Milo brand marked 25 years of sponsorship of junior cricket (Nestlé 2017). A Nestlé press release stated that in 2016, 78,000 children aged between 5 and 12 years took part in MILO In2Cricket and MILO T20 Blast. Milo is a powdered chocolate-flavoured drink of which a typical serving includes 12.6 grams of sugar (just under two teaspoons). For children aged 5–12 years, one serving is likely to constitute around 50 per cent of the maximum advised daily consumption of sugar. The product has been criticised by public health advocates in Malaysia for its high-sugar content, but, as in many other similar instances, the company refutes these charges and makes health claims for the minerals and vitamins contained in the drink (Wan 2018).

McDonald's has similarly sponsored grassroots football in the United Kingdom for 20 years since 2002 (Ireland and Boyland 2019). Its programme promotes football experiences for children and it actively uses its social media account @FunFootballUK as a means of securing brand engagement. Food companies have been sponsoring physical activity campaigns for many years and are eager to deflect current concerns about childhood obesity by asserting that this relates to a lack of physical activity rather than the overconsumption of their HFSS food and beverage products, which is much more significant. And, of course, the language used in discourses around childhood obesity emphasises parental responsibility rather than what has been called the obesogenic environment in which unhealthy food is marketed relentlessly (Swinburn et al. 2011).

Digital food marketing to young people represents a substantial new public health challenge in which marketeers use brand personalities, peer engagement and emotion and entertainment to persuade young people to engage and respond (Boyland et al. 2020). Academic studies consider sport sponsorship as a cause of obesity (Dixon et al. 2019) and clearly more research needs to be undertaken into the targeting of children through sports sponsorship and marketing, which should be considered a child-rights issue (Gokani et al. 2021).

As has been described in previous chapters, sporting collectibles promoting unhealthy products such as tobacco and alcohol have been popular for over a century and engage children as well as adults. These too now use both traditional and digital approaches to promote brands. Australian Rules football has provided collectible cards, and these have been associated with tobacco companies and chewing gum over the years (Wikipedia 2021). McDonald's long-term sponsorship of the Australian Football League (Australian Rules) featured a Captain Game card obtainable from the fast food company's outlets in 2021. The front of the card shows the McDonald's logo with the image of an AFL team captain, with the reverse having a 'Footy Trumps Quiz' and a link to www.teamcoach.com.au for "game instructions". Sport's easy acceptance of sponsorship from food and drink corporations contributes to the obesogenic environment that children are exposed to globally and the subsequent levels of overweight and obesity as a result mainly of poor nutrition.

From the traditional to the digital – Guinness and rugby

Television has been pivotal in enabling sport to achieve global penetration. In the twenty-first century, digital media platforms have further revolutionised the mediation of sport and its culture, providing a new platform for marketing to fan-consumers. Social media has been at the centre of these developments (Lamberton and Stephen 2016), enabling direct two-way communication between brand

and consumer (Newman *et al.* 2017). Sports marketing literature describes how consumers develop and maintain relationships both with their clubs and with their clubs' sponsors. Companies have to link their sponsorship with other promotional tools to leverage as much attention as possible (Bűhler and Nufer 2013). Academic literature has reported an association between exposure to alcohol marketing and increased consumption (Brown 2016), and the Irish-based alcohol brand Guinness provides an example of marketing methods developing over an extended period from 1999 as the transnational corporation has sought to affirm its global identity through the sport of rugby (Amis 2008).

Guinness is currently the title sponsor and the official beer of the Six Nations tournament. This is an annual men's rugby union competition between the teams of England, France, Ireland, Italy, Scotland and Wales. The tournament's website declares that "The brand (Guinness) is... continuing its commitment and promotion of responsible drinking by maintaining its reputation as Official Responsible Drinking Partner" (Guinness Six Nations Rugby 2020). A content analysis of Guinness-branded marketing during the 15 games of the 2019 Guinness Six Nations tournament estimated that 122.4 billion Guinness-related brand impressions were delivered to the UK population (Barker *et al.* 2021). The Guinness brand was superimposed on to the centre of the pitch and also appeared on the sidelines, sponsor walls and goal and flag posts.

Guinness was one of the global sponsors of the Rugby World Cup in 1999 (Heineken is the current alcohol sponsor). Guinness was clear about its target market for consumption, which focused on men (particularly those aged between 18 and 34 years) (Rines 2002). The alcohol brand saw the World Cup as a strong communication platform to address its audience, who were "inextricably linked through social drinking" (Rines 2002 p.82). Aside from advertising during the broadcast matches, Guinness ran themed press and radio campaigns, on-pack promotions, game cards linked with prizes such as holidays to rugby-playing nations and merchandise rewards for purchase (Rines 2002). The supporting public relations campaign was intended to develop an emotional bond between the fans and the brand (Rines 2002). Guinness claimed increased consumption of its products in France, Australia, South Africa and Great Britain as a direct result of its sponsorship as well as a reinforcement of its brand awareness (Rines 2002). The marketing at the Rugby World Cup and other events was designed to strengthen the brand identity as "masculine, strong, genuine and independent" (Amis 2008 p.155). The brand used the same approach, albeit less successfully, in the 'Born of Our Land' campaign to accompany Ireland's participation in the Six Nations tournament of 2009 (Kearns 2020).

The studies of Guinness's sponsorship of rugby reveal the methods of the sponsorship mix used to directly engage fans and encourage them to consume more of its (unhealthy) products. In Guinness's case, the claimed identity as "Responsible Drinking Partner" rings hollow when the brand is clearly trying to encourage increased sales through its sponsorship. In 2015, Three Ireland (the Irish branch of the international telecommunications brand) used a much more nuanced approach to promote its sponsorship of the Irish team in the Six Nations tournament by augmenting the usual posters, billboards and internet banner advertisements with three mini-documentary videos featuring Irish players, which were broadcast via Three Ireland's YouTube channel, gaining considerable viewing figures (Kearns 2020). This use of digital technologies to support Irish rugby sponsorship reflects wider changes in marketing, which is moving from 'traditional to digital', from the conventional, defined as TV, print and billboards, to digital connections through "horizontal webs of communities" (Kotler et al. 2017 p.47), in which brands seek to develop relationships with their consumers through customer connectivity. As companies seek to gain influence over their customers, both the traditional and digital will be employed to promote customer engagement.

Social media activation

In digital communications, social media is seen as an important method of nurturing customer relationships in the sport industry (Williams and Chinn 2010; Abeza and O'Reilly 2013) and publications in academic journals based on social media data have rapidly increased in number (Pedersen 2014; Filo et al. 2015; Alalwan et al. 2017). The social media service and micro-blogging platform Twitter was launched in 2006 and has been used by clubs to promote news about football and by fans wanting to vent their feelings and views about matches (Price et al. 2013). There is limited research regarding Twitter conversations about corporate sponsors, however. Jensen et al. (2015) carried out a study related to football fans at the FC Barcelona and Juventus 2015 UEFA Champions' League final. They used a visual analysis method to gather tweets that contained images to evaluate key metrics from Twitter conversations about two sponsors. This included tweets, retweets, favourites, impressions and hashtags. This study concluded that one sponsor (Qatar Airways) was more effective in engaging fans, as measured by the number of times fans clicked to retweet and share tweets amongst their followers. In other metrics, such as the volume of tweets, the other sponsor (Jeep) was more successful. However, the authors were unable to volunteer reasons for their findings, and there seems to be considerable space for further research around how clubs and sponsors engage with fans. There is a suggestion that a younger demographic is engaging with football, and sponsors will want to be present on the digital platforms they access (Sartori 2020). The richest EPL clubs provide sponsors with a global online community to leverage and activate (Sartori 2020). KPMG Football Benchmark calculated that EPL clubs represented six of the top ten football clubs across Europe in terms of their accumulated social media following across Facebook, Instagram, Twitter and YouTube in a period between 1 September 2015 and 20 July 2020 (Sartori 2020). Manchester United had 135 million followers, Chelsea 87 million and Tottenham Hotspur 31 million (the other three EPL clubs in this list are Manchester City, Arsenal and Liverpool).

These social media platforms are used by sports organisations as marketing and communication tools to gain greater audience reach and to increase commercial revenue through this engagement with fans (McGillivray and McLaughlin 2019). Twitter is now used in everyday communication by individuals as well as corporations (Weller *et al.* 2014). It has a huge take-up amongst sports fans as well as footballers, and clubs use the platform as a promotional tool and publishing platform (Price *et al.* 2013). Media platforms such as Twitter enable brands and sponsors to reach fans both physically and digitally, building relationships and awareness (Karg and Lock 2014). Indeed, a third of the population are now reported to use social media while watching sport (Britton 2022). Generation Z (those born between about 1996 and 2011) have been born into a digital world and marketers are already using a wide assemblage of virtual, images, voices and texts to engage with these new consumers (Witt and Baird 2018).

Apps such as Fanzo (formerly MatchPint) (see www.fanzo.com) are set up as fan engagement platforms for brands, broadcasters and rights holders. Fanzo's broadcasting and rights partners in July 2022 were Foxtel, Canal Plus, Sky Sports and the NFL. Its brand partners included Budweiser, Carlsberg, Heineken and Coca-Cola. The downloadable app works to enable sports fans to find bars where they can watch their teams play. The app boasts that it converts brand engagement into measurable commercial returns. The website quotes Rowan Chidgey, marketing director of AB InBev, Europe, as saying

> Working with FANZO ensures Budweiser connects authentically with a large audience of football fans to activate key sponsorships like the FIFA World Cup and Premier League. Through reactive offers, gamification, and a vast network of venues, FANZO helps us to convert brand engagement into commercial return, driving sales increase of 15% at a 2:1 ROI.
>
> (Fanzo 2022)

Fanzo had a promotion with Guinness in 2022, in which you could win a pint if you predicted a correct match score during the 2022 Guinness Six Nations rugby tournament.

The gamblification of sport

If television provided a gateway to the commodification of sport in the second half of the twentieth century, the innovations in machine intelligence and the invention of targeted advertising (Zuboff 2019) have enabled unhealthy corporations to take brand engagement in sport to an entirely new level. Quite simply, the development of computer systems has enabled companies to mine data and to aim advertising based on social media usage, past online purchases and media interests direct to consumers on their handheld and desktop digital devices. Nowhere is this more obvious in sport than in the alarming growth of the online gambling industry. Whilst gambling and sport have a very long history (Clapson 1992;

Schwartz 2006), the transition of gambling from pools coupons and high street shops to sporting arenas and smartphones has been rapid and extremely profitable for the industry (Rogan 2021; Davies 2022).

Sport and gambling have a very close relationship. Sports such as horse racing and cricket owed their development, and indeed the standardisation of their rules to the need to make it easier for gamblers to bet on match and race outcomes (Birley 2013). However, the development of mobile app technologies has enabled sports fans to bet on all aspects of matches 24 hours a day, seven days a week (McGee 2020). Gambling is ceaselessly promoted in many sports, whether Australian rugby league (Lindsay et al. 2013) or European football (Lopez-Gonzalez and Tulloch 2015). It is particularly prevalent in British football (Bunn et al. 2018), where one EPL match, televised during the coronavirus pandemic in 2021, offered 716 gambling brand exposures (Ireland and Bunn 2021), with an impact on gambling behaviour far beyond its shores (Bunn et al. 2020). Many of these exposures were for Bet365, a British-based gambling company.

Bet365 developed an online betting model which, arguably, changed the way sport is consumed (Samuel 2019). The technology that Bet365 uses enables betting at any time during a match. For example, you can now bet on which team has the first corner, which player receives the first yellow card, and who scores the first goal. The company is owned by a Stoke-on-Trent family, the Coates. The huge profits made by the company – its CEO, Denise Coates, is the richest woman in England, with her pay and dividends for the year ending in March 2020 being recorded as £421 million (Davies 2022) – enabled the founder, Peter Coates, to buy Stoke City FC and name its ground the Bet365 stadium, generating even more mentions for the Bet365 brand.

One academic has described the ubiquity of gambling brand mentions in sport (both during live action and in the paid advertising that accompanies commercial broadcasting) as enabling gambling to become "a normalised aspect of sports fandom for male youth demographics, many of whom view the casual wagering of money as vital to their enjoyment of sport" (McGee 2020 p.89). McMullan and Miller argued much the same in a paper which described how the high volume, attractiveness and pervasiveness of gambling messages has embedded betting into popular sport culture and made it part of "the fun ethic of contemporary consumer culture" (2008 p.230). McGee (2020) argued that the cultural normalisation of gambling is linked to advances in mobile phone technology and that companies such as Bet365 have aligned gambling with culturally embedded sporting activities including football. The gambling industry uses celebrities, excitement and humour in its marketing to suggest that online gambling is a risk-free entertainment business in which skill is more important than luck (McMullan and Miller 2008). Further studies of gambling advertising show a male-dominated world with individual betting using mobile devices, often linked to emotionally charged situations such as when teams score goals (Lopez-Gonzalez and Tulloch 2015). Constant exposure to marketing for sports betting products has removed the stigma traditionally associated with betting by creating a perception that gambling on sport is a normal activity. Sports betting advertisements incorporate existing rituals associated with young male sports fans' behaviours (e.g., watching sport with peers in a pub) and seek to add gambling to these behaviours (Deans et al. 2017; Lopez-Gonzalez et al. 2018; Jones et al. 2020).

And the advertising works. Many studies have shown that children are aware of sports betting advertising, which clearly therefore has the capacity to influence their attitudes and potentially encourage them to try gambling. These studies include a qualitative study of children aged 8–16 years in Melbourne (Pitt et al. 2017). These young people were able to recall gambling advertising in detail, highlighting the humour, and noting that the advertisements showed how someone would place a bet. A further study also carried out in Australia showed that 11–16-year olds recruited from community basketball stadiums also had a high recall and awareness of gambling brands, with most able to name a brand (Nyemcsok et al. 2018). And finally, a mixed-methods study carried out in London showed a raised level of awareness of gambling brands, particularly amongst young people who watched a lot of football on television (Djohari et al. 2019).

Whilst the gambling companies frame betting as a 'fun' and harmless leisure activity, others are recognising gambling as a public health concern (Wardle et al. 2019; van Schalkwyk et al. 2021). In this, advocates argue that targeting those who have suffered harm from gambling is likely to be ineffectual and may be stigmatising. They argue that, as with the tobacco industry, a series of measures is required to reduce harm, including regulation, legislation and funding. In the United Kingdom, individuals who have direct experience of gambling harm are arguing for more effective government policy in tackling gambling industry marketing, using high-profile campaigns such as the Big Step (see https://the-bigstep.com/home), which aims to kick gambling advertising out of British football, to draw attention to their concerns.

Case Study: Red Bull

Red Bull is an energy drink that was launched in Austria in 1987 and in the American market in 1997 (Tejwani 2020). To sports business practitioners, the brand represents an outstanding example of entrepreneurship through sports marketing (Gorse et al. 2010); to public health specialists, energy drink consumption represents a global public health problem (Ibrahim and Iftikhar 2014). In the history of marketing, many companies have made health claims for their products which have later been comprehensively disproved. The tobacco industry, as ever, set the standard for this, making fraudulent claims about the so-called health benefits of filtered, low-tar and menthol cigarettes, for example (Blum and Novotny 2018). In the twenty-first century, energy drink companies claim that their products boost energy and improve cognitive and physical performance (Ibrahim and

Iftikhar 2014). However, independent research often contradicts research which is industry-sponsored (Higgins *et al.* 2018). Industry research on sports drinks is generally conducted on highly trained young athletes, and results should not be generalised to non-athletic sedentary populations (Heneghan *et al.* 2012).

A report by the American Academy of Pediatrics in 2011 concluded that both sports and energy drinks were being marketed to children and young people for a wide variety of inappropriate uses (Schneider and Benjamin 2011). A later report by the American College of Sports Medicine also focused on energy drinks, their ingredients and problems associated with their consumption (Higgins *et al.* 2018). A major concern is the level of caffeine contained in most energy drinks. A 250 millilitre can of Red Bull energy drink contains 80 mg of caffeine, approximately the same as in a cup of coffee. Coffee is not generally considered a drink for adolescents, and adverse side-effects of energy drink consumption such as trouble sleeping, anxiety and even death are beginning to be observed (Goetz 2013). And there are further issues concerning the multiple ingredients in many energy drinks such as taurine, ginseng extracts and sugar. The 250 millilitre can of Red Bull contains 27.5 grams of sugar or just under seven teaspoons. This is around the maximum daily level of sugar intake recommended for young teenagers globally, and most will consume sugar in other ways daily including in processed foods. Level of sugar intake is closely associated with both weight gain and dental health, and the World Health Organisation recommend controls on the consumption of sugar (World Health Organization 2015).

There is insufficient space in this book to consider all the evidence around food and drink products, but it is safe to say that most medical experts do not see sufficient scientific evidence to support the claims about performance made on behalf of energy or sports drinks companies, and most would argue that water is the most appropriate drink for rehydration for all except elite athletes (Schneider and Benjamin 2011; Ibrahim and Iftikhar 2014; Higgins *et al.* 2018). It might also be argued that energy drinks have essentially been invented to meet a previously unidentified need, and that a market had to be found for them. The Austrian founder of the brand, Dietrich Mateschitz, has been quoted as saying exactly that: "When we first started, we said there is no existing market for Red Bull … But Red Bull will create it" (Dolan 2005). And Red Bull has been very successful at this, aiming its marketing at people and students, and using extreme sports and the purchase of sports teams to guarantee the brand regular exposure. By 2020, it was reported that global energy drinks sales had reached US$57.4 billion, with Red Bull still the market leader (Green Seed 2022).

As with many other types of sports marketing, Red Bull's primary audience is young, and its marketing has evolved a generation-defining product for Generation Y, those born in the 1980s and onwards (Gorse *et al.* 2010).

As with tobacco, the search to find new consumers started with the young, to try and embed a habit for life. Red Bull's first marketing was around individually focused extreme adventure activities, often described as action sports (such as snowboarding, BMX and downhill mountain biking). This married well with the unhealthy commodity industry framing of personal responsibility and individual risk. As Browne (2004) has commented, multi-national corporations have tapped into the money to be made from non-traditional sports framed around individualistic forms of expression. Mountain Dew's recent approach to marketing is similar and was described in Chapter 2. Red Bull invited engagement with its customers by presenting original video content online through its own YouTube channel (Saleh et al. 2019). In 2012, Red Bull supported Felix Baumgartner's 39,045-metre jump to Earth from the edge of space. By March 2022, a 90-second highlights video of the jump featuring multiple exposures to Red Bull's brand on Baumgartner's helmet, suit and parachute had received over 47 million views (Red Bull 2012). At the same time, Red Bull's YouTube channel had 10.4 million consumer subscribers. The videos show snowmobiles, skiing and wingsuit flying. They also feature the 2022 Formula 1 world champion, Max Verstappen. One film shows Verstappen driving his racing car on ice. This is a world which endorses conventional masculine identities, risk-taking behaviour and energy drink consumption (Miller 2008).

Red Bull's move into Formula 1 motor racing came in 2005 (it entered with two teams, Red Bull and Toro Rosso) and might be viewed as an exemplar of adding emotion to a brand through its motorsport sponsorship (Percival 2010). Fans who attend motorsports events can sample the product and engage with the 'World of Red Bull'. Those who watch on television or online will see a mobile advertising hoarding, but, arguably more importantly, they will hear constant repetition of the name of the driver and his (it's invariably a man) Red Bull car and team. Formula 1's mediated spectacle highlights a masculine world of fast cars, high-tech, risk and glamour (Sturm 2014), a heady mix for an energy drink company to associate with. Young collectors can buy model cars and many other mementos featuring the energy drink brand's logo. And the marketing works. Red Bull's global sales figures nearly quadrupled between 2002 and 2008 to US$4.4 billion (Percival 2010). Red Bull's marketing strategy has placed it as "both a premium and a lifestyle product" (Percival 2010 p.337). The successes of its lead drivers, currently Max Verstappen, and previously Sebastian Vettel, who won four consecutive F1 titles from 2010 to 2013, has led to even greater recognition for the brand.

Red Bull has taken a very similar approach to football, and as in Formula 1 racing, the brand's name and logo, slogan ("Red Bull gives you wings") and red and white colours were seen as essential to the development of its corporate identity (Gorse et al. 2010). First the company acquired SV Austria Salzburg in 2005, controversially changing the name of the club to FC Red Bull

Salzburg and the team's colours from its traditional violet and white to red and white (Gorse et al. 2010). Red Bull aggressively maintained this strategy, subsequently acquiring football clubs in New York, São Paulo and Sogakope (Tejwani 2020). Red Bull purchased the playing licence of a village team from Markranstäst in Germany, and despite seemingly robust rules on commercial entities in the Deutsche Bundesliga (the German football league), it established the new team of RasenBallsport (which translates into English as lawn ball sport) Leipzig e.V. These initials provided a convenient means for the team to become RB Leipzig, but this attracted criticism from fans of other German football teams (Schoenfeld 2020). RB Leipzig has now competed in the UEFA Champions League in its new Red Bull Arena.

Red Bull's approach is generally lauded by business students and entrepreneurs, whilst being decried by public health practitioners and 'traditional' sports fans. Kunz and Elsässer have characterised Red Bull's approach as "sport-related branded entertainment" (Kunz et al. 2016 p.520). Whilst marketeers see Red Bull as a successful integration of branding and sponsorship in sport, others criticise the way in which an international brand has been successful in creating a huge youthful market for a product no one needed 35 years ago. Red Bull is just one brand amongst many that might be argued to have contributed negatively to the health of its consumers.

Red Bull's approach to the rules of the Bundesliga was to bypass them. The same approach was used by FIFA, working on behalf of its alcohol sponsor to demand that beer was sold at the World Cup despite local national laws. As shown in Chapter 4, this is a well-used playbook first employed by the tobacco corporations when they were banned from advertising their products on television in the United States and the United Kingdom. They simply found another way to market their brands using an entirely complicit sports industry. It seems that money generally speaks louder than the health needs of populations. The next chapter considers whether sport can be regulated to improve our health rather than damage it.

References

Abeza, G. and O'Reilly, N. (2013) 'Relationship marketing and social media in sport', *International Journal of Sport Communication*, 6, 120–142.

Alalwan, A.A., Rana, N.P., Dwivedi, Y.K. and Algharabat, R. (2017) 'Social media in marketing: A review and analysis of the existing literature', *Telematics and Informatics*, 34, 1177–1190.

Amis, J. (2008) 'Guinness, sport and the positioning of a global brand' in Chadwick, S. and Arthur, D., eds., *International Cases in the Business of Sport*, Oxford: Butterworth-Heinemann.

Barker, A.B., Bal, J. and Murray, R.L. (2021) 'A content analysis and population exposure estimate of Guinness branded alcohol marketing during the 2019 Guinness Six Nations', *Alcohol and Alcoholism*, 1, 4.

Birley, D. (2013) *A Social History of English Cricket*, London: Aurum.
Blum, A. and Novotny, T. (2018) 'The filter fraud: Debunking the myth of "Safer" as a key new strategy of tobacco control', *Tobacco induced diseases*, 16(1), available: http://dx.doi.org/10.18332/tid/83988.
Boyland, E., Thivel, D., Mazur, A., Ring-Dimitriou, S., Frelut, M.-L. and Weghuber, D. (2020) 'Digital food marketing to young people: A substantial public health challenge', *Annals of Nutrition and Metabolism*, 76(1), 6–9.
Brandt, A.M. (2007) *The Cigarette Century*, New York: Basic Books.
Britton, A. (2022) 'As sponsorship evolves, sports marketing is no longer a game', *The Drum*, 20 July 2022, available: https://www.thedrum.com/opinion/2022/07/20/sponsorship-evolves-sports-marketing-no-longer-game [accessed 19 August 2022].
Broadbent, A. (2015) 'Brand activation and its role in driving consumer engagement and awareness', available: https://econsultancy.com/brand-activation-and-its-role-in-driving-consumer-engagement-and-awareness/ [accessed 19 October 2020].
Brown, K. (2016) 'Association between alcohol sports sponsorship and consumption: A systematic review', *Alcohol and Alcoholism*, 51(6), 747–755.
Browne, D. (2004) *Amped: How Big Air, Big Dollars, and a New Generation Took Sports to the Extreme*, New York: Bloomsbury.
Bühler, A. and Nufer, G. (2013) *Relationship Marketing in Sport*, Abingdon: Routledge.
Bunn, C., Ireland, R., Minton, J., Holman, D., Philpott, M. and Chambers, S. (2018) 'Shirt sponsorship by gambling companies in the English and Scottish Premier Leagues: Global reach and public health concerns', *Soccer and Society*, 17 Jan 2018, available: http://dx.doi.org/17 Jan 2018.
Bunn, C., Mtema, O., Songo, J. and Udedi, M. (2020) 'The growth of sports betting in Malawi: Corporate strategies, public space and public health', *Public Health*, 184, 95–101, available: http://dx.doi.org/https://doi.org/10.1016/j.puhe.2020.03.022.
Carrigan, M. and Carrigan, J. (1997) 'UK Sports Sponsorship: Fair Play or Foul?', *A European Review*, 6(2), 59–64.
Chanavat, N., Desbordes, M. and Lorgnier, N. (2017) 'Sports sponsorship and professional football' in Chanavat, N., Desbordes, M. and Lorgnier, N., eds., *Routledge Handbook of Football Marketing*, Abingdon: Routledge.
Clapson, M. (1992) *A bit of a flutter. Popular gambling and English society, c.1823–1961*, Manchester: Manchester University Press.
Collin, J. (2003) 'Think Global, Smoke Local: Transnational Tobacco Companies and Cognitive Globalization' in Lee, K., ed., *Health Impacts of Globalization. Towards Global Governance*, Basingstoke: Palgrave Macmillan.
Cornwell, T.B. (1997) 'The Use of Sponsorship-Linked Marketing by Tobacco Firms: International Public Policy Issues', *The Journal of Consumer Affairs*, 31(2), 238–254.
Cornwell, T.B. (2019) 'Less "Sponsorship as Advertising" and More Sponsorship-Linked Marketing As Authentic Engagement.', *Journal of Advertising*, 48(1), 49–60.
Cornwell, T.B. (2020) *Sponsorship in Marketing. Effective Partnerships in Sports, Arts and Events*, Second ed., Abingdon: Routledge.
Davies, R. (2022) *Jackpot. How Gambling Conquered Britain*, London: Guardian Faber.
Deans, E.G., Thomas, S.L., Derevensky, J. and Daube, M. (2017) 'The influence of marketing on the sports betting attitudes and consumption behaviours of young men: Implications for harm reduction and prevention strategies', *Harm Reduction Journal*, 14(1), 1–12.
Dixon, H., Lee, A. and Scully, M. (2019) 'Sports sponsorship as a cause of obesity', *Current Obesity Reports*, 31 October 2019, 480–494.

Djohari, N., Weston, G., Cassidy, R., Wemyss, M. and Thomas, S. (2019) 'Recall and awareness of gambling advertising and sponsorship in sport in the UK: A study of young people and adults', *Harm Reduction Journal*, 16(1), 1–12.

Dolan, K.A. (2005) 'The soda with buzz', *Forbes*, 28 March 2005, available: https://www.forbes.com/forbes/2005/0328/126.html?sh=2b149c0d3d60 [accessed 2 March 2022].

Dunlop, S., Freeman, B. and Jones, S.C. (2016) 'Marketing to youth in the digital age: The promotion of unhealthy products and health promoting behaviours on social media', *Media and Communication*, 4(3), 35–49.

Dwivedi, A. (2015) 'A higher-order model of consumer brand engagement and its impact on loyalty intentions', *Journal of Retailing and Consumer Services*, 24, 100–109.

Fanzo (2022) *Testimonials*, available: www.fanzo.com [accessed 14 July 2022].

Filo, K., Lock, D. and Karg, A. (2015) 'Sport and social media research: A review', *Sport Management Review*, 18, 166–181.

Gambetti, R., C. and Graffigna, G. (2010) 'The concept of engagement. A systematic analysis of the ongoing marketing debate', *International Journal of Market Research*, 52(6), 801–826.

Goetz, G. (2013) 'FDA to investigate safety of added caffeine', *Food Safety News*, 30 April 2013, available: https://www.foodsafetynews.com/2013/04/fda-to-investigate-caffeine-as-food-additive/#:~:text=The%20U.S.%20Food%20and%20Drug, Wrigley%2C%20which%20hit%20markets%20Monday [accessed 2 March 2022].

Gokani, N., Garde, A., Philpott, M., Ireland, R., Owens, R. and Boyland, E. (2021) 'UK Nutrition Research Partnership 'Hot Topic' workshop report: A 'game changer' for dietary health – addressing the implications of sport sponsorship by food businesses through an innovative interdisciplinary collaboration', *Nutrition Bulletin*, n/a(n/a), available: http://dx.doi.org/https://doi.org/10.1111/nbu.12535.

Gorse, S., Chadwick, S. and Burton, N. (2010) 'Entrepreneurship through sports marketing: A case analysis of Red Bull in sport', *Journal of Sponsorship*, 3(4), 348–357.

Green Seed (2022) *Energy Drink Market Trends, Growth and Growth Rate in 2022*, available: https://greenseedgroup.com/energy-drink-market-trends-growth/#:~:text=in%20the%20World-, How%20much%20is%20the%20energy%20drink%20market%20worth%3F, and%20%2453.01%20billion%20in%202018 [accessed 2 March 2022].

Guinness Six Nations Rugby (2020) *Guinness*, Internal Report, unpublished.

Hagstrom, R. G. (2001) *The NASCAR Way: The Business That Drives the Sport*, New York: John Wiley & Sons.

Heneghan, C., Howick, J., O'Neill, B., Gill, P.J., Lasserson, D.S., Cohen, D., Davis, R., Ward, A., Smith, A. and Jones, G. (2012) 'The evidence underpinning sports performance products: A systematic assessment', *BMJ Open*, 2(4), e001702.

Higgins, J.P., Babu, K., Deuster, P.A. and Shearer, J. (2018) 'Energy drinks: A contemporary issues paper', *Current Sports Medicine Reports*, 17(2), 65–72, available: http://dx.doi.org/10.1249/jsr.0000000000000454.

Hollebeek, L. (2011) 'Exploring customer brand engagement: Definition and themes', *Journal of Strategic Marketing*, 19(7), 555–573.

Ibrahim, N.K. and Iftikhar, R. (2014) 'Energy drinks: Getting wings but at what health cost?', *Pakistan Journal of Medical Sciences*, 30(6), 1415.

Ireland, R. and Boyland, E. (2019) 'Sports sponsorship and young people: Good or bad for health?', *BMJ Paediatrics Open*, 3(1), e000446.

Ireland, R. and Bunn, C. (2021) 'Euro 2020: Football's promotion of unhealthy consumption must end', *The Conversation*, 14 June 2021, available: https://theconversation.com/

euro-2020-footballs-promotion-of-unhealthy-consumption-must-end-162552 [accessed 22 June 2021].

Jensen, R.W., Limbu, Y.B. and Spong, Y. (2015) 'Visual analytics of Twitter conversations about corporate sponsors of FC Barcelona and Juventus at the 2015 UEFA final', *International Journal of Sports Marketing & Sponsorship*, July 2015, 3–9

Jones, C., Pinder, R. and Robinson, G. (2020) 'Gambling sponsorship and advertising in British Football: A critical account', *Sport, Ethics and Philosophy*, 14(2), 163–175.

Karg, A. and Lock, D. (2014) 'Using new media to engage consumers at the Football World Cup' in Frawley, S. and Adair, D., eds., *Managing the Football World Cup*, Basingstoke: Palgrave Macmillan.

Kearns, C. (2020) 'From Team of Aliens to #TeamofUs: The evolution of Irish-rugby advertising, 2007–17' in O'Boyle, N. and Free, M., eds., *Sport, the Media and Ireland: Interdisciplinary Perspectives*, Cork: Cork University Press.

Kelly, B., Baur, L.A., Bauman, A.E., King, L., Chapman, K. and Smith, B.J. (2011) '"Food company sponsors are kind, generous and cool": (Mis)conceptions of junior sports players', *International Journal of Behavioral Nutrition and Physical Activity*, 8(95), 1–7.

Kotler, P., Kartajaya, H. and Setiawan, I. (2017) *Marketing 4.0. Moving from Traditional to Digital*, Hoboken: John Wiley.

Kunz, R.E., Elsässer, F. and Santomier, J. (2016) 'Sport-related branded entertainment: The Red Bull phenomenon', *Sport, Business and Management: An International Journal*, 6(5), 520–541, available: http://dx.doi.org/10.1108/SBM-06-2016-0023.

Lamberton, C. and Stephen, A.T. (2016) 'A thematic exploration of digital, social media, and mobile marketing: Research evolution from 2000 to 2015 and an agenda for future inquiry', *Journal of Marketing: AMA/MSI Special Issue*, 80(November 2016), 146–172.

Lardinoit, T. and Derbaix, C. (2001) 'Sponsorship and recall of sponsors', *Psychology & Marketing*, 18(2), 167–190.

Leckie, C., Munyaradzi, W.N. and Johnson, L.W. (2016) 'Antecedents of consumer brand engagement and brand loyalty', *Journal of Marketing Management*, 32(5–6), 558–578.

Lindsay, S., Thomas, S., Lewis, S., Westberg, K., Moodie, R. and Jones, S. (2013) 'Eat, drink and gamble: Marketing messages about 'risky' products in an Australian major sporting series', *BMC Public Health*, 13(1), 1–11.

Lopez-Gonzalez, H., Guerrero-Solé, F. and Griffiths, M.D. (2018) 'A content analysis of how 'normal' sports betting behaviour is represented in gambling advertising', *Addiction Research & Theory*, 26(3), 238–247.

Lopez-Gonzalez, H. and Tulloch, C.D. (2015) 'Enhancing media sport consumption: Online gambling in European football', *Media International Australia*, 155(1), 130–139, available: http://dx.doi.org/10.1177/1329878X1515500115.

Madrigal, R. (2004) 'A review of team identification and its influence on consumers' responses towards corporate sponsors' in Kahle, L. R. and Riley, C., eds., *Sports Marketing and the Psychology of Marketing Communication*, Mahwah: Lawrence Erlbaum.

McGee, D. (2020) 'On the normalisation of online sports gambling among young adult men in the UK: A public health perspective', *Public Health*, 184, 89–94, available: http://dx.doi.org/https://doi.org/10.1016/j.puhe.2020.04.018.

McGillivray, D. and McLaughlin, E. (2019) 'Transnational digital fandom. Club media, place, and (networked) space' in Lawrence, S. and Crawford, G., eds., *Digital Football Cultures. Fandom, Identities and Resistance*, Abingdon: Routledge.

McMullan, J.L. and Miller, D. (2008) 'All in! The commercial advertising of offshore gambling on television', *Journal of Gambling Issues*, (22), 230–251.

Meenaghan, T. (2001) 'Understanding sponsorship effects', *Psychology & Marketing*, 18(2), 95–122.

Miller, K.E. (2008) 'Wired: Energy drinks, jock identity, masculine norms, and risk taking', *Journal of American College Health*, 56(5), 481–490, available: http://dx.doi.org/10.3200/JACH.56.5.481-490.

Nestlé (2017) *Cricket Australia and Milo Celebrate 25 Years of Junior Cricket* [press release], 17 September 2017, available: https://www.nestle.com.au/en/media/cricket-aust-milo-celebrate-junior-cricket [accessed 3 March 2022].

Newman, T., Peck, J.F., Harris, C. and Wilhide, B. (2017) *Social Media in Sport Marketing*, Abingdon: Routledge.

Nyemcsok, C., Thomas, S.L., Bestman, A., Pitt, H., Daube, M. and Cassidy, R. (2018) 'Young people's recall and perceptions of gambling advertising and intentions to gamble on sport', *Journal of Behavioral Addictions*, 7(4), 1068–1078, available: http://dx.doi.org/10.1556/2006.7.2018.128.

O'Keefe, R., Titlebaum, P. and Hill, C. (2009) 'Sponsorship activation: Turning money spent into money earned', *Journal of Sponsorship*, 3(1), 43–53.

Pedersen, P.M. (2014) 'A Commentary on Social Media Research From the Perspective of a Sport Communication Journal Editor', *Communication & Sport*, 2(2), 138–142.

Percival, B. (2010) 'The misuse of motor racing and the sport's true potential', *Journal of Sponsorship*, 3(4), 333–337.

Petticrew, M., Shelmit, I., Lorenc, T., Marteau, T.M., Melendez-Torres, G.J., O'Mara-Eves, A., Stautz, K. and Thomas, J. (2017) 'Alcohol advertising and public health: Systems perspectives versus narrow perspectives', *Journal of Epidemiology and Community Health*, 71, 308–312.

Pitt, H., Thomas, S.L., Bestman, A., Daube, M. and Derevensky, J. (2017) 'What do children observe and learn from televised sports betting advertisements? A qualitative study among Australian children', *Australian and New Zealand Journal of Public Health*, 41(6), 604–610, available: http://dx.doi.org/https://doi.org/10.1111/1753-6405.12728.

Pracejus, J.W. (2004) 'Seven psychological mechanisms through which sponsorship can influence consumers' in Kahle, L. R. and Riley, C., eds., *Sports Marketing and the Psychology of Marketing Communication*, Mahwah: Lawrence Erlbaum.

Price, J., Farrington, N. and Hall, L. (2013) 'Changing the game? The impact of Twitter on relationships between football clubs, supporters and the sports media', *Soccer & Society*, 14(4), 446–461.

Red Bull (2012) *Felix Baumgartner's Supersonic Freefall from 128k' - Mission Highlights*. Video, available: https://www.youtube.com/watch?v=FHtvDA0W34I [accessed 19 August 2022].

Rines, S. (2002) 'Guinness Rugby World Cup sponsorship; A global platform for meeting business objectives', *International Journal of Sports Marketing & Sponsorship*, December/January 2002, 79–95.

Rogan, A. (2021) *Punters. How Paddy Power Bet Billions and Changed Gambling Forever*, Dublin: HarperCollins.

Saleh, A., Chefor, E. and Babin, B. (2019) 'An action-based approach to retail brand engagement' in Granata, G., Tartaglione, A. M. and Tsiakis, T., eds., *Predicting Trends and Building Strategies for Consumer Engagement in Retail Environments*, Hershey: IGI Global, 27–43.

Samuel, M. (2019) 'How the mastermind of Bet365 changed how we consume sport - and not for the better', *GQ*, 16 June 2019, available: https://www.gq-magazine.co.uk/article/bet365-denise-coates-success [accessed 1 March 2022].

Sartori, A. (2020) 'The changing face of football sponsorship - key trends', *FootballBenchmark*, 21 July 2020, available: https://footballbenchmark.com/library/the_changing_face_of_football_sponsorship_key_trends [accessed 4 August 2020].

Schneider, M.B. and Benjamin, H.J. (2011) 'Sports drinks and energy drinks for children and adolescents: Are they appropriate?', *Pediatrics*, 127(6), 1182–1189.

Schoenfeld, B. (2020) 'Why RB Leipzig is the most hated soccer team in the Bundesliga', *ESPN*, available: https://www.espn.co.uk/football/german-bundesliga/story/4029702/why-rb-leipzig-is-the-most-hated-soccer-team-in-the-bundesliga [accessed 3 March 2022].

Schwartz, D.G. (2006) *Roll the Bones: The History of Gambling*, New York: Gotham Books.

Smith, R., Kelly, B., Yeatman, H. and Boyland, E. (2019) 'Food marketing influences children's attitudes, preferences and consumption: A systematic critical review', *Nutrients*, 11(4), 875.

Sturm, D. (2014) 'A glamorous and high-tech global spectacle of speed: Formula One motor racing as mediated, global and corporate spectacle' in Dashper, K., Fletcher, T. and McCullough, N., eds., *Sports Events, Society and Culture*, Abingdon: Routledge, 68–82.

Swinburn, B.A., Sacks, G., Hall, K.D., McPherson, K., Finegood, D.T., Moodie, M.L. and Gortmaker, S.L. (2011) 'The global obesity pandemic: Shaped by global drivers and local environments', *The Lancet*, 378(9793), 804–814.

Tejwani, K. (2020) *Wings of Change: How the World's Biggest Energy Drink Manufacturer Made a Mark in Football*, Worthing: Pitch Publishing.

Tonietto, G.N. and Barasch, A. (2020) 'Generating content increases enjoyment by immersing consumers and accelerating perceived time', *Journal of Marketing*, 10 September 2020, available: http://dx.doi.org/https://doi.org/10.1177%2F0022242920944388.

van Schalkwyk, M.C., Petticrew, M., Cassidy, R., Adams, P., McKee, M., Reynolds, J. and Orford, J. (2021) 'A public health approach to gambling regulation: Countering powerful influences', *The Lancet Public Health*, 6(8), e614–e619.

Vivek, S.D., Beatty, S.E. and Morgan, R.M. (2012) 'Customer engagement: Exploring customer relationships beyond purchase', *Journal of Marketing Theory and Practice*, 20(2 (Spring 2012)), 127–145.

Wan, L. (2018) 'Nestlé Malaysia defends Milo over viral video accusations about sugar content', *Food Navigator*, 14 February 2028, available: https://www.foodnavigator-asia.com/Article/2018/02/14/Nestle-Malaysia-defends-Milo-over-viral-video-accusations-about-sugar-content [accessed 3 March 2022].

Wardle, H., Reith, G., Langham, E. and Rogers, R.D. (2019) 'Gambling and public health: We need policy action to prevent harm', *BMJ*, 365, l1807, available: http://dx.doi.org/https://doi.org/10.1136/bmj.l1807.

Weller, K., Bruns, A., Burgess, J., Mahrt, M. and Puschmann, C. eds. (2014) *Twitter and Society*, Oxford: Peter Lang.

Wikipedia (2021) 'Australian rules football card'. Available: https://en.wikipedia.org/wiki/Australian_rules_football_card#:~:text=An%20Australian%20rules%20football%20card, more%20Australian%20rules%20football%20players [accessed 19 August 2022].

Williams, J. and Chinn, S.J. (2010) 'Meeting relationship-marketing goals through social media: A conceptual model for sport marketers', *International Journal of Sport Communication*, 3, 422–437.

Witt, G.L. and Baird, D.E. (2018) *The Gen Z Frequency. How Brands Tune in & Build Credibility*, London: Kogan Page.

World Health Organization (2015) *Guideline: Sugars Intake for Adults and Children*, Geneva: World Health Organization.

Zuboff, S. (2019) *The Age of Surveillance Capitalism: The Fight for a Human Future at the New Frontier of Power*, London: Profile Books.

Chapter 9

The regulation of sport

Introduction

Sport is often only considered from the perspective of results and records rather than in terms of power and legitimacy, with no consideration of the costs and benefits to wider society. Thus, sport has traditionally only been subjected to self-governance. Given how the marketing of gambling, alcohol and unhealthy food and beverage brands saturates sport today, the sports industry should be considered like any other in which regulation might be required if an unfettered marketplace impacts on people's health. Although industries such as alcohol and gambling have always been involved with sport (Vamplew 2021), in today's highly commodified sports arenas the brands of unhealthy commodities saturate the mediated space, creating a powerful and highly visible presence amongst sport's followers (Crawford 2004). As many areas of the stadiums, pitch surrounds, players' and coaching staff uniforms as possible have been commodified and display multiple logos. Cricket boundaries came about when traditional playing areas were enclosed, but Marqusee (2016) has argued that they have become in more recent years simply a vehicle for brands. The driver for sport sponsorship is to increase brand recognition and commercial income wherever possible. In a neoliberal capitalist world, this marketplace is scarcely moderated or regulated in any way, allowing transnational corporations unfettered capacity to market unhealthy brands across media platforms.

However, the events of 2020 and 2022 showed very clearly that governments and governing bodies are perfectly willing and able to intervene in the day-to-day running of elite sport whenever it is deemed necessary. The beginning of the coronavirus pandemic at the end of 2019 and in the first few months of 2020 brought a temporary end to sporting activities almost worldwide and created much debate about when it would be safe to resume. In the United Kingdom, the government's decision to allow Liverpool FC's Champions League match against Atletico Madrid to go ahead on 11 March 2020, and the Cheltenham Festival (horse racing) in the same week, was widely criticised, with a report suggesting that 78 people died as a result (Skysports 2021). Prime Minister Boris Johnson ordered a national lockdown (including all sport) on 23 March. When the English Premier

League resumed on 16 June 2020, it was with many strictures in place, and no spectators were allowed into grounds so as to prevent the spread of the virus (ITV News 2020). Clearly this was a public health emergency, but it provides an example of a government acting to protect health.

The ownership of the clubs in the English Premier League reflects the growth of economic capital in football in the twenty-first century and has been described as a metric of globalisation (Giulianotti and Robertson 2009). Where once clubs were owned by local businessmen, they are now controlled by oligarchs such as Roman Abramovich, a Russian billionaire, who took control of Chelsea FC in June 2003 (Montague 2018). The Premier League's list of owners in 2020 (Beard 2020) showed 14 clubs in foreign control, reflecting the fact that the EPL has become a global commercial empire (Robinson and Clegg 2019). However, the Russian invasion of Ukraine in 2022 led the UK government to freeze Abramovich's economic interests, including Chelsea FC, calling into question the Premier League's owners' and directors' governance assessments (Conn 2022). It is hard for anyone to deny the association between sport and politics, or that sport is simply a reflection of society. Whilst football in particular is extensively used for sportswashing, to enable nation-states to improve their reputations (Goldblatt 2022), the same process is also used by transnational brands to associate their products with a seemingly healthy activity. This has been described in other settings as using a 'health halo' to give a false impression of the healthfulness of a product or a process of public relations to mislead shoppers (Peloza and Montford 2015). In sport, transnational corporations use this approach to gain a 'halo effect' for an unhealthy brand through sponsorship (Dixon et al. 2019).

Ethical marketing?

In considering the ethics of marketing and taking into account the activities of the tobacco industry, it is tempting to suggest that the concept of advertising ethics is an oxymoron (Beltramini 2003). Eagle et al. (2021) noted how the corporate behaviour of some multi-nationals such as Nestlé has been regularly called into question. Nestlé has been repeatedly criticised for its marketing tactics in the Global South in which its sales representatives have promoted bottle feeding of babies and infants rather than breast feeding (Sasson 2016). The ethical debate around marketing practices has moved on to many widely available yet harmful products such as sugar and alcohol, gambling and tobacco still, although cigarette advertising has mainly been banned globally (Lužar et al. 2020). The tobacco industry now actively promotes electronic cigarettes (Doward 2021) and continues to produce snuff (a form of smokeless tobacco) in some countries. The World Health Organization has stated clearly that all forms of tobacco are harmful (World Health Organization 2021), and yet it was still possible to buy snuff from Bayern Munich's online store in 2022, branded with FC Bayern's logo (https://fcbayern.com/shop/en/snuff/28341/). Bayern Munich is one of the most successful teams in world football, having won the German Bundesliga a record 31 times.

As ever, the tobacco industry is an exemplar of marketing tactics, including being an early innovator of sports sponsorship as described in Chapter 4. Allan Brandt's book *The Cigarette Century* (2007) provides an excellent account of how marketing was used by Big Tobacco to promote its lethal products to new consumers including young people, to construct controversy about the damage to health caused by smoking, to challenge regulation intended to reduce consumption and, finally, to export the epidemic of smoking globally. By the mid-1950s, clinicians and researchers were mainly convinced of the links between cancer and cigarettes, and the US Surgeon General's report in 1964 was unequivocal: "No reasonable person should dispute that cigarette smoking is a serious health hazard" (quoted in Brandt 2007 p.210). And yet, as we have seen, tobacco companies sought to circumvent advertising regulation, using sports sponsorship as both to encourage new consumers, and to reassure existing smokers with images of healthy, active sporting events and athletes. Indeed, the growth of sports sponsorship in the 1970s has been argued by many academics (Crompton 1993; Cornwell 1997) to have been a direct result of the tobacco industry seeking new ways to promote its brands following the ban on cigarette advertising and promotion in broadcast media.

The publication of 'The Cigarette Papers' in 1995 by Stanton Glantz and colleagues (Glantz *et al.* 1995) detailed key aspects of the tactics of the tobacco industry, obtained from the internal documents of Brown & Williamson (a former subsidiary of British American Tobacco whose brands included Lucky Strike, State Express and Viceroy) and other companies. These tactics included marketing cigarettes to young smokers, using ultracool and humorous cartoon characters such as Joe Camel to emphasise the desirable psychological effects of smoking, whilst seeming to support the developing self-image of the young person and making smoking seem fun (Brandt 2007). These tactics are very familiar to those who have studied the marketing approaches used by Red Bull and Monster Energy in the promotion of 'energy' drinks or of the numerous gambling companies such as Paddy Power (now Flutter Entertainment, which also owns Betfair) or Bet365.

Cornwell (2020) discusses how sport contributes to society and considers its corporate social responsibility when it comes to 'controversial products' including tobacco, gambling and alcohol, and food and non-alcoholic drinks. As has been described in this book, all these industries have been criticised at some point for their sponsorship programmes in sport. As Cornwell indicates, central concerns often revolve around the ability of sports sponsorship to reach youth audiences, sometimes, as with alcohol and gambling, underage consumers. Cornwell suggests that the gains expected from marketing communications can be lost if brands are viewed as being commercial or inauthentic in their sponsorship. She provides an example in which Kentucky Fried Chicken sponsored the Susan G. Komen Race for the Cure cancer charity in the United States. The charity was heavily criticised for this sponsorship because of the relationship between unhealthy diets and the incidence of breast cancer (McVeigh 2012). Whilst unhealthy brands promote consumption, consumers are tasked with behaving responsibly. A recent

Australian study (Donaldson and Nicholson 2020) showed that the majority of sports organisation members believed that their organisation should not be accepting junk food sponsorship, particularly when these companies were sponsoring children's sport.

Fans also have objected to overt commercialisation in some situations. In France, some rugby fans and citizens objected when the French Federation of Rugby Union decided to carry a sponsor's logo on the national team shirt in 2018 (Chanavat and Bodet 2020). In English football, the fans of Norwich City FC forced the club to change its policy in 2021 after accepting shirt sponsorship from an Asian-based gambling company that had used "provocative" posts on its social media channels (BBC News 2021). There is clearly a potential for campaign groups, or even social movements, to challenge unhealthy sponsorships. Freudenberg, for example, in describing his experiences as a "public health researcher, practitioner, and activist" (Freudenberg 2021 p.6), argued that only social movements can "create alternatives to the world created by twenty-first century capitalism" (p.299) and thus address the impact of corporations on health.

A business ethics study carried out in the late 1990s considered sport sponsorship by alcohol and tobacco brands (McDaniel *et al.* 2001). It investigated the perceptions of this type of sponsorship amongst American and Australian students who expected to work in the marketing industry in the future. The results found that the further the students were in their education, the less difficulty they saw in the ethics of alcohol or tobacco sponsorship. The authors suggested a socialisation effect in which the more the students studied the practices of alcohol and tobacco sponsorship, the more they became accepting of such sponsorship. This socialisation or normalisation effect has been described in particular in relation to gambling industry sponsorship of British football (McGee 2020). As one would expect, industry places the profits of its shareholders before the health of its consumers, as Nestlé (2015) has described in the case of the soft drinks industry, long-standing sponsors of sport.

Who owns sport?

There is a long-standing argument around the funding of mass participation sport and elite sport, with the latter traditionally winning state support in the United Kingdom whilst drawing on an economic case to trump the potential health benefits of the former (Wynne 2019). This book has focused on elite sport, as it is on professional sport's television audience that the tobacco, alcohol, gambling and junk food industries have focused their marketing. Many sports such as cricket do not necessarily see themselves as a business, but of course they have always been commercial in some way (Marqusee 2016). Similarly, football clubs have unusual features as businesses in that they often lose money (Szymanski and Kuypers 1999). In addition, there is a philosophical question in terms of understanding 'Who owns sport?' Is it a question of who owns the assets of a particular football club or a sport such as cricket? Is it a collection of disembodied property rights? Or is it the 'imagined community' of football fans, whether in the United Kingdom or watching on a television set in Nigeria (Adams 2019)? There are complex relations between sports fans and their clubs in which concepts of tradition and authenticity have been challenged by the injection of sponsorship revenue following major broadcasting contracts.

The platitudes of FIFA's 'football family' draw on an imagined amateur world where governing bodies, leagues, club owners and fans share common interests in their sport (Parrish 2011). A qualitative research study carried out in 2019 interviewed informants from different sections of the British football industry to ascertain their views on sponsorship and marketing in the English Premier League by unhealthy commodity industries (Ireland 2021). The analysis drew on Bourdieu's work (1988, 1999) and showed how the positions occupied by representatives of social groups in the field of football reflected their dispositions and their respective orientations towards economic and cultural capital. The owners of football clubs and the management of the English Premier League often pretend that they share a common interest with those who follow football. This is transparently not the case when economic capital is at stake and fan-consumers are placed in a difficult position in which their love for their club is placed against commercial partnerships that they often prefer not to think too closely about. Whilst fans' concerns are more likely to be voiced about the political practices of their owners (Bland and Ahmed 2018), there has been growing concern about the commercial partnerships formed by football clubs with the gambling industry in particular, and ethical issues are beginning to be raised (Jones et al. 2020).

Walsh and Giulianotti (2007) reflected on the commodification of elite sport in which commercial interests play a high price to access global audiences. Inevitably the huge increase in commercial income is not evenly distributed across leagues and clubs, and competition may suffer, with results often being predictable, such as in European soccer or North American baseball. However, like most other sports sociologists, Walsh and Giulianotti do not consider the ethics of using sport to promote unhealthy brands. They mention the way in which income from gate money has been reduced whilst income from sports sponsorship has increased, giving the example of the Washington Redskins (now known as the Washington Commanders) in the NFL, which more than doubled their annual revenues within five years. This included sponsorship deals with Anheuser-Busch and PepsiCo. Walsh and Giulianotti do touch on gambling, but only in terms of how the increased revenues in cricket have led to match-fixing, such as in the case of Hanse Cronje, the former South African cricket captain, who took money from Indian bookmakers. They were of course writing before gambling marketing exploded into sport, and football in particular (Bunn et al. 2018), and before it was widely appreciated that gambling marketing had the capacity to harm as well as to normalise gambling amongst children and adolescents (Monaghan et al. 2008). Sadly, the NFL in North America now seems to be taking the same path as the EPL, with many teams developing commercial partnerships with gambling brands (Levant 2022).

As Walsh and Giulianotti suggested, corporate sponsorship will continue without some kind of state intervention, and "advertisers will continue to dictate the shape and structure of sport" (2007 p.17). However, whilst some levels of commercialisation are acknowledged and generally accepted, there are areas of sport which should be protected from commercialisation and constrained by regulation.

Complex problems

Every industry claims that it operates in a complex and challenging environment and this is often used as an excuse to avoid regulation. Petticrew *et al.* (2017) referenced the tobacco industry when examining the tactics of the food, beverage, alcohol and gambling industries in using the concept of complexity to undermine effective public health policies. Unhealthy commodity industries argue that the aetiology of NCDs is too complex to allow individual products to be blamed and that policy interventions cannot be effective in addressing complex problems.

It is clear that any attempt to address unhealthy sponsorship and marketing will be aggressively opposed by the commercial interests that it would most affect. The review of the 2005 Gambling Act in the UK-led campaigners, such as the charity Gambling With Lives, to call for reforms particularly around industry advertising. The response of the chief executive of the Betting and Gaming Council (BGC) was aggressive, suggesting that critics were "prohibitionists" and that working-class gamblers would not welcome state interference in personal freedoms (Orme-Claye 2022). This language is strongly resonant of that used by the tobacco industry to oppose tobacco control interventions (Cohen *et al.* 2000). Similarly, the BGC suggested that controls on legitimate gambling would simply send gamblers off to the unregulated black market (Gibbs 2022). Once again, this argument about illicit products was used by the tobacco industry against regulation such as the introduction of plain packaging for tobacco products (Brandt 2007) and, even now, against plans to protect future generations from smoking in New Zealand (Neilson 2021).

Options for regulation

Bruyninckx (2012) argued that historically the world of sport and the world of government have been perceived as separate, and he characterised the sports administrator as having an obsession with the rules and regulation of their sport, whilst having an aversion to being ruled and regulated (e.g., by the government). As the amounts of money get higher, so do the stakes, and issues around independent regulation are raised regularly, from the Indian Premier League (Sekhri 2016) to the ongoing discussions around ownership in the English Premier League which has resulted in the publication of a fan-led review of football governance (DCMS 2021). Whilst the latter does consider the financing of British football, there is no mention of commercial sponsorship and, indeed, the report recommends a relaxation of the Sporting Events (Control of Alcohol, etc.) Act 1985 which prohibits the sale of alcohol in sight of the pitch, in the interests of bringing more income into the game.

In 2015, the Cabinet Office in the United Kingdom published *Sporting Futures* (HM Government 2015). In the section entitled 'Supporting a more productive, sustainable and responsible sport sector' on page 54, there is a statement:

> Sponsorship is an area where a number of sports, and individual clubs, have adopted a responsible approach, for example around sponsorship by companies marketing alcohol or high fat sugar and salt (HFSS) foods. We will continue to discuss with sports the scope for voluntary agreements in this area.

This was followed in 2017 by a "set of principles for sports bodies to consider when entering into relationships that relate to HFSS products". These principles were set out in Sport England's wider guidance to sports bodies on commercial sponsorship in May 2017 (Sport England 2017).[1] Under 'Sponsorship from high fat salt and sugar products', it is noted that sports bodies enter into commercial partnerships and sponsorship arrangements to enable them to find the funding to make more physical activity opportunities available in return for the marketing of food and drink products which are high in fat, salt and sugar (HFSS). Sport England advised that these products might be checked against the UK government's Nutrient Profile Model (Department of Health and Social Care 2011). However, in this document, Sport England avoided the obvious contradiction between the promotion of physical activity opportunities (often to counteract obesity) and the marketing of 'junk' food. In Chapter 7, I noted UK charity Street Games' relationship with Coca-Cola. This is by no means unusual. Indeed, Sport England provides a ready-made excuse in its toolkit: "This is an essential source of income into sport especially at a time when funding from central and local government sources is under pressure". No mention here of the accompanying pressure on the health services caused by rising levels of obesity and type 2 diabetes. And the document is indicative of the standard framing of sport as being able to make its own 'responsible' agreements.

It seems entirely inappropriate that unhealthy brands are being promoted through sport and are benefiting from an association with its rich cultural capital, and the 'health halo' it provides. It is possible that the sheer incongruence and inauthenticity of linking a healthy activity with an unhealthy brand (such as an 'energy' drink) may make this type of sponsorship unacceptable if it is challenged sufficiently either by sports fans or by the general public (Cornwell 2020).

Individual papers and public health advocates have called for regulation of gambling advertising in sport (Bunn *et al.* 2018; Purves *et al.* 2020), of alcohol marketing at football matches (Purves *et al.* 2017) and of sports sponsorship by unhealthy food brands (Bragg *et al.* 2018; Dixon *et al.* 2019). The impact of COVID-19 is likely to have a long-lasting effect on sport as in all other areas of society and may have provided an opportunity for wider reflection on public health. There is a strong case to be made for applying a health impact assessment to all forms of commercial sponsorship in sport to assess how they might affect population health. In 1983, the UK's Central Council of Physical Recreation (CCPR) launched a Committee of Inquiry into Sports Sponsorship (The Central Council of Physical Recreation 1983). It is surely time for inquiries such as these to consider the impact of sport sponsorship on health? The CCPR published its recommendations in terms of ethical considerations. It stated, "The Voluntary Agreement concluded between the government and the tobacco industry is the right way to regulate sponsorship of sport by tobacco interests" (1983 p.110). Its report considered sports sponsorship by the alcohol, tobacco and gambling industries and took the view that "what is lawful must also be presumed to come within the ambit of personal choice and freedom" (1983 p.93). The CCPR noted the tax revenue gained from alcohol, gambling and tobacco, but once again did not consider the health and social costs generated by these industries.

Sponsorship should not be separated from advertising in considering regulation that helps to protect children and young people from developing unhealthy habits, whether related to diet and alcohol or gambling. Sponsorship of sport reaches and is likely to influence large audiences including children and young people (Pitt *et al.* 2016, 2017; Newall *et al.* 2019) and reinforces gambling as a socially acceptable form of entertainment (Binde 2009; Buil *et al.* 2015). Exposure of gambling brands through sport encourages risky behaviour amongst young people, causing potential public health problems (Lamont *et al.* 2011).

Public policy has only just begun to consider the commercial determinants of health. Consideration of their application in sport is also recent and might be partly constrained by an individual compartmentalised industry approach (gambling, food and drink HFSS and alcohol), as it might have been previously in its approach to tobacco regulation (McCambridge and Morris 2019). Collin argued for policy coherence in addressing NCDs in moving beyond "tobacco exceptionalism" (Collin 2012 p.277). He proposed a governance model to address the regulation of corporate conduct in the tobacco industry but also partnerships with the food and alcohol industries. In considering corporate power, Hastings wrote, "The marketing campaigns of multi-national corporations are harming our physical and mental wellbeing" (2012 p.26). He urged the public health movement to take action. I would endorse this call and ask public health practitioners and advocates to consider more carefully the marketing of unhealthy commodities in sport at all levels, from grassroots to professional, and the impact this marketing may have on population health.

As with many other public health challenges, there is usually much to learn from the experience with the tobacco industry. As observed in this and earlier chapters, controls on the advertising of tobacco products in the 1960s and 1970s led tobacco companies to invest in sport to make up for lost advertising revenue (Dewhirst 2004). For example, sponsorship of Formula 1 motor racing was associated with tobacco advertising from 1968 and the industry continued with indirect marketing techniques even after the 2005 European Union Tobacco Advertising Directive (Grant-Braham and Britton 2011). As in motor racing, sport has shown its ability to generate alternative sources of income.

The World Health Organization is in an ideal position to lead global enquiry and advocacy into the impact of the marketing of unhealthy commodities in sport. In 2019, the WHO agreed a four-year collaboration with FIFA to "promote healthy lifestyles through football globally" (World Health Organization 2019). Whilst the policy of ensuring tobacco-free stadiums at FIFA events is to be commended, this collaboration seems to ignore the fact that FIFA's partners and sponsors for the World Cup in Qatar include Coca-Cola, Budweiser and McDonald's (FIFA 2021). It would seem to be impossible to claim that the World Cup is promoting "healthy lifestyles" whilst the competition is being used to market sugary drinks, beer and HFSS food and beverages (as described more fully in Chapter 5).

It is difficult to make overarching recommendations, as these are complex issues. But rather than ducking them, my initial recommendation would be to take sport more seriously. If we accept its positive force for the economy, so we should also consider the impact it can have on health, both positive and negative. Sport certainly gets a free ride from the market checks that periodically have to be made in the interests of population health. The recommendations below are likely to engender as much discussion as solutions, but that is fine. Too often sponsorship is simply accepted as a necessary commercial evil for sport and not questioned.

Recommendations for sports' governing bodies

- *Further attention should be given to finding alternative sources of income in professional and amateur sport.*
- *Establishing an ethical framework for sponsorship should be considered as part of any overview of sport's governance.*
- *Sports' governing bodies should not accept sponsorship from unhealthy commodity industries.*
- *Particular attention should be given to the funding of children's sport.*

Recommendations for governments

- *Governments should establish inquiries to consider the impact of sport sponsorship on health.*
- *Any reviews and policies designed to protect children from the advertising of unhealthy brands in broadcasting and online media should include sport sponsorship in their remit.*
- *Sport sponsorship from the gambling and alcohol industry should be banned, together with sponsorship that promotes the consumption of HFSS food and beverages.*

Recommendations for public health

- *Public health practitioners and advocates should challenge the commercial relationships and marketing agreements between unhealthy commodity industries and sports organisations at all levels.*
- *The World Health Organization should lead a public health inquiry into the impact of the marketing of unhealthy commodities in sport.*
- *The World Health Organization should review its relationship with FIFA.*

Recommendations for researchers

- *The effect of unhealthy sponsorship on consumption should be further examined.*
- *More studies should be undertaken to explore the views of sports fans on unhealthy sponsorship.*
- *All aspects of sport should be included in the above research – junior sport, women's as well as men's, disability sport and amateur sports.*
- *Trends in brand engagement, such as through the use of social media, should be monitored closely.*

Note

1 This guidance is no longer in the public domain and was obtained through a UK Freedom of Information request by the author.

References

Adams, A. (2019) 'Towards a framework for understanding who owns sport' in Adams, A., ed., *Who Owns Sport?* Abingdon: Routledge.
BBC News (2021) *Norwich City name Lotus Cars as New Shirt Sponsor*, available: https://www.bbc.co.uk/news/uk-england-norfolk-57617452 [accessed 25 March 2022].
Beard, B. (2020) 'Foreign ownership of premier league clubs', *Myfootballfacts.com*, 30 April 2020, available: https://www.myfootballfacts.com/2020/04/article-foreign-ownership-of-premier-league-clubs/ [accessed 1 October 2020].
Beltramini, R.F. (2003) 'Advertising ethics: The ultimate oxymoron?: JBE', *Journal of Business Ethics*, 48(3), 215–216, available: http://dx.doi.org/http://dx.doi.org/10.1023/B:BUSI.0000005847.39154.69.
Binde, P. (2009) 'Exploring the impact of gambling advertising: An interview study of problem gamblers', *International Journal of Mental health and Addiction*, 7(4), 541–549.
Bland, B. and Ahmed, M. (2018) 'Chinese investors take route one out of European football', *Financial Times*, 30 July 2018, available: https://www.ft.com/content/fb11b9c0-93c8-11e8-b67b-b8205561c3fe [accessed 22 October 2020].
Bourdieu, P. (1988) 'Program for a sociology of sport', *Sociology of Sport Journal*, 5, 153–161.
Bourdieu, P. (1999) 'The state, economics and sport' in Dauncey, H. and Hare, G., eds., *France and the 1998 World Cup. The National Impact of a World Sporting Event*, London: Frank Cass, 15–21.

Bragg, M.A., Roberto, C.A., Harris, J.L., Brownell, K.D. and Elbel, B. (2018) 'Marketing food and beverages to youth through sports', *Journal of Adolescent Health*, 62(1), 5–13.

Brandt, A.M. (2007) *The Cigarette Century*, New York: Basic Books.

Bruyninckx, H. (2012) 'Sports governance. Between the obsession with rules and regulation and the aversion to being ruled and regulated' in Segaert, B., Theeboom, M., Timmerman, C. and Vanreusel, B., eds., *Sports Governance, Development and Corporate Responsibility*, Abingdon: Routledge.

Buil, P., Moratilla, M.J.S. and Ruiz, P.G. (2015) 'Online gambling advertising regulations in Spain. A study on the protection of minors', *Adicciones*, 27(3), 198–204.

Bunn, C., Ireland, R., Minton, J., Holman, D., Philpott, M. and Chambers, S. (2018) 'Shirt sponsorship by gambling companies in the English and Scottish Premier Leagues: Global reach and public health concerns', *Soccer and Society*, 17 Jan 2018, available: http://dx.doi.org/17 Jan 2018.

Chanavat, N. and Bodet, G. (2020) 'Ethics within sponsorship' in Eagle, L., Dahl, S., De Pelsmacker, P. and Taylor, C. R., eds., *The SAGE Handbook of Marketing Ethics*, London: Sage, 444–456.

Cohen, J.E., Milio, N., Rozier, R.G., Ferrence, R., Ashley, M.J. and Goldstein, A.O. (2000) 'Political ideology and tobacco control', *Tobacco Control*, 9(3), 263–267, available: http://dx.doi.org/10.1136/tc.9.3.263.

Collin, J. (2012) 'Tobacco control, global health policy and development: Towards policy coherence in global governance', *Tobacco Control*, 21, 274–280.

Conn, D. (2022) 'Football ignored the truth about Roman Abramovich's oligarch money for too long', *The Guardian*, 10 March 2022, available: https://www.theguardian.com/football/2022/mar/10/football-ignored-the-truth-about-roman-abramovichs-oligarch-money-for-too-long [accessed 25 March 2022].

Cornwell, T.B. (1997) 'The use of sponsorship-linked marketing by tobacco firms: International public policy issues', *The Journal of Consumer Affairs*, 31(2), 239–254.

Cornwell, T.B. (2020) *Sponsorship in Marketing. Effective Partnerships in Sports, Arts and Events*, Second ed., Abingdon: Routledge.

Crawford, G. (2004) *Consuming Sport. Fans, Sport and Culture*, Abingdon: Routledge.

Crompton, J.L. (1993) 'Sponsorship of sport by tobacco and alcohol companies: A review of the issues', *Journal of Sport & Social Issues*, 73, 148–167.

DCMS (2021) *Fan-Led Review of Football Governance: Securing the Game's Future*, London, available: https://www.gov.uk/government/publications/fan-led-review-of-football-governance-securing-the-games-future/fan-led-review-of-football-governance-securing-the-games-future#chap9 [accessed 27 March 2022].

Department of Health and Social Care (2011) *The Nutrient Profiling Model*, London: UK Government, available: https://www.gov.uk/government/publications/the-nutrient-profiling-model [accessed 15 July 2022].

Dewhirst, T. (2004) 'Smoke and ashes: Tobacco sponsorship of sports and regulatory issues in Canada' in Kahle, L. R. and Riley, C., eds., *Sports Marketing and the Psychology of Marketing Communication*, Mahwah: Lawrence Erlbaum.

Dixon, H., Lee, A. and Scully, M. (2019) 'Sports sponsorship as a cause of obesity', *Current Obesity Reports*, 31 October 2019, 480–494.

Donaldson, A. and Nicholson, M. (2020) 'Attitudes of sports organisation members to junk food sponsorship', *Public Health*, 185, 212–217, available: http://dx.doi.org/https://doi.org/10.1016/j.puhe.2020.04.043.

Doward, J. (2021) 'Tobacco firms accused of using Formula One to flout ads ban on e-cigarettes', *The Observer*, 26 July 2021, available: https://www.theguardian.com/business/2019/may/11/formula-one-ferrari-mclaren-e-cigarette-advertising#:~:text=Britain's%20biggest%20tobacco%20firm%20and, they%20are%20banned%20from%20advertising [accessed 29 March 2022].

Eagle, L., Dahl, S., De Pelsmacker, P. and Taylor, C.R. (2021) 'Introduction to marketing ethics' in Eagle, L., Dahl, S., De Pelsmacker, P. and Taylor, C. R., eds., *The Sage Handbook of Marketing Ethics*, London: Sage, 3–19.

FIFA (2021) *FIFA World Cup Qatar 22. Partners and Sponsors*, available: https://www.fifa.com/worldcup/organisation/partners/ [accessed 27 April 2021].

Freudenberg, N. (2021) *At What Cost. Modern Capitalism and the Future of Health*, New York: Oxford University Press.

Gibbs, E. (2022) *Betting and Gaming Council Warns Against 'Naïve Changes' to UK Gambling Law*, available: https://www.casino.org/news/betting-and-gaming-council-warns-against-naive-changes-changes-to-uk-gambling-law/ [accessed 27 March 2022].

Giulianotti, R. and Robertson, R. (2009) *Globalization & Football*, London: SAGE.

Glantz, S.A., Barnes, D.E., Bero, L., Hanauer, P. and Slade, J. (1995) 'Looking through a keyhole at the tobacco industry: The Brown and Williamson documents', *JAMA*, 274(3), 219–224, available: http://dx.doi.org/10.1001/jama.1995.03530030039032.

Goldblatt, D. (2022) 'Abramovich is but one in a long list of tainted owners. Is there no end to sportswashing?', *The Guardian*, 13 March 2022, available: https://www.theguardian.com/commentisfree/2022/mar/13/still-believe-politics-football-dont-mix-tell-that-to-dictators-oligarchs [accessed 25 March 2022].

Grant-Braham, B. and Britton, J. (2011) 'Motor racing, tobacco company sponsorship, barcodes and alibi marketing', *Tobacco Control*, 21, 529–535.

Hastings, G. (2012) 'Why corporate power is a public health priority', *British Medical Journal*, 345(7871), 26–29.

HM Government (2015) *Sporting Future: A New Strategy for an Active Nation*. London, available: https://assets.publishing.service.gov.uk/government/uploads/system/uploads/attachment_data/file/486622/Sporting_Future_ACCESSIBLE.pdf [accessed 12 June 2020].

Ireland, R. (2021) *Commercial Determinants of Health in Sport. The Example of the English Premier League*, unpublished thesis (PhD), University of Glasgow.

ITV News (2020) *Premier League 'Project Restart': Everything You Need to Know*, available: https://www.itv.com/news/2020-06-16/premier-league-project-restart-everything-you-need-to-know [accessed 25 March 2022].

Jones, C., Pinder, R. and Robinson, G. (2020) 'Gambling sponsorship and advertising in British football: A critical account', *Sport, Ethics and Philosophy*, 14(2), 163–175.

Lamont, M., Hing, N. and Gainsbury, S. (2011) 'Gambling on sport sponsorship: A conceptual framework for research and regulatory review', *Sport Management Review*, 14, 246–257.

Levant, H. (2022) 'Upon further review: The NFL'S gambling strategy is a risk to public health and congress must act', *Gaming Law Review*, 26(2), 98–102, available: http://dx.doi.org/10.1089/glr2.2021.0040.

Lužar, K., Greenland, S. and Low, D. (2020) 'Ethical marketing of harmful products: Sugar, alcohol and tobacco' in Eagle, L., Dahl, S., De Pelsmacker, P. and Taylor, C. R., eds., *The SAGE Handbook of Marketing Ethics*, London: Sage, 339–354.

Marqusee, M. (2016) *Anyone But England: Cricket, Race and Class*, London: Bloomsbury Publishing.

McCambridge, J. and Morris, S. (2019) 'Comparing alcohol with tobacco indicates that it is time to move beyond tobacco exceptionalism', *European Journal of Public Health*, 29(2), 200–201.

McDaniel, S.R., Kinney, L. and Chalip, L. (2001) 'A cross-cultural investigation of the ethical dimensions of alcohol and tobacco sports sponsorships', *Teaching Business Ethics*, 5(3), 307–330.

McGee, D. (2020) 'On the normalisation of online sports gambling among young adult men in the UK: A public health perspective', *Public Health*, 184, 89–94, available: http://dx.doi.org/https://doi.org/10.1016/j.puhe.2020.04.018.

McVeigh, K. (2012) 'Susan G Komen's 'pinkwashing' problem a black mark on charity', *The Guardian*, 15 February 2012, available: https://www.theguardian.com/world/2012/feb/15/komen-pinkwashing-problem-planned-parenthood [accessed 29 March 2022].

Monaghan, S., Derevensky, J. and Sklar, A. (2008) 'Impact of gambling advertisements and marketing on children and adolescents: Policy recommendations to minimise harm', *Journal of Gambling Issues*, (22), 252–274.

Montague, J. (2018) *The Billionaires Club. The Unstoppable Rise of Football's Super-Rich Owners*, London: Bloomsbury.

Neilson, M. (2021) 'Fears smoking ban could lead to black market', *NZ Herald*, 9 December 2021, available: https://www.newstalkzb.co.nz/news/politics/smoking-ban-fears-smokefree-2025-legislation-could-lead-to-black-market/ [accessed 27 March 2022].

Nestle, M. (2015) *Soda Politics. Taking On Big Soda (and Winning)*, Oxford: Oxford University Press.

Newall, P.W.S., Moodie, C., Reith, G., Stead, M., Critchlow, N., Morgan, A. and Dobbie, F. (2019) 'Gambling marketing from 2014 to 2018: A Literature review', *Current Addiction Reports*, 6(2), 49–56, available: http://dx.doi.org/10.1007/s40429-019-00239-1.

Orme-Claye, T. (2022) *Michael Dugher: Ministers 'walking a tightrope' on Gambling Act Balancing*, available: https://sbcnews.co.uk/sportsbook/2022/01/04/michael-dugher-ministers-walking-a-tightrope-on-gambling-act-balancing/ [accessed 27 March 2022].

Parrish, R. (2011) 'Europe: The transformation of football' in Niemann, A., García, B. and Grant, W., eds., *The Transformation of European Football. Towards the Europeanisation of the National Game*, Manchester: Manchester University Press, 23–39.

Peloza, J. and Montford, W. (2015) 'The health halo: How good PR is misleading shoppers', *The Guardian*, 11 March 2015, available: https://www.theguardian.com/sustainable-business/2015/mar/11/know-what-you-eat-health-halo#:~:text=The%20health%20halo%20effect%20refers,the%20overconsumption%20of%20certain%20foods [accessed 25 March 2022].

Petticrew, M., Katikireddi, S.V., Knai, C., Cassidy, R., Hessari, N.M., Thomas, J. and Weishaar, H. (2017) 'Nothing can be done until everything is done: The use of complexity arguments by food, beverage, alcohol and gambling industries', *Journal of Epidemiology and Community Health*, 71, 1078–1083.

Pitt, H., Thomas, S.L., Bestman, A., Daube, M. and Derevensky, J. (2017) 'What do children observe and learn from televised sports betting advertisements? A qualitative study among Australian children', *Australian and New Zealand Journal of Public Health*, 41(6), 604–610, available: http://dx.doi.org/https://doi.org/10.1111/1753-6405.12728.

Pitt, H., Thomas, S.L., Bestman, A., Stoneham, M. and Daube, M. (2016) '"It's just everywhere!" Children and parents discuss the marketing of sports wagering in Australia', *Australian and New Zealand Journal of Public Health*, 40(5), 480–486, available: http://dx.doi.org/https://doi.org/10.1111/1753-6405.12564.

Purves, R.I., Critchlow, N., Morgan, A., Stead, M. and Dobbie, F. (2020) 'Examining the frequency and nature of gambling marketing in televised broadcasts of professional sporting events in the United Kingdom.', *Public Health*, 184, 71–78.

Purves, R.I., Critchlow, N., Stead, M., Adams, J. and Brown, K. (2017) 'Alcohol marketing during the UEFA EURO 2016 football tournament: A frequency analysis', *International Journal of Environmental Research and Public Health*, 14(704), available: http://dx.doi.org/10.3390/ijerph14070704.

Robinson, J. and Clegg, J. (2019) *The Club. How the Premier League Became the Richest, Most Disruptive Business in Sport*, London: John Murray.

Sasson, T. (2016) 'Milking the third world? Humanitarianism, capitalism, and the moral economy of the Nestlé Boycott', *The American Historical Review*, 121(4), 1196–1224, available: http://dx.doi.org/10.1093/ahr/121.4.1196.

Sekhri, D.G. (2016) *Not Out! The Incredible Story of The Indian Premier League*, Gurgaon: Penguin UK.

Skysports (2021) *Coronavirus: MPs Report Links Cheltenham Festival and Liverpool Champions League tie to 78 Deaths*, available: https://www.skysports.com/football/news/11669/12432371/coronavirus-mps-report-links-cheltenham-festival-and-liverpool-champions-league-tie-to-78-deaths [accessed 25 March 2022].

Sport England (2017) *Sponsorship Toolkit*. No longer available. Personal copy obtained by author after Freedom of Information request.

Szymanski, S. and Kuypers, T. (1999) *Winners and Losers. The Business Strategy of Football*, London: Viking.

The Central Council of Physical Recreation (1983) *Committee of Enquiry into Sports Sponsorship. "The Howell Report"*, London: The Central Council of Physical Recreation.

Vamplew, W. (2021) *Games People Played. A Global History of Sport*, London: Reaktion Books.

Walsh, A. and Giulianotti, R. (2007) *Ethics, Money and Sport. This Sporting Mammon*, Abingdon: Routledge.

World Health Organization (2019) *WHO and FIFA Team Up For Health* [Press Release], available: https://healthpolicy-watch.news/who-and-fifa-team-up-for-health/ [accessed 22 March 2021].

World Health Organization (2021) *Tobacco*, available: https://www.who.int/news-room/fact-sheets/detail/tobacco [accessed 29 March 2022].

Wynne, C. (2019) 'Politics, policy and the ownership of sport' in Adams, A. and Robinson, L., eds., *Who Owns Sport?*, Abingdon: Routledge, 59–69.

Chapter 10

Conclusions and discussion

This concluding chapter begins by considering how sport and public health were treated during the coronavirus pandemic and goes on to consider whether there are alternatives to unhealthy sports sponsorship.

This book was mainly written during the COVID-19 pandemic when articles from different disciplines and perspectives were considering the future of various sports and the impacts and challenges for the future (Evans *et al.* 2020; Edgar 2021; Skinner and Smith 2021; Parnell *et al.* 2022). Many of these papers took a health protection stance in discussing how sport could reduce the risks of contracting the virus for athletes and spectators (McCloskey *et al.* 2020). When some sports started to appear once again on our screens, though fans were not allowed into stadiums, academics and journalists alike questioned the place of sports such as football in society without the physical presence of spectators (Liew 2020; Bond *et al.* 2022).

At the bottom line for many during the pandemic was the binary choice offered by many politicians of health versus wealth. In other words, should lockdowns be permitted with the accompanying jolt to the economy in order to protect people from contracting the virus? A report published in the United Kingdom (Aked *et al.* 2021) argued that this was a false dichotomy and that economies should prioritise public health as a valuable social asset. The economic policies implemented in the United Kingdom and many other Western countries prior to the pandemic were linked to austerity measures and helped to increase social inequalities (Schrecker and Bambra 2015).

Rather than promoting health in any way, it was clear that many sports prioritised the needs of their sponsors during lockdown in the United Kingdom in 2021. As briefly mentioned in Chapter 8, in the football match between Newcastle United and Wolverhampton Wanderers played in the English Premier League on 27 February 2021, there were 716 gambling brand exposures alone, more than six logos per minute. With the stands empty (although the sounds of the absent spectators were simulated), Newcastle United used every space imaginable to display the brands of the gambling companies FUN88 and Bet365, two of its sponsors (Ireland and Bunn 2021). When some football fans were permitted to return in May 2021, Tottenham Hotspur placed them in the upper tier of the stands to keep sponsorship banners (including those for BetWay and Cadbury) next to the pitch and in view of television cameras (Nagle 2021). Indeed, this behaviour was not unique to sport; transnational corporations undermined public health messages during the pandemic by aggressively marketing ultra-processed food and drinks (Global Health Advocacy Incubator 2020), even whilst concerns were raised about growing levels of overweight and obesity (Noguchi 2021; Beaumont 2022) and the links between this and risks from COVID (Kwok *et al.* 2020; Sanchis-Gomar *et al.* 2020).

This practice of colonising every available sporting space with brand logos has developed at an alarming pace over the past 50 years. As we have seen, the idea of a sports consumer is not new. We have consumed sport ever since we first paid to enter grounds and go pitchside at the end of the nineteenth century. But the scale of hyper-commodification since the Los Angeles Olympics of 1984 (Payne 2006), the launch of the English Premier League in 1992 (Elliott 2017), the Football World Cup in Los Angeles in 1994 (Evans 2022; Tennent and Gillett 2022) and the Indian Premier League in 2007 (Sekhri 2016) has been staggering. Coronavirus has allowed some of the few remaining commercial barriers to be overcome. The International Cricket Council only permitted Test cricket shirt sponsorships in 2020 during the pandemic (Bassam 2020). The brands remain on the cricketers' shirts in 2022.

This book has shown how the development of sports sponsorship was led by the tobacco, alcohol and sugary drinks companies. In the twenty-first century, they have been joined by gambling, 'energy' drink and 'junk food' corporations. As has been illustrated, these transnationals are adept at avoiding national laws in promoting their brands. They are assisted in doing so by their huge financial assets. Companies such as Coca-Cola, AB InBev (including Budweiser) and Mondelez International (the owners of Cadbury) have annual turnovers that dwarf some countries' GDP. Coca-Cola's net operating revenues were reported as US$38.66 billion in 2021 (Ridder 2022), AB InBev's at US$54.3 billion (AB InBev 2022) and Mondelez International's as US$28.7 billion (Mondelez International 2022). Whilst the gambling industry is a small player in comparison to these behemoths, it is growing at an alarming rate. Flutter Entertainment (Rogan 2021), the owner of Paddy Power, SportsBet, Betfair and Fox Bet, declared revenue of £2.1 billion in 2021 and has aspirations to grow globally (Flutter Entertainment 2022).

All these corporations colonise our sporting worlds, with their brands displayed on our televisions, our computer screens, in sporting arenas, on our smartphones and on bus shelters and in supermarkets. They have developed skills of brand engagement to accompany the opportunities for consumption that digital technology has permitted, with the gambling industry being an exemplar of the cynical exploitation of these technologies (Cassidy 2020; Davies 2022). Companies want their brands and products to be associated with sport's excitement and passion. They want to be in front of young fans to promote consumption and to increase their net operating revenues. They use the language of personal responsibility, "drink responsibly", "snack right" and "when the fun stops, stop", whilst encouraging fans to consume more. There's always an advertisement to order a pizza for half-time, to buy a chocolate bar at the supermarket, to place a bet when the match gets exciting and to celebrate when your team has won (or drown your sorrows when it loses). It never ends.

In Chapter 2, I introduced the concept of the commercial determinants of health, and how the practices of transnational corporations have the potential to impact (usually negatively) on population health. This book has focused on the marketing practices of these corporations within sport. The previous chapter considered regulatory approaches to these marketing practices. Regulatory approaches are generally about controlling marketing, but is there also an argument for altering markets and improving health (Liber 2022)? Indeed, are there healthier options to unhealthy sponsorship? In the last chapter, the UK's Committee of Inquiry Into Sports Sponsorship (The Central Council of Physical Recreation 1983) was mentioned, introduced in the 1980s when there were already concerns about the increasing amounts of sponsorship coming into UK sport (much of it from the tobacco industry). At the same time, David Player of the then Health Education Council wrote a paper entitled, 'Health Promotion Through Sponsorship: The State of the Art' (1986). Player neatly summed up the rewards of sponsorship in a piece which is still resonant today: value for money; increased awareness of logo, name, company colours etc.; association of product with an attractive sport or lifestyle; improvement in public image; a way of circumventing the law (1986 pp.18–19). He went on to argue that we should use sponsorship to promote healthy activities and to encourage greater participation in physical activity. He gave three examples: cycling events, fun runs and football promotions. For example, in 1982, Scotland's World Cup team was officially a 'non-smoking team' (NHS Scotland 2022). The team was sponsored by the Scottish Health Education Group to enhance the image of non-smoking. The sponsorship was supported by merchandise, work with primary schools and involved the funding of football training and competitions for girls and boys (Player 1986).

There are few positive contemporary examples of public health funding or funding by healthy industries for sport, possibly because health budgets are even more squeezed than in the 1980s. Whilst English netball was being sponsored by Jaffa Fruit in 2018 (England Netball 2018), Australian netball was considering gambling industry sponsorship in 2022 (Australian Associated Press 2022). Some events have adopted an ethical sponsorship approach, such as the ParkRun running movement (Hindley 2022), which organises free, timed, five-kilometre events in 22 countries (ParkRun 2022) whilst promoting healthy exercise across communities (Stevinson and Hickson 2013). In the Netherlands, an organisation called JOGG-Teamfit (www.jogg-teamfit.nl/sport) works to help make both sports locations and events healthier. A systematic review of sports sponsorship for public health and social marketing published in 2018 (Kubacki et al. 2018) found only 17 examples, of which all but two were in Australia. The Australian examples involved the health agencies VicHealth (in Victoria) and Healthway (Western Australia) and provided examples of initiatives such as holiday football clinics (Corti et al. 1997) aimed at harder to reach communities, but these are now quite dated. The Healthy Stadia movement has also used sport to "promote the health of visitors, fans, players, employees and the surrounding community" (Parnell *et al.* 2017)

It is evident that whilst there is considerable debate about "sportswashing" (Ronay 2019; Dooley 2022), the use of sport to improve tarnished national reputations (by no means a new phenomenon (Ellis 2020)), there has been very little thus far about the impact of unhealthy sport sponsorship on public health. In *Greenwashing Sport* (Miller 2017), Miller argued that professional sports promoted their green credentials and yet were responsible for significant carbon footprints through travel, media coverage (including electricity usage) and event construction. Questions about sustainability and the impact on climate change are now levelled at both the Olympics (Darcy and Taylor 2013) and the FIFA World Cup (Orr *et al.* 2022). As argued in this book, Coca-Cola's nearly 100-year-long association with sport, in order to promote its sugary drinks, has encouraged increased consumption, contributing both to obesity and tooth decay. At the same time, the corporation was reported as producing a huge plastic pollution footprint, calculated at 200,000 tonnes of plastic waste, or about 8 billion bottles, per year (Sandra 2020). Similarly, alcohol has a large environmental footprint. For example, one bottle of beer uses 148 litres of water in its manufacture (Hamilton 2021). And whilst transnational corporations such as AB InBev use sport to target young people, in particular, the most recent Global Burden of Diseases study shows that alcohol carries significant health risks and no benefits for young people (Gregory 2022).

There is certainly a need for new research into unhealthy sports sponsorship across various disciplines and interests (Lamont *et al.* 2011; Dixon *et al.* 2019; Gokani *et al.* 2021). In the introduction to this book, I noted that it had taken a long time for academics to address sport seriously. It seems to be taking even longer for public health to consider the use of sport to promote unhealthy consumption. If people are (rightly) concerned about the human rights records of Qatar or China, or the environmental practices of Shell or BP, surely they should also be concerned about the activities of Red Bull, Budweiser, Bet365 or Cadbury in sport? Is this 'healthwashing'? In other words, a way of using the positive health associations of sport, and its accompanying excitement and passion, to promote the opposite, that is, unhealthy consumption?

References

AB InBev (2022) *AB InBev Annual Report 2021*, available: https://www.ab-inbev.com/assets/pdfs/AB%20InBev_FY_European_financials_statements_FINAL.pdf [accessed 12 July 2022].

Aked, H., Bridger, E., Carter, D.J., Mehta, S., Sharman, M., Talwar, H., Thoburn, M. and Uthayakumar-Cumarasamy (2021) *Health versus Wealth? UK Economic Policy and Public Health during COVID-19*, London, available: https://www.medact.org/2021/resources/briefings/health-versus-wealth-uk-economic-policy-and-public-health-during-covid-19/ [accessed 11 July 2022].

Australian Associated Press (2022) 'Netball Australia could turn to gambling cash to solve financial woes', *The Guardian*, 17 June 2022, available: https://www.theguardian.com/sport/2022/jun/17/netball-australia-could-turn-to-gambling-cash-to-solve-financial-woes#:~:text=Netball%20Australia%20could%20turn%20to%20gambling%20cash%20to%20solve%20financial%20woes, -CEO%20says%20accepting&text=Netball%20Australia%20says%20it%20is, bid%20to%20generate%20more%20revenue [accessed 12 July 2022].

Bassam, T. (2020) *Test Cricket Shirt Sponsorships Approved by ICC*, available: https://www.sportspromedia.com/news/test-cricket-shirt-sponsorships-icc/ [accessed 12 July 2022].

Beaumont (2022) *Has the Pandemic Affected Obesity Rates?*, available: https://www.beaumont.org/health-wellness/blogs/has-the-pandemic-affected-obesity-rates [accessed 13 July 2022].

Bond, A.J., Cockayne, D., Ludvigsen, J.A.L., Maguire, K., Parnell, D., Plumley, D., Widdop, P. and Wilson, R. (2022) 'COVID-19: The return of football fans', *Managing Sport and Leisure*, 27(1–2), 108–118, available: http://dx.doi.org/10.1080/23750472.2020.1841449.

Cassidy, R. (2020) *Vicious Games. Capitalism and Gambling*, London: Pluto Press.

Corti, B., Donovan, R.J., J. Holman, C.D.A., Coten, N. and Jones, S.J. (1997) 'Using sponsorship to promote health messages to children', *Health Education & Behavior*, 24(3), 276–286.

Darcy, S. and Taylor, T. (2013) 'Managing Olympic venues' in Frawley, S. and Adair, D., eds., *Managing the Olympics*, Basingstoke: Palgrave Macmillan, 99–126.

Davies, R. (2022) *Jackpot. How Gambling Conquered Britain*, London: Guardian Faber.

Dixon, H., Lee, A. and Scully, M. (2019) 'Sports sponsorship as a cause of obesity', *Current Obesity Reports*, 8(4), 480–494.

Dooley, B. (2022) *Sportswashing: The 2022 Beijing Olympics*, available: https://sk.sagepub.com/cases/sportswashing-the-2022-beijing-olympics [accessed 2022/07/13].

Edgar, A. (2021) 'Sport and Covid-19', *Sport, Ethics and Philosophy*, 15(1), 1–2, available: http://dx.doi.org/10.1080/17511321.2021.1862478.

Elliott, R. ed. (2017) *The English Premier League. A Socio-Cultural Analysis*, Abingdon: Routledge.

Ellis, J. (2020) *Sportswashing and Atrocity: The 1978 FIFA World Cup*, available: https://yetagainuk.com/sportswashing-and-atrocity-the-1978-fifa-world-cup/ [accessed 13 July 2022].

England Netball (2018) *Juicy New Partnership with Jaffa Fruit* [press release], available: https://www.englandnetball.co.uk/jaffafruitpartnership/ [accessed 12 July 2022].

Evans, A.B., Blackwell, J., Dolan, P., Fahlén, J., Hoekman, R., Lenneis, V., McNarry, G., Smith, M. and Wilcock, L. (2020) 'Sport in the face of the COVID-19 pandemic: Towards an agenda for research in the sociology of sport', *European Journal for Sport and Society*, 17(2), 85–95, available: http://dx.doi.org/10.1080/16138171.2020.1765100.

Evans, M. (2022) *USA 94. The World Cup that Changed the Game*, Chichester: Pitch Publishing.

Flutter Entertainment (2022) *Flutter Entertainment plc Annual Report & Accounts 2021*, available: https://www.flutter.com/media/dvvn0ith/flutter-entertainment-plc-annual-report-2021.pdf [accessed 12 July 2022].

Global Health Advocacy Incubator (2020) *Facing Two Pandemics. How Big Food Undermined Public Health in the Era of COVID-19*, available: https://advocacyincubator.org/wp-content/uploads/2020/11/GHAI-Facing-Two-Pandemics-Report-November-2020.pdf [accessed 10 February 2022].

Gokani, N., Garde, A., Philpott, M., Ireland, R., Owens, R. and Boyland, E. (2021) 'UK Nutrition Research Partnership 'Hot Topic' workshop report: A 'game changer' for dietary health – addressing the implications of sport sponsorship by food businesses through an innovative interdisciplinary collaboration', *Nutrition Bulletin*, n/a(n/a), available: http://dx.doi.org/https://doi.org/10.1111/nbu.12535.

Gregory, A. (2022) 'Alcohol is never good for people under 40, global study finds', *The Guardian*, 14 July 2022, available: https://www.theguardian.com/society/2022/jul/14/alcohol-is-never-good-for-people-under-40-global-study-finds?CMP=Share_iOSApp_Other [accessed 16 July 2022].

Hamilton, I. (2021) 'It's not just a bad hangover – this is how alcohol affects the environment', *The Independent*, 5 March 2021, available: https://www.independent.co.uk/climate-change/opinion/alcohol-climate-crisis-environment-b1812946.html [accessed 16 July 2022].

Hindley, D. (2022) *Parkrun: An Organised Running Revolution*, Abingdon: Routledge.

Ireland, R. and Bunn, C. (2021) 'Euro 2020: Football's promotion of unhealthy consumption must end', *The Conversation*, 14 June 2021, available: https://theconversation.com/euro-2020-footballs-promotion-of-unhealthy-consumption-must-end-162552 [accessed 22 June 2021].

Kubacki, K., Hurley, E. and Rundle-Thiele, S.R. (2018) 'A systematic review of sports sponsorship for public health and social marketing', *Journal of Social Marketing*, 8(1), 24–39, available: http://dx.doi.org/10.1108/JSOCM-01-2017-0001.

Kwok, S., Adam, S., Ho, J.H., Iqbal, Z., Turkington, P., Razvi, S., Le Roux, C.W., Soran, H. and Syed, A.A. (2020) 'Obesity: A critical risk factor in the COVID-19 pandemic', *Clinical Obesity*, 10(6), e12403, available: http://dx.doi.org/10.1111/cob.12403.

Lamont, M., Hing, N. and Gainsbury, S. (2011) 'Gambling on sport sponsorship: A conceptual framework for research and regulatory review', *Sport Management Review*, 14, 246–257.

Liber, A.C. (2022) 'Using regulatory stances to see all the commercial determinants of health', *The Milbank Quarterly*. ISSN: 0887-378X.

Liew, J. (2020) 'Fans without football have been left staring into a howling void', *The Guardian*, available: https://www.theguardian.com/football/2020/nov/02/fans-without-football-have-been-left-staring-into-a-howling-void [accessed 11 July 2022].

McCloskey, B., Zumla, A., Ippolito, G., Blumberg, L., Arbon, P., Cicero, A., Endericks, T., Lim, P.L. and Borodina, M. (2020) 'Mass gathering events and reducing further global spread of COVID-19: A political and public health dilemma', *The Lancet*, 395(10230), 1096–1099.

Miller, T. (2017) *Greenwashing Sport*, Abingdon: Routledge.

Mondelez International (2022) *Mondelez International 2021 Annual Report*, available: https://www.mondelezinternational.com/-/media/Mondelez/PDFs/MONDELEZ-INTERNATIONAL-INC_10K_2021.pdf [accessed 12 July 2022].

Nagle, B. (2021) 'Tottenham fans fume at Daniel Levy and owners ENIC for putting returning fans in the upper tier in order to keep sponsorship banners next to pitch... while charging them £60 for the privilege - the most expensive of any team in the Premier League', *Mail Online*, 20 May 2021, available: https://www.dailymail.co.uk/sport/football/article-9599565/Tottenham-fans-SLAM-Daniel-Levy-owners-ENIC-decision-returning-fans-upper-tier.html [accessed 11 July 2022].

NHS Scotland (2022) *Historical Facts*, available: http://www.ournhsscotland.com/65-years/65-facts/historical-facts [accessed 12 July 2022].

Noguchi, Y. (2021) *Obesity Rates Rise During Pandemic, Fueled By Stress, Job Loss, Sedentary Lifestyle*, available: https://www.npr.org/sections/health-shots/2021/09/29/1041515129/obesity-rates-rise-during-pandemic-fueled-by-stress-job-loss-sedentary-lifestyle?t=1657697468216 [accessed 13 July 2022].

Orr, M., Murfree, J.R., Anahory, A. and Edwabne, R.E. (2022) 'Environment and sustainability in FIFA World Cups' in Chadwick, S., Widdop, P., Anagnostopoulos, C. and Parnell, D., eds., *The Business of the FIFA World Cup*, Abingdon: Routledge, 106–118.

ParkRun (2022) *Countries*, available: https://www.parkrun.com/countries/ [accessed 12 July 2022].

Parnell, D., Curran, K. and Philpott, M. (2017) 'Healthy stadia: An insight from policy to practice', *Sport in Society*, 20(2), 181–186, available: http://dx.doi.org/10.1080/17430437.2016.1173914.

Parnell, D., Widdop, P., Bond, A. and Wilson, R. (2022) 'COVID-19, networks and sport', *Managing Sport and Leisure*, 27(1–2), 78–84, available: http://dx.doi.org/10.1080/23750472.2020.1750100.

Payne, M. (2012) *Olympic Turnaround: How the Olympic Games stepped Back from the Brink of Extinction to Become the World's Best Known Brand*, Oxford: Infinite Ideas.

Player, D. (1986) 'Health promotion through sponsorship: The state of the art' in S, L. D., Hastings, G. B., O'Reilly, K. M. and Davies, J. K., eds., *Health Education and the Media II*, Oxford: Pergamon Press, 17–22.

Ridder, M. (2022) *The Coca-Cola Company's Net Operating Revenues Worldwide from 2007 to 2021*, Statista, available: https://www.statista.com/statistics/233371/net-operating-revenues-of-the-coca-cola-company-worldwide/ [accessed 12 July 2022].

Rogan, A. (2021) *Punters. How Paddy Power Bet Billions and Changed Gambling Forever*, Dublin: HarperCollins.

Ronay, B. (2019) 'Sportswashing and the tangled web of Europe's biggest clubs', *The Guardian*, 15 February 2019, available: https://www.theguardian.com/football/2019/feb/15/sportswashing-europes-biggest-clubs-champions-league-owners-sponsors-uefa [accessed 19 August 2020].

Sanchis-Gomar, F., Lavie, C.J., Mehra, M.R., Henry, B.M. and Lippi, G. (2020) 'Obesity and outcomes in COVID-19: When an epidemic and pandemic collide', *Mayo Clinic Proceedings*, 95(7), 1445–1453, available: http://dx.doi.org/https://doi.org/10.1016/j.mayocp.2020.05.006.

Sandra, L. (2020) 'Report reveals 'massive plastic pollution footprint' of drinks firms', *The Guardian*, 31 March 2020, available: https://www.theguardian.com/environment/2020/mar/31/report-reveals-massive-plastic-pollution-footprint-of-drinks-firms#:~:text=-Coca%2DCola%20creates%20the%20biggest, 33%20football%20pitches%20every%20day [accessed 16 July 2022].

Schrecker, T. and Bambra, C. (2015) *How Politics Makes Us Sick: Neoliberal Epidemics*. London: Palgrave Macmillan.

Sekhri, D.G. (2016) *Not Out!: The Incredible Story of The Indian Premier League*, Gurgaon: Penguin UK.

Skinner, J. and Smith, A.C.T. (2021) 'Introduction: Sport and COVID-19: Impacts and challenges for the future (Volume 1)', *European Sport Management Quarterly*, 21(3), 323–332, available: http://dx.doi.org/10.1080/16184742.2021.1925725.

Stevinson, C. and Hickson, M. (2013) 'Exploring the public health potential of a mass community participation event', *Journal of Public Health*, 36(2), 268–274, available: http://dx.doi.org/10.1093/pubmed/fdt082.

Tennent, K.D. and Gillett, A. (2022) 'A brief history of the FIFA World Cup as a business' in Chadwick, S., Widdop, P., Anagnostopoulos, C. and Parnell, D., eds., *The Business of the FIFA World Cup*. Abingdon: Routledge, 5–27.

The Central Council of Physical Recreation (1983) *Committee of Enquiry into Sports Sponsorship. "The Howell Report"*, London: The Central Council of Physical Recreation.

Index

Note: **Bold** page numbers refer to tables and *italic* page numbers refer to figures.

AB InBev (Anheuser Busch) 5, 24, 66, 68, 81, 118, 145, 147
Adorno, T. 75, 78, 80
advertising: brands and 26; ethics 131–133; LED pitchside 26; perimeter 27–28, 30; of tobacco 31, 40–42, 137; *see also* marketing; sponsorship
affect transfer 114
AFL *see* Australian Football League (AFL)
alcohol 8, 10–12; business 24; industry 11–12, 24, 29, 42, 58, 81, 137; marketing 116, 136
Ali, M. 86
Allen, L. N. 45
Anderson, B. 96
Anheuser Busch, A. Jr. 24, 66
Anheuser-Busch brewery 24, 57, 81, 112, 134
Archetti, E. P. 81
Armstrong, G. 81
Australian Football League (AFL) 26, 31–33, 85, 100, 115
Australian Rules football 30–33, 104, 115

Baimbridge, M. 95
Barney, R. K. 65
baseball 22, 24, 40–42, 104, 134
BAT *see* British American Tobacco (BAT)
Bayern Munich 42, 131
Beck, D. 79
Benson and Hedges 41–42, 64, 84, 94
Best, G. 94
Bet365 62, 119, 132, 144, 147

betting 23, 24, 83, 100–102, 119–120
Betting and Gaming Council (BGC) 135
Big Bash League 85–86
Big Step 9, 120
Birley, D. 83
Board of Control for Cricket in India (BCCI) 86
Bosshart, L. 79
Bourdieu, P. 57, 76–78, 80, 82, 87, 105, 134
Bovril 23
Boykoff, J. 66–67
brands: activation 66, 104, 113–114; congruence (coherence) 26, 27; engagement 32, 34, 112–123, 139, 145; unhealthy 1–3, 8, 10–12, 29, 34, 42, 58–59, 130–132, 134, 136
Brandt, A. M. 41, 44–46, 132
Brazil 29, 56, 58, 67
"bread and circuses" 67
British American Tobacco (BAT) 44, 47, 132
British Code of Advertising Practice (BCAP) 101
British football 2, 5, 22–24, 41, 76, 78, 93–96, 119–120, 133–135
Broadcasters' Audience Research Board (BARB) 59
Browne, D. 122
Brundage, A. 64
Bruyninckx, H. 135
BSkyB 78–79, 95–96
Bud Bowl 24

Budweiser 4, 9, 57–59, 62, 65–66, 79, 81, 96, 118, 138, 145, 147
Bunn, C. 98–99
Burstyn, V. 81

Cadbury 103–106, 145
Cadbury, J. 103
Camel brand 57
capital 76
Carrigan, J. 29
Carrigan, M. 29
Cashmore, E. 3
Castells, M. 78, 98
CDOH *see* commercial determinants of health (CDOH)
Central Council of Physical Recreation (CCPR) 137
Chanavat, N. 27
Charlton, B. 94
Chevrolet 29, 97–98
Chidgey, R. 118
China 3, 29, 32, 58, 59, 61, 66, 100, 147
cigarettes 4, 26, 40–48, 57, 61, 63–64, 94, 104, 113, 120, 131–132; *see also* smoking
Circus Maximus 62, 67
Clapson, M. 24
club shirt sponsorships 98–100, 99
Coca-Cola 5, 8, 12–15, 32, 41, 54, 56–57, 59, 61–68, 79, 85, 96, 101–103, 112, 118, 136, 138, 145, 147
Collin, J. 12, 43, 137
Collins, T. 22, 77–78, 83
commercial determinants of health (CDOH) 2, 8–15, 9, 53, 77, 137, 146
commercialisation 30–33, 53, 57, 60, 64–65, 77–78, 82–83
commercial origins 22–26
Commission on the Social Determinants of Health (CSDH) 7
commodification 1, 4–5, 60, 62, 64, 68, 77–78, 80, 82–87, 95, 118, 134, 145
Confederación Sudamericana de Fútbol (CONMEBOL) 56
Conn, D. 67
consumption 66, 78–80
Coolidge, C. 44
Cornwell, T. B. 102, 132

corporate social responsibility (CSR) 102–103, 105, 132
Coubertin, B. P. de 62
COVID-19 105, 136, 144, 145
Crawford, G. 80
cricket 23; commodification of 82–87; limited over 84, 85, 87
Cricket World Cup 84–85
Crompton, J. L. 10, 48
Cronje, H. 134
Crosbie, E. 12
CSDH *see* Commission on the Social Determinants of Health (CSDH)
CSR *see* corporate social responsibility (CSR)
cultural capital 76

darts 41, 94
Dassler, H. 57, 64–65, 84
Dees, W. 14
Deloitte Sports Business Group 98
Dick, Kerr Ladies F.C. 60
Dixon, K. 96
Durkheim, E. 80

Eagle, L. 131
Eastman Kodak 63
economic capital 76
Elias, N. 75–76, 82
Elsässer, F. 123
energy drinks 14–15, 45, 58, 120–122, 132, 136, 145
England 22–23, 25, 41, 59–61, 83, 85, 87, 93–95, 103–104
England and Wales Cricket Board (ECB) 87
English football *see* British football
English Premier League (EPL) 5, 12, 26–27, 28, 55–56, 78–80, 86–87, 94–98, 100–103, 106, 117, 119, 131, 134–135, 144–145
ethical marketing 131–133
European Cup 93

Fanzo 118
FCTC *see* Framework Convention on Tobacco Control (FCTC)
Fédération Internationale de Football Association (FIFA) 4–5, 9, 28, 53–62,

58, 64–67, 79, 84, 96, 101, 118, 123, 134, 138
FIFA World Cup 4–5, 9, 28, 53–62, **58,** 64–67, 79, 84, 96, 101, 118, 123, 134, 138
FIFA Women's World Cup 60–62
Flutter Entertainment 132, 145
football: Australian Rules 30–33, 115; British 2, 5, 22–24, 41, 76, 78, 93–96, 119–120, 133–135; clubs 2, 22, 24–25, 29, 32, 76, 99–100, 104–105, 133–134; women's 60–62
Foulkes, G. 41
Framework Convention on Tobacco Control (FCTC) 4, 10, 44, 48
Frawley, S. 68
Freudenberg, N. 10, 12

Gallahers 42
gamblification 118–120
gambling 118–119; problem 45; sponsorship 100, 137
Giulianotti, R. 54–55, 75–76, 80–81, 95, 134–135
globalisation 8, 12, 26, 43, 53–57, 82, 84, 131
Godfrey Phillips 64, 86
Goldblatt, D. 66
golf 42, 84, 96
Gruneau, R. 23, 62, 65, 67
Guinness 115–118

habitus 76–77
Hamm, M. 61
Harris, J. L. 14
Hastings, G. 11–12, 68
Havelange, J. 56–57, 64–65, 67
Haynes, R. 2
health halo 29, 131, 136
health inequalities 7, 12
Healthy Stadia 1, 147
high in fat, salt and sugar (HFSS) 87, 115, 136–138
Hill, J. 23, 79, 93, 96
Hill & Knowlton 45–46, 67
Hillsborough disaster 2–3, 94, 105
Hope, W. 81–82
Howell, D. 42

Hutchins, B. 80
hyper-commodification 80, 95, 145
hyperconsumption 10

India 66, 84–87, 100
Indian Premier League (IPL) 85–87
International Cricket Conference (ICC) 83–84
International Olympic Committee (IOC) 54–56, 64–67
International Sports Leisure Marketing (ISL) 65
Ireland, R. 12

Jägermeister 25
Jennings, A. 64
Jensen, P. M. 48
Jernigan, D. H. 12
John Player Special League 83, 87
Johnson, B. 130
Jordan, M. 61

Kellogg 114; swimming badges 7
KFC 85, 132
Kfouri, J. 68
Kickbusch, I. 9
King, A. 2, 96
King, B. J. 46–48
Knai, C. 11–12
Kunz, R. E. 123

Lacy-Vawdon, C. de 10–11
Lash, S. 75, 78
Law, D. 94
Lawrence, S. 80
LED pitchside advertising 26, 29, 100
Lee, K. 12
Liverpool F.C. 2, 25, 93, 94, 97, 100, 102, 117, 130
Livingstone, C. 10–11
London Olympic Games 12, 68, 102
Lopez, S. 60
Los Angeles Games 63, 65
Lury, C. 75

Maani, N. 13
McDonald's 12, 27, 32–33, 54, 57–59, 65, 68, 85, 102, 115, 138

McGee, D. 119
McMillan, N. A. 41
McMullan, J. L. 119
Maguire, K. 101
Manchester United 29, 40, 44, 80, 82, 93–94, 97–100, 102, 117
marketing 26–33; ethical 131–133; relationship 11, 29; tobacco 44–45; of unhealthy brands 10–12, 58–59
Marmot, M. 10
Marqusee, M. 86, 130
Marylebone Cricket Club (MCC) 83–84
masculinity 81
Mason, T. 23, 93
Mateschitz, D. 121
Matthews, S. 93–94
media *see* social media
Meenaghan, T. 27, 113
mega-events 54–55
mental health 4, 8, 10, 11
Messi, L. 58
Mialon, M. 10–11
Millar, J. S. 9
Miller, D. 119; *Official History of the Olympic Games* 62–63
Miller, T. 147
Millward, P. 98
Milsom, P. 11
Mitchell and Kenyon 40
M&M's Cup 61
Modi, L. 86
Mondelez International 5, 103, 104, 105, 145
motor racing 12, 25, 41, 43, 45, 94, 113, 122, 137, 138
Mountain Dew 13–15, 122
Mûller, M. 54
Murdoch, R. 78, 85, 95

Nally, P. 57, 65
National Association for Stock Car Auto Racing in the United States (NASCAR) 5, 14, 42, 81, 104, 112
National Football League (NFL) 24, 118, 134
NCDs *see* non-communicable diseases (NCDs)
neoliberalism 7, 86

Nestlé 114, 131
Nestle, M. 103, 133
New Zealand 61, 81, 83, 85, 135
Nixon, R. 46
non-communicable diseases (NCDs) 7–8, 10–11, 42, 49, 135, 137
North American Basketball League (NBA) 15, 25
Numerato, D. 3

Official History of the Olympic Games (Miller) 62–63
Olympic Games 12, 53–55, 62–66, 68, 84, 96, 102–103
The Olympic Partner (TOPS) worldwide sponsorship programme 55

Packer, K. 84–86
Park Drive cigarette packets 42
Pelé 41
Peñarol 25
Pepsi 8, 97
PepsiCo 14, 32, 102, 134
personal responsibility 13, 43, 45, 122, 145
Petticrew, M. 10, 48, 135
Philip Morris tobacco company 41, 44, 46–48, 61, 86, 112
pleasurable excitement 76
Pollay, R. W. 44
pools (football) 119
Pracejus, J. W. 114
Professional Footballers' Association (PFA) 93
'Programme for a Sociology of Sport' (Bourdieu) 77
public health 1–5, 44, 48, 49, 67, 68, 105, 115, 120, 123, 131, 133, 135, 137; advocates 27, 47, 102, 136, 139, 144–147; sport 7–15
public houses 24
Purves, R. 59, 136

Qatar 3, **58**, 138, 147

RB Leipzig 123
Red Bull 5, 15, 44, 120–123, 132, 147
Reemsta cigarette company 63–64
relationship marketing 11, 29

responsibilization 12
R. J. Reynolds Tobacco Company 42, 45, 57, 81
Robertson, R. 54–55, 79, 96
Robertson, W. 45
Roche, M. 54, 61
Ronaldo, C. 41
Rose, N. 12
Rothmans International 41, 94
Rowe, D. 80
Royal College of Physicians of London 43
rugby league 31, 77, 119
rugby union 5, 77, 116
Rumford, C. 86
Ruth, B. 41

Samaranch, J. A. 64–65, 67
Sartori, A. 32
Semens, A. 27
Serazio, M. 80
shirt sponsorship 12, 25–27, 97–100, 99, 113, 133, 145
Simson, V. 64
Sinclair, C. 61
Sky Sports 96
smoking 8, 40–41, 43–48, 67, 104, 132, 135, 146
social media 66, 79–80, 87, 98–99, 114–115, 117–118, 133
sponsorship: gambling 100, 137; promotional assemblage 30; pyramid 27–28, 28; shirt 98–100, 99; tobacco 4, 33, 41–42, 113, 133
'Sport and Social Class' (Bourdieu) 76
Sport England 136
Sporting Events (Control of Alcohol, etc.) Act 1985 135–136
'The Sports Business' (Wilson) 42
sportswashing 131, 147
Stillerman, J. 26
Suárez, L. 58
symbiotic relationship 79
symbolic capital 76
symbolic violence 78
systems thinking approach 11

Taylor, I. 94
Taylor, R. 2

television 24–25; audience 24, 31, 33, 47, 54, 61, 81, 84, 99–101; broadcasts 31, 33, 55; coverage 30, 34, 56, 98, 112
tennis 41, 42, 45, 46–48, 61, 94
Thatcher, M. 94
Three Ireland 116–117
tobacco: advertisement 31, 40–42, 137; industry 1, 4, 10, 12–13, 25–26, 31, 34, 40–48, 57–58, 67, 104, 113–114, 120, 131–132, 135, 137, 146; marketing 44–45, 131–133; playbook 13, 43–48; sponsorship 4, 33, 41–42, 113, 133
Tomlinson, A. 54, 63
totemic principle 80
Tottenham Hotspur 95, 97, 117, 144–145
transnational corporations 1, 8–9, 12, 26, 31, 43–45, 53–56, 59, 64–65, 68, 78, 80, 100, 102–103, 113–114, 116, 130–131, 145–147
Turner, M. 96
Twenty20 (T20) cricket 85
Twitter 117–118

UK Rugby Football League 42
unhealthy brands 1–3, 8, 10–12, 29, 34, 42, 58–59, 130–132, 134, 136
unhealthy commodity industries (UCIs) 9–13, 29, 99
Union des Associations Européennes de Football (UEFA) 56, 61, 97, 100, 117, 123
The United Kingdom 5, 10, 13, 41, 43, 59, 64, 66, 78–79, 83, 100, 114–115, 120, 123, 130, 133–134, 136, 144
The United States 5, 13–14, 25, 40, 42–43, 46, 61–63, 78, 81, 86, 100, 112, 123, 132
US Lawn Tennis Association 46

Varela, O. 25
Verstappen, M. 122
VicHealth 146
Victorian Football League 31
Virginia Slims 4, 46–48, 61

Wagg, S. 68
Wagner, H. 40

Walsh, A. J. 80, 95, 134–135
Whannel, G. 24, 25, 41, 56, 78, 83, 84, 94, 100
Wheaties 23
W.D. & H.O. Wills 31, 40, 84
WHO *see* World Health Organization (WHO)
Williams, J. 60–61
Williams, S. B. 25
Women's Football Association 60
World Health Organization (WHO) 7, 10, 13, 44, 48, 68, 121, 131, 138
World Series Cricket (WSC) 84–85
Wrack, S. 61

Young, C. 54, 66